The Transition of Religion to Culture in Law and Public Discourse

This book explores the recent trend toward the transformation of religious symbols and practices into culture in Western democracies. Analyses of three legal cases involving religion in the public sphere are used to illuminate this trend: a municipal council chamber; a town hall; and town board meetings. Each case involves a different national context—Canada, France and the United States—and each illustrates something interesting about the shape-shifting nature of religion, specifically its flexibility and dexterity in the face of the secular, the religious and the plural. Despite the differences in national contexts, in each instance religion is transformed into culture or heritage by the courts to justify or excuse its presence and to distance the state from the possibility that it is violating legal norms of distance from religion. The cultural practice or symbol is represented as a shared national value or activity. Transforming the 'Other' into 'Us' through reconstitution is also possible. Finally, anxiety about the 'Other' becomes part of the story of rendering religion as culture, resulting in the impugning of anyone who dares to question the putative shared culture.

The book will be essential reading for students, academics and policy-makers working in the areas of sociology of religion, religious studies, socio-legal studies, law and public policy, constitutional law, religion and politics, and cultural studies.

Lori G. Beaman, Ph.D., F.R.S.C., is the Canada Research Chair in Religious Diversity and Social Change, Professor in the Department of Classics and Religious Studies at the University of Ottawa and Principal Investigator of Understanding Nonreligion in a Complex Future. She is the author of numerous books and articles, a regular participant in public discussions about religion and the public sphere and is the principal investigator of the multi-site study Nonreligion in a Complex Future.

ICLARS Series on Law and Religion

Series Editors:

Silvio Ferrari, University of Milan, Italy, Russell Sandberg, Cardiff University, UK, Pieter Coertzen, University of Stellenbosch, South Africa, W. Cole Durham, Jr., Brigham Young University, USA, and Tahir Mahmood, Amity International University, India

The *ICLARS Series on Law and Religion* is a new series designed to provide a forum for the rapidly expanding field of research in law and religion. The series is published in association with the International Consortium for Law and Religion Studies, an international network of scholars and experts of law and religion founded in 2007 with the aim of providing a place where information, data and opinions can easily be exchanged among members and made available to the broader scientific community. The series aims to become a primary source for students and scholars while presenting authors with a valuable means to reach a wide and growing readership.

Regulating Religion
State Governance of Religious Institutions in South Africa
Helena Van Coller

Religious Rights within the Family
From Coerced Manifestation to Dispute Resolution in France, England and Hong Kong
Esther Erlings

Religion, Law, Politics and the State in Africa
Applying Legal Pluralism in Ghana
Seth Tweneboah

Law and Religious Diversity in Education
The Right to Difference
Kyriaki Topidi

The Transition of Religion to Culture in Law and Public Discourse
Lori G. Beaman

For more information about this series, please visit: www.routledge.com/ICLARS-Series-on-Law-and-Religion/book-series/ICLARS

The Transition of Religion to Culture in Law and Public Discourse

Lori G. Beaman

Routledge
Taylor & Francis Group
LONDON AND NEW YORK

First published 2020
by Routledge
2 Park Square, Milton Park, Abingdon, Oxon OX14 4RN

and by Routledge
52 Vanderbilt Avenue, New York, NY 10017

Routledge is an imprint of the Taylor & Francis Group, an informa business

British Library Cataloguing in Publication Data
A catalogue record for this book is available from the British Library

Library of Congress Cataloging-in-Publication Data
Names: Beaman, Lori G. author.
Title: The transition of religion to culture in law and public discourse / Lori Beaman.
Description: Abingdon, Oxon ; New York, NY : Routledge, 2020. | Series: ICLARS series on law and religion | Includes bibliographical references and index.
Identifiers: LCCN 2019055076 (print) | LCCN 2019055077 (ebook) | ISBN 9780367440534 (hardback) | ISBN 9781003007319 (ebook)
Subjects: LCSH: Religion and state. | Church and state--Québec (Province). | Church and state--France. | Church and state--United States.
Classification: LCC K3280 .B43 2020 (print) | LCC K3280 (ebook) | DDC 306.6--dc23
LC record available at https://lccn.loc.gov/2019055076
LC ebook record available at https://lccn.loc.gov/2019055077

ISBN: 978-0-367-44053-4 (hbk)
ISBN: 978-1-003-00731-9 (ebk)

Typeset in Galliard
by Taylor & Francis Books

Contents

Acknowledgments

This book has benefitted from conversations with many people. In particular, I wish to thank the following key research and conversation partners who have made invaluable suggestions, given generously of their time and energy, and have challenged my arguments: Helge Årsheim, Peter Beyer, Dia Dabby, Frédéric Dejean, Doug Ezzy, Inger Furseth, Anna Halafoff, David Koussens, Bertrand Lavoie, Mia Lövheim, Julia Martínez-Ariño, Damon Maryl, Paula Montero, Mary Jo Neitz, Sheryl Reimer-Kirkham, Jennifer Selby, Sonia Sikka, Teemu Taira, Juan Marco Vaggione and Linda Woodhead.

Thank you to Amélie Barras, Gary Bouma, Anna Salonen and Leo Van Arragon for reading and commenting on a full draft of the manuscript.

Huguette Bourgeois has checked in regularly to make sure I was not too deep in the abyss of work. And in the final draft to help me with a translation puzzle.

Solange Lefebvre is a cherished friend, collaborator and conversation partner. Her willingness to enter into vigorous debate with a generous spirit has enabled me to see issues more clearly from multiple vantage points. Merci, chère amie.

Marianne Abou-Hamad and Christine Cusack provided research assistance on early drafts of the manuscript. Cory Steele has been a meticulous research assistant with a sharp eye for inconsistencies and an insistence on perfection in referencing, even as I insist on creating my own style. Thank you Cory for giving so much care and energy to this manuscript.

The Annual Law and Religion Roundtable generously invited me to present this book as work in progress at their 2017 meeting at the University of Pennsylvania Law School. Their comments, questions and suggestions were vital to the analysis in Chapter 4.

I am also grateful to the organisers and participants of 2018 *Democracy, Citizenship, and Constitutionalism* conference at the University of Pennsylvania. Heather Sharkey and Jeffrey Green made comments on a portion of the manuscript that will appear as a chapter in their forthcoming book.

Matthias Koenig, along with the participants in the 2017 *Religious Freedom and Varieties of Religious Establishment: National Identities, Public Morals and Cultural Values* meeting at the Göttingen Institute for Advanced Study in the Humanities and Social Sciences, Göttingen, Germany commented especially on the framework that guides my analysis.

I have taken advantage of the generosity of my hosts as a keynote speaker in a number of venues, using the opportunity they provided me to test the ideas I was developing. Thank you to each of you for your generous engagement with my ideas.

The intellectual environment offered through the Religion and Diversity Project, as well as the privileges and obligations attached to the Canada Research Chair in Religious Diversity and Social Change, have provided key support for this project. Funding for both comes from the Social Sciences and Humanities Research Council of Canada, with support in various forms from the University of Ottawa.

Last but not least, thank you to my partner Derek Mac Donald for his patience and support as my "just a few more minutes" inevitably turns into another hour or two at my desk.

1 Introduction

> In February, 2017 the crucifix in Saint-Sacrement hospital in Quebec, which had lain increasingly mute for 90 years (with the exception of some private whispering with the devout and desperate), suddenly began to speak: it spoke to the contribution of the Sisters of Charity who had founded and supported the hospital; it spoke to the history of the hospital and the community; it articulated the heritage of the province; it declared its loyalty to "our" culture; it testified to universal values that it represented. What caused this revival, this sudden need to speak?

The religious landscape is changing rapidly in Western democracies, creating a new diversity that frames the context within which social actors interact and institutions operate. The number of people in who self-describe as "nonreligious" is at an all-time high (and likely to increase), sometimes comprising over half of the population.[1] More importantly, nonreligion, or being a "none", has moved from being a marginal category to being one that represents a legitimate position or identity.[2] "Nones" is a complex category that includes a broad spectrum of belief, unbelief and worldviews,

1 The nonreligious account for the following percentages of the populations in various countries: Canada (23.9 per cent), the United States (19.6 per cent), Australia (30 per cent), the UK (46 per cent), France (28 per cent), the Czech Republic (76.4 per cent), Estonia (59.6 per cent) and Sweden (59 per cent). See Statistics Canada (2011); Pew Research Center (2012a; 2012b: 45–50); YouGov (2015); Woodhead (2016a); Australian Bureau of Statistics (2017); Gallup International (2015); and Zuckerman (2008). Nones make up a significant portion of the population in other areas of the world as well—Hong Kong (56 per cent), China (52 per cent) and Japan (57 per cent)—though the complexity of imposing the notion of religion requires another layer of analysis. See Josephson (2012). A Gallup International (2012, 15–16) report found that more than half of the populations in Vietnam, France and Ireland consider themselves "not a religious person" or atheist. Survey wording is variable: For example, Statistics Canada provides the option of "no religious affiliation", which is further sub-categorised to include: "agnostic", "atheist", "humanist", "no religion" and "no religious affiliation, n.i.e.". Pew Research Center uses the term "religiously unaffiliated", while the Australian Bureau of Statistics uses "no religion". YouGov uses the term "none" in its surveys.

2 See Woodhead (2016a; 2016b). This phenomenon does not include the massive number of people who claim a religious affiliation but who, for the most part, have almost no involvement or engagement with that tradition.

including the spiritual but not religious, atheist, humanist and the indifferent. There is a growing yet incomplete literature on this group.[3]

Predictably and logically, there is a simultaneous decline in affiliation with organised religion, with a much-reduced number of people regularly participating in religious services and rituals.[4] Grace Davie (2007; 2015) has described this as believing without belonging, arguing that a small number of people are performing religion for those who do not participate. In Canada, this has had tangible effects: one frequently sees church buildings for sale, as well as the demolition or transformation of such buildings into condominiums, restaurants and senior citizens' complexes.[5] Congregations are merging in order to survive. Churches are opening to circuses, concerts and sharing their space with other religions.[6] In other countries like Sweden the impact is less visible because of the robust state support for church assets such as buildings. This spatial shift is only one example of the shifts resulting from declining affiliation with traditional institutional religion.

Migration to these same countries has also increased, bringing with it an acceleration of numbers of minority religious groups. While historically present, increased visibility has brought heightened attention to these groups.[7] In the decade between 2001 and 2011 the percentage of those who identify as Hindus, Sikh, Buddhist and Muslim in Canada increased from 4.9 per cent to 7.2 per cent. They made up one third of the immigrants who arrived during that decade (Statistics Canada 2013a; 2013b).[8] A similar increase was experienced in Australia.[9] In the United Kingdom,

3 A number of pioneers in the field of nonreligion include Campbell (1971); Lee (2015; 2012); Day (2011); Zuckerman (2008); Quack (2014); Cragun et al. (2015); Beaman and Tomlins (2015); Beyer (2015); Wallis (2014); and Day et al. (2013). Contrary to Korie Edwards' (2019) argument, this acknowledgment does not diminish the importance of studying religion: to the contrary, it is only by understanding both religion and nonreligion that there is any hope of understanding how to live well together.

4 Brian Clarke and Stuart Macdonald observe that 55 per cent of the Canadian population is de- and non-churched (Clarke and Macdonald 2017, 209).

5 See, for example, Grigore Dovlete and Beaman (2017).

6 A CBC News article by Kate McKenna (2019) reports on how St. Jax church in Montreal, Canada has partnered with Le Monastère, a circus cabaret show, to help fund its "daily operations". See also Beaman (2018).

7 The precise dimensions of the shift are tempered by the fact that survey questions are not always consistent across time. The other challenge is that decennial survey data gives a slow-moving picture at best and, by the time data are released, they are often several years old. To complicate matters further, accurate historical data is not always available. Subtleties in terms of reference are also important: as Steven Green explains, Church historians and apologists often exaggerate historical church affiliation and attendance in the United States. Contemporary scholars refute historical numbers by noting that church affiliation and attendance never exceeded approximately 30 per cent of the population in the United States (Green 2015, 212). For an examination of the history of Muslims in Canada, see chapter 2 in Selby et al. (2018). See also Kazemipur (2014).

8 The Angus Reid Institute (2017) reports that growth in faith communities is attributable to immigrants, "many of whom are non-white and non-Christian". Approximately 3.2 per cent of the Canadian population identifies as Muslim (Statistics Canada 2011).

9 In Australia, there has been a steady increase in non-Christian religions with Hindus, Buddhists and Muslims increasing from 3.9 per cent of the population in 2001 to 6

the number of Buddhists, Muslims, Sikhs and Hindus similarly rose from 5 per cent of the population in 2001 to 7.5 per cent of the population in 2011 (Office for National Statistics 2012a; 2012b). These statistics are similar in many Western countries.[10] Migration and its entanglement with religion is nothing new: there is a long history of migration that has involved religious groups, including Jews, Muslims, radical Protestants, Hindus and Mormons.[11] These migrations each have a unique history and trajectory. However, with increased numbers often comes increased public visibility.

A fourth element of the new diversity that will receive less attention in coming pages of this book is the increased visibility of Indigenous peoples in considerations of spiritual diversity. In Canada, Australia, Sweden and Norway, for example, there is a renewed awareness in Indigenous populations and the impact of state policies on them. In Canada, the state constituted the Truth and Reconciliation Commission of Canada to identify and respond to the devastating impact of colonialization on Indigenous peoples. The recommendations from that Commission are extensive and call for meaningful reconciliation initiatives to address the harm caused by the attempted eradication of Indigenous culture and spirituality (Truth and Reconciliation Commission of Canada 2015).

In short, the presence of what might be described as a critical mass of those identifying as nonreligious, the decline in affiliation with organised religion, the significantly enhanced visibility of non-Christian newcomers coupled with existing minorities and renewed attention to Indigenous spiritual practices (in some contexts) have created the context within which a reshaping of previously (and arguably still) hegemonic religion is being recast as culture and as vital to the heritage of some countries. This reimagining of religion is occurring within social institutions such as law, education, media and in broader public discourse.[12] It is occurring particularly in relation to practices and symbols that occupy space, literally or figuratively,

per cent in 2011. See Australian Bureau of Statistics (2006; 2012). See also Bouma and Halafoff (2017).

10 In the United States, individuals who identify as belonging to non-Christian faiths increased from 4.7 per cent in 2007 to 5.9 per cent in 2014. Similarly, the Pew-Templeton (2015a) Global Religious Futures Project has projected that France's Muslim population will increase from 7.5 per cent (in 2010) to 10.9 per cent (in 2050) because of migration. From 2010 to 2050, Sweden's Muslim population is estimated to increase from 4.6 per cent to 12.4 per cent (Pew-Templeton 2015b).

11 See James A. Beckford (2016a; 2016b) for a more detailed discussion of these migrations. There is some argument to be made that in the Syrian refugee crisis orthodox Christians in addition to Muslims are migrating for religious reasons. However, there are some qualifiers to be made on this, including the overemphasis of religion in public policy. See Beaman et al. (2017).

12 This reimagining work has a number of forms, from the lived religion focus of Robert Orsi (2005), the concept of the secular sacred by Kim Knott et al. (2013), Linda Woodhead's (2016b) everyday religion, and Courtney Bender (2003), and Helge Årsheim (2015), following Dressler and Mandair (2011), with the notion of religion-making. Sullivan (2005) and Hurd (2015) have challenged the stability of the concept of religion.

in the public sphere, such as the presence of crucifixes and crosses[13] and the practice of prayer at public meetings and in legislative bodies.[14]

Part and parcel of the shifting social and cultural context in rising "none" countries is social anxiety about what is perceived to be rapid change.[15] The fear that "our" culture is somehow being lost is a recurring theme in discussions about prayer in public places, negotiations around food and drink, holiday celebrations and so on.[16] To be sure, fear is only one current in a sea of responses, but it is manifesting in a variety of ways, one of which is the insistence that practices previously understood as being religious constitute an integral part of culture and are thus effectively exempt from human rights frameworks related to religion that might curtail their presence. While the nonreligious, particularly atheists, are sometimes challenging the presence of religion in the (ostensibly "secular") public sphere, observant religious minorities are asking for greater flexibility in the public presence and practice of their symbols. As a result, there is a concurrent challenging of hegemonic religious symbols combined with an increased presence of minority religious symbols and practices.[17] This is taking place in a context in which majoritarian religion is in decline.

This book does not focus on a comparative approach to Muslim versus Christian symbols in the public sphere. Rather, the focus is on the reconfiguration of practices like prayer and symbols, such as crucifixes, taking into account the broader contexts in which those transformations occur. Fear of the other is primarily, but not exclusively, directed at Muslims. There is indeed a rich literature that analyses symbols and practices associated with Muslims, including the hijab, niqab and the presence of minarets.[18] But, anxiety about loss of culture or values is multi-causal, and also has links to economic and technological causes.

13 While I use the crucifix and the cross somewhat interchangeably in this work, there is a difference that has significance for those who consider these symbols as meaningful. The crucifix that is the focus of debate in Quebec is a Catholic crucifix as it has the corpus on it (emphasis on sacrifice/crucifixion). Protestant crosses less frequently display the body of Christ, symbolising the emphasis on resurrection. In Quebec, Protestants were historically a minority, associated with the Anglophone population, although this distinction is, like all divisions, not entirely accurate.

14 In Canada, a prayer is recited before Parliament's doors are opened to the public (Parliament of Canada 2009). In April 2017, MP Ted Falk delivered an Easter message in the House of Commons, declaring, "it's important to reflect on the Judeo-Christian principles that played such a key role in Canada's formation" (The Christian Institute 2017). Similarly, the Australian Senate recites a prayer before sitting (Parliament of Australia 2009). In the United States, both the House of Representatives and Senate employ an official chaplain that opens sessions with a prayer (Brudnick 2011).

15 As Ulrich Beck (2009) puts it, "Fear determines the attitude towards life" (8).

16 See Paul Scheffer (2011, 24) for a discussion of immigration in particular, and the notion of "losing our culture". He takes seriously this sentiment, arguing that whatever we might think of it, fear must be addressed. Scheffer argues that "A vague and unrealistic concept of world citizenship has encouraged a return to parochialism" (26).

17 The decline of churches and the concomitant loss of churches, artefacts and practices as part of the heritage of Quebec has been the focus of scholarly attention, including Bernier (2015), Lefebvre (2009) and Turgeon (2005).

18 See Abu Odeh (1993), Alvi et al. (2003), Bakht (2012), Beaman (2013a), Bracke and Fadil (2012), Clarke (2013), Dot-Pouillard (2007), Shakeri (2000), McGoldrick (2006),

In his book *Immigrant Nations*, Paul Scheffer (2011) argues that it is important to take seriously the fears about loss of culture in countries experiencing rapid rates of settlement. He notes the tendency to frame newcomers, as well as subsequent generations, as "perpetuating a particular culture" and the emerging self-designation of lower and middle-class whites as a "minority" and "victims" (29). This frequently translates as "we're losing our culture" (24).[19] To be sure, as Sonia Sikka (2012) points out, this group has produced a particular version of what "our culture" consists of, which is itself only a partial representation of the members of any given society from which minority groups are excluded. But, pointing that out has little traction with the dominant producers of culture and does little to address their sense of culture under threat. The challenge to prayer and religious symbols in public spaces has acted as a lightning rod for anxieties about social change more generally. Cloaking religion as culture is one defensive or protective strategy.

Zygmunt Bauman (2011) summarises three major phases in migration in his book *Culture in a Liquid Modern World*: first, the migration of 60 million Europeans to "empty lands"; second, resettlement which was accompanied by the assimilation model, "created in the early phase of nation-building as a way of dealing with ethnic minorities, linguistic or cultural" (35); third,

> currently in full flow and gathering momentum despite frenetic attempts to hold it back, introduces the age of diasporas: an infinite archipelago of ethnic, religious and linguistic settlements, heedless of the pathways marked out and paved by the imperial/colonial episode, and steered instead by the logic of the global redistribution of living resources and the chances of survival peculiar to the current stadium of globalization. (35)

In this current phase, "native pretensions to the primacy of local needs, demands and entitlements" are ignored, and dual citizenship and multiple loyalties pervade (35). From all of this we arrive at a place in history where the "'art of living with difference' has become an everyday problem" (36). Here Bauman makes a key point: that this problem could only materialise "at a point when the differences between people had ceased to be perceived merely as transitory irritants" (36–37). Assimilation is shredded and "cultural relations are no longer vertical but horizontal: no culture can demand or be entitled to subservience, humility or submission on the part of any other simply on account of its own assumed superiority or 'progressiveness'" (37). Nor, I would add, its foundational status, though this is a battle that is currently being fought.

Howard (2009), Bacquet (2009), Khan (2009), Fadil (2011), Hoodfar (1997), Jouili (2011), Jiwani and Rail (2010), Mossière (2013), Korteweg and Yurdakul (2014), Brems (2014), Berg and Lundahl (2016), Oliva (2016), Moore (2007), Alghafli et al. (2017), Selby et al. (2018); Selby (2014a); Barras (2017); and Alibhai (forthcoming).

19 One Pew study links national belonging and Christianity: 15 per cent of Canadians indicated that religion, specifically Christianity, is important to national identity, compared with 32 per cent of Americans (Stokes 2017).

It is precisely this state of affairs, bolstered and perhaps created by human rights (which Bauman reduces to "the right to difference"), that is at the crux of the transformation of religion to culture and heritage. It is the challenge by human rights to religious and cultural primacy that puts privilege to the test by pushing toward a model in which majoritarian religions are one among many. The move from religion to culture is precisely because of this: the protection of religious freedom[20] has created a horizontal relationship between religions. No religion can legitimately claim superiority. The move to culture is a protective strategy, an attempt to reframe majoritarian religion as a heritage to be protected against both religious "others" and the nonreligious. This is not to say there are not and will not be reversions, resistances and even rebellions (as we will see in the chapters that follow), but that, at least in theory, the playing field has been graded to be even. Law, attached as it is to cultural hegemony, is in the paradoxical role of enforcing the protections and great equalisers at the same time as it protects the cultural generator of those same protections, at least in their current form.

The case that initially sparked my interest in religion's transformation to culture and heritage was the Italian case of *Lautsi*.[21] In brief, the case involved an atheist parent and her objection to a crucifix hanging on the walls of her children's public school classroom. The state and a number of interveners argued that the crucifix is an integral part of Italy's culture and heritage and is a passive symbol that does not force anyone to do or to believe anything. The decision of the European Court of Human Rights in 2009 held that the display of crucifixes violated religious freedom and the parents' right to educate their children. The decision was met with public and political outcry that reflects a sense of "culture under threat" (BBC News 2009). The Italian Minister of Education noted: "No one, not even some ideologically motivated European court, will succeed in rubbing out our identity" (*The Guardian*, Hooper 2009). Post-decision discussion included concern about the erasure of Christianity from European history and some characterised it as an anti-Christian backlash (Beaman 2012/3).[22] The Italian government appealed the decision to the Grand Chamber of the European Court of Human Rights, which decided in 2011 that the crucifixes were passive symbols that did not violate the right to education nor religious freedom. The theme of cultural threat recurred in the arguments before the Grand Chamber and in the decisions of some of the judges:

> A court of human rights cannot allow itself to suffer from historical Alzheimer's. It has no right to disregard the cultural continuum of a nation's flow through time, nor to ignore what, over the centuries, has served to mould and define the profile of a people. No supranational court has any business substituting its own ethical mock-ups for those qualities that history has imprinted on the national identity. On a human rights court falls the function

20 For critical discussions on the notion of religious freedom, see Sullivan et al. (2015), Hurd (2015), Mauldin (2016) and Philpott and Shah (2016).

21 *Lautsi and others v. Italy* 2011. ECHR. No. 30814/06. Hereinafter "*Lautsi*".

22 See Iovino (2010). For thorough analysis on *Lautsi*, reactions, and crucifix debates in Italy more generally, see Ozzano and Giorgi (2013), Mancini (2010) and Fokas (2017).

> of protecting fundamental rights, but never ignoring that "customs are not passing whims". They evolve over time, harden over history into cultural cement. They become defining, all-important badges of identity for nations, tribes, religions, individuals. (Justice Bonello in *Lautsi*, p. 38, 1.1)

A strong current running through the arguments and some parts of the decision was the idea that the crucifix is not religious or representative of any particular religion: the crucifix emerges as representative of universal values, a symbol of Italy's culture and heritage.

The Grand Chamber decision was framed around the legal exit door of the "margin of appreciation",[23] though the narrative of cultural preservation was woven through the decision: "A European court should not be called upon to bankrupt centuries of European tradition.[24] No court, certainly not this Court, should rob the Italians of part of their cultural personality" (Justice Bonello in *Lautsi*, p. 38, 1.2).

The *Lautsi* case encapsulates many of the arguments that recur across countries with majoritarian religious symbols and practices when those come under question, including during the public discussion of the Saint-Sacrement hospital incident that opened this book.

In his discussion of the culturalisation of religion, Christian Joppke (2018) notes that the only way states can associate with religion (presumably because of human rights guarantees and claims to secularity by European and North American states) is to transform religion into culture. He argues that *Lautsi* "sent the right political message" in that it acknowledged the historically dominant position of Christianity. However, Joppke goes on to state:

> As long as the preferences of this majority are not minority-repressing, they should be respected, and the court rightly refused to subdue them for the sake of a legally correct but politically contentious principle of strict secularity. This is achieved by means of the culturalization of religion, which allows favoring

23 See Fokas (2016) and Koenig (2015a).

24 Robert Schuman, referred to as the Father of Europe, is quoted as saying: "We are called to bethink ourselves of the Christian basics of Europe by forming a democratic model of governance which through reconciliation develops into a 'community of peoples' in freedom, equality, solidarity and peace and which is deeply rooted in Christian basic values" (as quoted in Fountain 2010, 5). During the 2004 European Union Constitution debates and negotiations, politicians debated whether the preamble should contain a reference to Christianity. Seven states—Italy, Poland, Lithuania, Malta, Portugal, the Czech Republic and Slovakia—called for the European Union to recognise a "historical truth" by including in the Constitution a reference to the "Christian roots of Europe". France, Sweden and Denmark were strong opponents to the idea (*The Guardian*, Ian Black 2004). In the end, no specific reference was included; the Preamble reads, "DRAWING INSPIRATION from the cultural, religious and humanist inheritance of Europe, from which have developed the universal values of the inviolable and inalienable rights of the human person, freedom, democracy, equality and the rule of law."

> the preferences of the majority without unduly compromising the liberal neutrality principle. (243)

Here is where Joppke and I part company. The removal of the crucifix from the classroom in *Lautsi*, from hospitals in Quebec, from state legislatures and parliaments as well as the end of Christian prayer before municipal, state and ceremonial investitures of police, for example, is necessary to preserve democracy and the credibility of states. This is not "strict secularity", a concept I will return to shortly, but an opening of the spaces of the performance of democracy to everyone who lives in diverse societies. "Historical" Christianity has, in many cases, contributed to the erasure of other histories that are vital to the stories of states and their peoples. In Canada, intertwining Christianity and "our culture and heritage" obscures the story of Indigenous peoples (and their forced conversion), the contributions of Jews, Muslims and Sikhs, as well as the nonreligious to contemporary Canadian society.[25] Fair and just societies are not about pleasing majorities, but creating inclusive narratives and realities and inscribing the desire to recognise and redistribute privilege when imbalances exist, rather than asserting superiority based on a constructed foundational position. This does not mean the erasure of recognition and of the significant contribution of Christianities (which comprise the majority religion in the countries I focus on here), but a renegotiation of their place in the story. This does not require the crucifix to leave the building, but it may require its repositioning.

The context of debates about religious symbols and practices such as prayer varies from country to country. The context also shapes both the definition and regulation of religious symbols and practices. Country specific features impact the contours of these processes and boundaries: In Canada multiculturalism is an important ideological driver of how diversity is understood (Griffith 2015). In France, *laïcité* and the constitutional imperatives of *liberté, fraternité* and *égalité* shape the public sphere in important ways. The separation of church and state both in the Constitution of the United States and as popular myth filters the conversation there.[26]

This focus is distinct from that of Olivier Roy (2013), another scholar who has considered the entanglement of religion and culture. Roy argues that religion has deterritorialised and has undergone deculturalisation. His focus is on the global

25 Laniel (2018) uses a similar approach to what he calls "cultural religion", arguing that the "revisibilization" of Catholic symbols is an "*affirmation* of culturally inspired and largely shared symbols and values" (37; emphasis in original). Asserting the largely shared nature of such symbols displaces those for whom they are not relevant or harmful.

26 Leigh Eric Schmidt (2016) comments on Supreme Court Justice Antonin Scalia's reshaping of the wall of separation, linking it to ongoing historical processes in the United States, and noting: "When it comes to conflicts between theists and atheists—whether over legislative prayers or the 'under God' phrase in the Pledge of Allegiance—the notion of neutrality is, for those holding Scalia's conservative views, a mistaken constitutional interpretation. Both the nation's religious history and its original political framing are on the side of God against the ungodly" (282).

circulation of religions and the reconfiguration of religion vis-à-vis purity and in relation to secular culture as pagan. Roy argues that religion can only circulate globally because of deculturation: "in order to circulate, the religious object must appear universal, disconnected from a specific culture that has to be understood in order for the message to be grasped" (6). In common with Roy, I centre on the role that universalisation has in religion, but Roy's articulation of religion and culture considers a different dynamic. Moreover, my argument is that religion is becoming more, rather than less, enmeshed with culture in the particular contexts I study. It is conceivable that the transformation of religion to culture and the deculturation of religion are simultaneous processes, thus illustrating the socially constructed nature of religion and culture in relation to both social action and power relations.

This book considers the transformation of religion to culture in legal and public discourse through three cases and the public discussion surrounding them: the *Mouvement laïque québécois v. Saguenay (City)* case from Canada, the *Vendée (N° 395223)* case from France and the *Town of Greece v. Galloway* case from the United States. The lessons to be learned from the cases transcend their specific geographic origins to illuminate a broader trend that is emerging globally. As the ancestral ghosts of majoritarian religion continue to haunt present-day iterations of the boundaries of religious freedom, it is important to consider the consequences for increasingly complex and diverse societies.[27] The cases have been chosen to facilitate the exploration of multiple angles of the process of transition of religion to culture.

At issue is not what is "really" religion or "really" culture: when religion mutates into culture it is not a matter of insisting that religion to reveal its "true" nature. Rather, it is important to ask what does this shift in the production of a particular set of symbols, practices and techniques enable? What are the consequences of such a shift? What is the work this configuration does on the ground? By constituting religion as culture, a different kind of imaginary about who "we" are is constructed that then makes possible the exclusion, scrutiny and regulation of what is designated as religion and the exemption of certain constituencies from it. Moreover, calling into question "our" culture or heritage is difficult: the challenger is immediately positioned on the margins, as an outsider who does not belong and is not one of "us" because culture is taken to be self-evident, as is also often the case with its frequent companion, "our values".

A key component of the construction of religion and culture is context: as Jewel Amoah (2011) argues, the designation of African Traditional Religions as culture has had the effect of diminishing their significance "in an international human rights context, where religious rights are more highly regarded than the right to culture" (37). The highly variable and shifting construction of culture as something to be either protected or dismissed and its relation to religion can also occur within the

27 Jessica Radin's (2016) "ghostly" language aptly captures the phenomenon I am mapping in this book. She says: "A ghost of the faithful forefathers always seems to linger. It is, in the world of the modern nation-state, usually a Christian ghost" (110).

same context. For example, the Canadian government attempted to construct the niqab as a cultural rather than a religious symbol in the *Ishaq* case[28] in which a Muslim woman wanted to wear her niqab while taking her citizenship oath.[29] In this instance, though, rather than a privileged status, the reference to "culture" served the same purpose it does in Africa, to diminish and to move the practice outside of human rights protections. Race, religion and culture are inextricably woven together,[30] as we will see in the cases that are the focus of this book.

This approach to religion relies on two underlying premises: first, drawing on the insights of James Beckford, religion (and I extend this to culture) is socially constructed at both the first and second order levels. By this Beckford (2003) means that religion is constituted both by those engaged in it (first order) and by those who analyse it (second order). Notions of religion are thus "constructed, negotiated and contested" and religion is conceptualised as a social construct whose meaning varies across time and place that (7). This fluid approach to religion is precisely the insight that underpins the discussion that follows, with the added dimension of a focus on power relations and the dynamics of shifting categorisation. In more precise terms, how is a crucifix a religious symbol in one instance and a nonreligious representative of universal values in the next? What are the drivers of such a transformation? What is the work that shifting the meaning of a symbol or practice does: what are the possibilities, exclusions and boundaries of such a transformation?

Beckford notes the parallel worlds of religion as it is lived and religion as it is conceptualised. It is worth reflecting a bit further on this as what counts as religion is embedded in the case studies that follow. Meredith McGuire's (2008) research emphasises the importance of studying the relational aspects of everyday religious practices that can at first seem like isolated or individualistic phenomena.[31] Monica

28 *Ishaq v. Canada* 2015 *(Citizenship and Immigration)*, FC 156. Hereinafter "*Ishaq*".

29 The then Conservative Prime Minister made a number of statements regarding the case, saying "it is offensive that someone would hide their identity at the very moment where they are committing to join the Canadian family" (*The Star*, Whittington 2015) and the Conservative Party's website said that covering one's face while being sworn in is "not the way we do things here" (Conservative Party of Canada 2015). The Prime Minister also called the niqab a "product of a culture that is antiwoman" (*The Globe and Mail*, Chase 2015). During his campaign for re-election in 2015 he promised to create a "Barbaric Cultural Practices" hotline. He was not re-elected (*CBC News*, Powers 2015).

30 Sherene Razack (2008) states that "who people are is formulated in terms of an unchanging essence derived from their histories, associations, and religious practices, a constellation of invariant characteristics inherited from a culture, religion, and region. A race fiction thus grounds the nation and inheres in the power of the state to decide who is part of the kin group and who is not" (28). Mayanthi Fernando (2014) argues that the concept of culture "depends on a racialized notion of difference that combines races, religion, and culture to produce the figure of the Muslim. It also, of course, produces the European as a figure—though always unmarked—of racial, religious, and cultural particularity" (138). Her comments have application beyond Europe.

31 Meredith McGuire's (2008) research acts as a powerful antidote to Robert Bellah et al.'s (1985) lament (which has been so dominant in American accounts of religion and society) for a socially cohesive and communal society that sees only one type of religious participation as contributing to that. She challenges Bellah et al.'s analysis of Sheila, that

Grigore (2015) discusses the structural shifts that can occur through the actions of women pilgrims in Romania. Using lived religion as her framework for understanding women's religiosity, Grigore links the role of the women's religious practices in creating a contemporary right-wing nationalism in Romania. Unexamined as legitimate religion or important sites of social action, such practices remain outside of scholarly attention as not being "real" religion.[32]

The notion of lived religion complicates the conceptual challenges even further. It also flags the complexity of the task at hand: religion is constituted in multiple forms and through diverse power relations. Kocku von Stuckrad (2010) argues that we should instead consider it a matter of discourse and episteme, focusing on the ways religion is enmeshed in other fields and as a phenomenon that is both produced and productive. This book takes such a discursive approach. The question is not whether prayer before a municipal council meeting is religious or yoga is a Hindu practice, but on the consequences of them being formulated as one rather than the other. Or, in some cases, as both at once.

The analysis in the pages that follow speaks to a debate about the very idea of religion itself and its usefulness in understanding anything at all about social life. Though the development of a critical approach to religion is most welcome, a complete abandonment of the idea of religion is not without consequences.[33] Aside from the arrogance of assuming we can simply eliminate categories by academic fiat, a key consideration is the ability of groups and individuals to shape and create narrative or to control its direction. In other words, understanding power relations is an important element of any analysis of the social construction of particular categories. Recasting prayer as culture or heritage potentially reconfigures religion in a manner that protects it from challenge. Transforming prayers and crucifixes as "cultural" and as representative of universal values cushions them from accusations of state support for religion. Culture, heritage and universal values are enshrined as societal "secular sacreds", which Kim Knott et al. (2013) describe as "those beliefs, values, practices, places, symbols and objects that are formally speaking 'non-religious' but

now famous nurse in their study who became the poster woman for individualism, religious self-indulgence, and the disconnectedness from community and civic responsibility that Bellah et al. worried about. McGuire offers another interpretation of the sort of religious practices Sheila engaged in, and also challenged the highly gendered nature of Bellah et al.'s analysis. The lament for cohesion has been reconstituted by Robert Putnam's (2000) *Bowling Alone: The Collapse and Revival of American Community*, which, combined with (a misreading of?) Pierre Bourdieu's work has resulted in the circulation of a discourse of "social and cultural capital" which, in turn, meshes nicely with a neoliberal imagining of social life deploying an economic logic.

32 See Nancy T. Ammerman (2007) and David D. Hall (1997) for helpful collections on lived religion. Lived religion has also been a focus of anthropologists. See the classic work by Robert Redfield (1956) as well as Barbara Myerhoff's (1978) research in California with elderly Jews and Celia Rothenberg's (2004) more recent ethnographic study in the Palestinian West Bank on interactions with *jinn* (spirit) possessions. See also Orsi (2005) who explores Catholicism and lived religion.

33 See, especially, Goldstein et al. (2016). Véronique Altglas and Matthew Wood (2018) offer a nuanced articulation of a critical approach to religion.

are nevertheless prioritized by people, deemed to be inviolable and non-negotiable, and often referred to as 'sacred'" (11).

Religious actors are not passive in the construction of religion as religion and religion as culture and heritage. Alberta Giorgi and Pasquale Annicchino (2017) found in their research under the Grassrootsmobilise project,[34] that religious actors "selectively mobilise the 'religion' identity: while in some cases they call themselves religion because it grants advantages, in other instances they prefer not to because it would be disadvantageous" (292). There are multiple social actors engaged in the process of producing practices and artefacts as religion, culture and heritage. Citing Michel de Certeau's (1974) argument that Christianity was becoming folklore which was detached from faith to become culture, Jean-François Laniel (2016) argues that this development opens Christian heritage to characterisations such as aesthetic, folklore, patrimony and emblem, all linked to the notion of culture (374).

As with religion, culture too is a constructed concept with variable meanings depending on context and the user.[35] And, like religion, culture is often used in a fixed manner that assumes a taken for granted aspect—that its definition is self-evident. Anthropology especially has built itself around the notion of culture, though there is a strong cultural turn in sociology as well.[36] Perhaps it is most productive to explore what the courts or public discussions seem to mean when they draw on the notion of culture to frame and defend religion and the maintenance of hegemonic practices and symbols in the public sphere as "culture". Though her focus is moral relativism, Sikka (2012) gets to the heart of the matter, noting the lack of clarity in the use of the term culture and its variable meaning. Most of the time, she argues, culture refers to

> the actual traditions, practices, norms, laws, institutions, language, literature and other aesthetic products of a society. Thus, when a privileged group or particular stratum of a society claims to be the primary representatives of that society's "culture", it may well be right, but only because it has been the dominant producer of that culture. (59)[37]

34 Grassrootsmobilise is a research programme at the Hellenic Foundation for European and Foreign Policy that examines the "grassroots level mobilisations 'in the shadow' of European Court of Human Rights religious freedoms jurisprudence". See http://grassrootsmobilise.eu/.

35 Jewel Amoah (2011) points out that there have historically been two competing views of culture, one which takes a more static approach and the other which sees culture as changing and dynamic (39–40).

36 See Anderson-Levitt (2012), Bauman (2011), Griswold (1987; 1992; 2013), Loader (2015), Roseneil and Frosh (2012) and Turner (2012).

37 Sonia Sikka (forthcoming) develops an equally nuanced position regarding religion, arguing that the ways in which religion is understood lead to different frameworks for the individual, social and political negotiations of religion, which in turn shape religion.

Culture, like religion, is contested and imagined (Bayart 2005). It is this attention to power and the claim to culture that are focus of this book. In the conclusion, we will return to the question of culture, the place of religion and what a more inclusive formulation of it might look like in relation to majoritarian religion and the public sphere. For the moment, it is the notion that "our culture" is under threat that forms a primary focus of this discussion.

The relationship between religion and culture, specifically where one ends and the other begins, is complex. Rhys Williams (2015) articulates this challenge, beginning with the observation that "religion, like language, is often considered a preeminent marker of culture, and thus in many ways, religion and culture may seem largely redundant" (607). Williams identifies the unique features of religion that distinguish it from culture:

> Religion, after all, is social organization, institutions, and networks as well as expressive meaning-making, ideational systems, and symbol generation. And even among those meaning-making aspects, religion is multidimensional. There are beliefs, values, rituals, and practices—which can vary from individual and internal, to necessarily social, to societal and public. (608)

He notes that the claim to universality and transcendent truth of a number of religions renders their relationship with culture especially ambiguous (608). In everyday life, the religion–culture relationship is fluid: "at times, religion or culture is a way of life that embeds personal identity within a social group, and at times it offers a distinction between things of a sacred or divine origin and things of a human, social origin" (609). Moreover, as Laniel (2016) points out, ruminations over the relationship between religion and culture are not new: Michel de Certeau observed that if Christianity is detached from faith it comes to belong to culture, which opens it to multiple uses, including "patrimony" (374).

> As social pressure increases, it is more and more difficult to establish whether social conformity or faith itself is being professed. Religion's cultural saturation is then at its peak, and it isn't uncommon for religious culture to be indistinguishable from culture at large. (376)

In his discussion of the religion to culture phenomenon, Peter Beyer links the shaping of practices and symbols to political practices. At the heart of these are power relations. Beyer also asks why these practices work and under what circumstances. An important aspect of these considerations is the historical intertwining of religion and culture in the imagination of nations. Part of this story is the construction of minorities who were, as Beyer (2019) puts it "less included". This book maps this continuing process through specific examples.

Key social institutions, including education, the media and law, shape the construction of symbols and practices as culture and heritage.[38] Law is uncontestably an important social institution that, some argue, has back-streaming or shadowing effects on society and social practices at large.[39] In short, law organises and regulates the lives of people in day-to-day life.[40] This focus, however, sometimes cedes too much power to law, and obfuscates other institutional lenses. In other words, no one lens will show us everything. Rather than focusing on law's regulatory power or radiating effect, I take the position that law offers a window onto points of friction in societies characterised by diversity. Moreover, legal cases leave behind detailed records of events and public debates in addition to legal opinions about the nature of religion, society and culture. Thus, I have drawn on them here not as a legal scholar (though I am trained as a jurist and in fact had a legal practice for 5 years), but as a sociologist whose concern is the conceptualisation of religion at a lived or everyday level, by groups and within social institutions. As Russell Sandberg (2014) suggests in his plea for an interdisciplinary approach to the analysis of religion, law and society:

> The moral panics of recent years concerning the place of religion in the public sphere have highlighted issues that have both legal and sociological dimensions. This suggests that neither the legal nor the sociological study of these debates exist in isolation from one another and that there is room for a cross-fertilisation of legal and sociological approaches. (219–220)

It is such an interdisciplinary approach I've taken here.

Legal texts constitute "data" which are not just the words on the page, but organising practices constituting a discourse. Case law offers an important opportunity to explore legal discourse, which is composed of texts, actions and interactions,

38 This is in no way intended to minimise the importance of social actors within social institutions, but rather acknowledges the ways that institutional sites shape social practices, an approach taken by Dorothy Smith (1987) in her foundational sociological research on schools.

39 Winnifred Sullivan (2013) writes on the juridification of life, noting the powerful influence of the law to shape life to suit the law beyond the courts. Benjamin Berger (2013b) has written on the aesthetics of law and their impact on religious freedom. In her project on grassroots mobilisation in the "shadow of the law" in Greece, Effie Fokas (2015; 2016) talks about operating under the shadow of the law and the "radiating effects" of court decisions. Robert Mnookin and Lewis Kornhauser (1979) have described the shadow the law casts in the case of negotiations and bargaining beyond the courtroom between divorcing couples. See also Beaman (2017, 175–177).

40 As Carol Smart (1989) says, "law exercises power not simply in its material effects (judgements) but also in its ability to disqualify other knowledges and experiences. Non-legal knowledge is therefore suspect and/or secondary. Everyday experiences are of little interest in terms of their meaning for individuals. Rather these experiences must be translated into another form in order to become 'legal' issues and before they can be processed through the legal system" (11).

recorded in judgments, facta, and submissions, all of which provide a detailed window on law's construction of religion, nonreligion and the state, among other things. Legal decisions incorporate arguments made by the parties to the case. These arguments do not come out of thin air, but rather may reflect previously successful arguments, or they may echo current anxieties, concerns and hopes. In some instances, these are obvious from the cases themselves and in others, excavation around the decisions is necessary to gain a better appreciation for the genealogies and drivers of the discourse of the decisions. In other words, law alone is not responsible for the religion to culture and heritage shift, but rather it folds in and elaborates on this mode of framing.

It is for this reason that law and public discourse are often coupled together in the pages that follow. In part, this is a strategy to emphasise the connectedness of the legal discussions and the conversations and debates that occurred in the public sphere. It also serves to decentre law as the only site of importance. I am interested in the arguments that people make to persuade courts that prayer is "universal", or that a crucifix is really a work of art and not a religious symbol or that history justifies continued practices of exclusion. I am also interested in how law processes these arguments—what conclusions does it reach about the meaning of such symbols and practices? Finally, how do people engage in these debates about the meaning of symbols and practices? How do they come to defend the crucifix, for example, as "culture and heritage"? What do these discussions reveal about public anxieties, values and imaginaries[41] about nation and citizenship and their links to religion and culture?

The chapters that follow consider the variable ways that law and public discourse define, conceptualise and understand religion and culture, particularly when adjudicating its presence in the public sphere.[42] What is the public sphere? This amorphous space has its own chameleon-like qualities and is a concept that is much used and infrequently defined or clarified. A great deal of the "public sphere" framing was generated by the Jürgen Habermas (2006) article "Religion in the Public Sphere", in which he fails to specify what he means by "the public sphere". However, in earlier writing he says,

> The public sphere can best be described as a network for communicating information and points of view (i.e., opinions expressing affirmative or negative attitudes); the streams of communication are, in the process, filtered and synthesized in such a way that they coalesce into bundles of topically specified *public* opinions. Like the lifeworld as a whole, so, too, the public sphere is reproduced through communicative action, for which

41 Benedict Anderson (2006) uses the concept of imagined communities to discuss aspects of social solidarity, and notes the importance of the museum in the creation of the national imaginary. If we regard the preservation of "historical and cultural artifacts" such as churches, crucifixes and crosses in this light we can then see even more clearly their importance to the project of nation building and maintenance.

42 For a clear articulation of the concept of religion see Linda Woodhead's (2011) article "Five Concepts of Religion".

mastery of a natural language suffices; it is tailored to the *general comprehensibility* of everyday communicative practice. (360; emphasis in original)[43]

One way to capture this network of communication is to examine media discussions (Lövheim 2014).[44] Thus, in the following pages media coverage, particularly that of print media, but also online communications found in blogs and other online communications, are considered as public engagement with the issues at hand in the cases. As Knut Lundby et al. (2018) convincingly argue, an examination of the media is a key component of the assessment of religion in the public sphere.[45] The media are also important evidence of the conceptualisation of national identity (Pottie-Sherman and Wilkes 2014) and responses to social change, including migration (Bleich et al. 2015; Park 2014). But, beyond evidence, the frameworks used by the media actively construct public conversation (Gamson and Modigliani 1989).[46]

The focal cases of this book involve three public sphere sites: a municipal council chamber in Quebec, Canada, in which is displayed a crucifix and a sacred heart statue (*Saguenay*); a town hall in Vendée, France, which, every December, hosts the display of a nativity scene (*Vendée*); and the opening ritual at a municipal council in Greece, upstate New York, in the United States (*Town of Greece*). These sites are different forms of networks for communicating information and points of view. Municipal council chambers and meetings are places in which, at least in theory, citizens can interact with each other and those they have chosen to govern their communities. Town halls serve as hubs of community activity and as symbolic spaces in which information is disseminated. Even in the absence of specific activities such as meetings, the space of the town hall serves to speak to who the members of a community are.

Implicated in these spaces is the notion of "the secular", a chameleon concept that is deployed as a standard of states and their corresponding institutions, and as

43 "The public sphere is a social phenomenon just as elementary as action, actor, association, or collectivity, but it eludes the conventional sociological concepts of 'social order.' The public sphere cannot be conceived as an institution and certainly not as an organization. It is not even a framework of norms with differentiated competences and roles, membership regulations, and so on. Just as little does it represent a system; although it permits one to draw internal boundaries, outwardly it is characterized by open, permeable, and shifting horizons" (Habermas 1996, 360). Klaus Eder (2013) writes: "The public sphere is hard to define in terms of boundaries—it has in principle no limits. We can try to separate it from the private sphere; yet even here claims abound that the private is political, thus undermining a clear separation of the sites where public communication takes place from sites where private communication takes place. We can try to separate it from the economic sphere or from other spheres; yet the porosity of the boundaries is obvious. Some sites succeed better than others in keeping the public sphere outside for a time. Often such attempts collapse. Boundaries move in and out of other spheres of social life, and no definition can be given that clearly delineates either a spatial boundary (as the concept of public space insinuates) or a functional boundary (private versus public) or a thematic one (things you do not talk about, i.e. tabooed topics, and things you talk about)" (530).

44 See also Myers and Caniglia (2004).

45 See also Hjarvard (2013) and Lövheim (2014).

46 On media, see Van Dijk (1993); Bauder (2008); and Korteweg and Yurdakul (2009).

a marker of the dividing line between acceptability and problematic.[47] Secularism, or more accurately the perception of it as a dominant paradigm (despite rejoicing about the arrival of a post-secular age),[48] has arguably been one of the driving forces in the reconstitution of religious practices and symbols as culture and heritage. This book is not a plea for an enhanced secular, or an erasure of religion. Rather it considers the deployment of that term as part of the process by which heritage and culture are used to describe particular symbols and practices in the public sphere. By emphasising cultural or heritage value as being paramount, symbols or practices are able to slip behind the protective barrier of the secular, passing the threshold of the acceptable. The binary "religious/secular" erases ambiguity and displaces necessary (and often difficult) conversations in diverse societies. In other words, if it is not religious it is secular. Though majoritarian practices and symbols are most commonly transmuted this way, as we will see in Chapter 4, sometimes minority practices are reshaped to fit the secular mould. Part and parcel of this is the transposition of the particular into the universal.

The universal occupies a strange place in this process: claiming that symbols and practices represent universal values transports them into the modern framework of human rights. Once allied with that framework, they are difficult to displace. They become part of the secular package of human rights. Jonathan Boyarin and Daniel Boyarin (1993) link universalism to the character of Christianity:

> If particularism plus power tends toward fascism, then universalism plus power produces imperialism and cultural annihilation as well as, all too often, actual genocide of those who refuse to conform. Our thesis is that Judaism and Christianity, as two different hermeneutic systems for reading the Bible, generate two diametrically opposed and mirror-image forms of racism—and also two dialectical possibilities of antiracism. The genius of Christianity is its concern for all the peoples of the world; the genius of Judaism is its ability to leave other people alone. And the evils of the two systems are the precise obverse of these genii. The genies all too easily become demons. Christian universalism, even at its most liberal and benevolent, has been a powerful force for coercive discourses of sameness, denying, as we have seen, the rights of Jews, women, and others to retain their difference. (707)

The peculiar paradox, though, is that the claim to universalism vis-à-vis religious symbols and practices is used to shore up nationalist discourses of who "we" are and "our" culture and values, which is in turn a particularist endeavour. Further complicating this narrative is the role of the state as both a broker and a protector

47 See Jakobsen and Pellegrini (2008); Berlinerblau et al. (2014); Connolly (1999); Calhoun et al. (2011); Berman et al. (2013); Zuckerman and Shook (2017). Jakobsen and Pellegrini (2008) in particular argue that Christianity is folded into the conceptualisation of the secular. For an elaboration of the intersection of law and secularisation, see Sandberg (2014).

48 See Beckford (2012) for a critical analysis of the "postsecular".

of that culture and values.[49] Moreover, as we shall see, the coercive force of Christianity identified by Boyarin and Boyarin is both present and deflected in each of the cases considered. To be sure, Christianity here is covered in broad strokes and might be better articulated as "Christianities" with a view to nuancing depending on theological specificities, as well as specific social contexts including degree of diversity, economic imperatives, political opportunities.[50]

One of the imperatives attributed to secularism is the notion of state neutrality. In some cases, as in the United States, this is constitutionally enshrined, what we might call "hard neutrality". France, too, makes constitutional reference to the nature of the state in Article 1 of the constitution and in its 1905 law on the separation of church and state.[51] Canada, on the other hand, has a more complicated approach, with no formal constitutional separation or requirement for state neutrality, but according to the Supreme Court of Canada, a duty of neutrality that is unfolding through case law. This "soft neutrality" is shaped by the *Canadian Charter of Rights and Freedoms*, which Bruce Ryder (2005) argues "suggests that the Canadian state should aim to secure a religiously positive pluralism in an even-handed manner. This is best accomplished by a secular state that is neutral between religions but not neutral about religion" (177).

Each state has its own version of religious establishment, which is not necessarily reliant on constitutional imperatives:

> Establishment focuses us on the background cultural assumptions, cosmologies, anthropologies and institutions used to manage religion, as well as both internal and external religious diversity; it is historically and culturally specific, and reveals difficulties with universal multicultural and interfaith models. (Beaman and Sullivan 2013, 8)

By deeming prayer and symbols such as the crucifix "culture and heritage", the state is then called upon to protect them by virtue of their critical role in society. The conceptualisation of neutrality is inextricably linked to the configuration of the nation. In settler societies such as Canada, Australia and the United States, "all people may belong to nationalism, not all people occupy the same tense of nationalism" (Povinelli 2011, 37), meaning that the settler citizen, configured as the non-native native and the non-foreign foreigner, "differentiates, localizes and

49 Rogers Brubaker (2012) considers the relationship between nationalism and religion, arguing, "'Religion' and 'nationalism' have long been contested terms. Both terms—on almost any understanding—designate large and multidimensional fields of phenomena. Given the lack of agreement on what we are talking about when we talk about religion, or nationalism, it is no surprise that one encounters seemingly antithetical assertions about the relation between the two—for example, the assertion that nationalism is intrinsically secular, or that it is intrinsically religious; that nationalism emerged from the decline of religion, or that it emerged in a period of intensified religious feeling" (2).

50 Thank you to Leo Van Arragon and Anna Salonen for their reminders about nuance here.

51 See Blandine Chelini-Pont (2005, 612) for a history of the use of *laïcité* in the French constitution as well as an analysis of state neutrality of France. See also Koussens (2015a).

temporalizes its territorial claims by creating two distinct and contrasting categories, the native and the foreigner, locating their territorial claims in the past (native) and future (foreigner)" (37). The precise configuration of these pasts and futures varies from context to context as does the relationship between religion and nationalism (38).

Jessica Radin (2016) summarises the effect of what she describes as the "lingering love" of the state for traditions that are so clearly religious and specifically Christian in nature:

> Defending the right to belief while extending unequal, ambiguous, and often unstable protections to practices reveals the Christian character of these ghosts. Under the veiled Christian regime of many secular governments, the *de facto* requirement of religious minorities is that, at least in public, they allow their distinctions to disappear. They may believe whatever they like, but the presence of those beliefs in a material form renders them subject to examination, and sometimes legislation. (111)[52]

The potential impact of this is relatively obvious: certain groups, particularly religious minorities and the nonreligious, are excluded from the narrative of "we" in the public sphere, and as contributors to nation in the present tense, the past, and potentially the future. What is worth preserving and protecting does not belong to them and does not originate with them. To be clear, not all Christianities are welcome in this "we". It is often a specific formulation of Christianity that provides a language, symbols and framework for a particular social order.[53] Moreover, narratives of values and community circulate to reinforce boundaries of belonging. A "we" can situate itself in alignment with culture and heritage, excluding those who do not share this tradition.

Radin's analysis is insightful in its identification of the lingering effects of a belief-based understanding of religion, but I want to argue that what is at stake is more than a lingering love of tradition and pesky ghostly apparitions. Rather, the reconstitution of symbols and practices that have traditionally been associated with religion as culture and heritage is part of a larger discursive pattern that affirms majoritarian religion, in this case Christianity, as deeply intertwined with and supported by the state. Other concepts such as "residual Christianity" and "shadow establishment" also capture this notion.[54]

52 Josephson (2012) also makes this point about religious freedom when discussing the Japanese-Dutch Supplementary Treaty from 1857. The treaty "seems to represent an intensely circumscribed toleration. It guarantees a kind of religious freedom that can be expressed only in Dutch buildings and cemeteries, and thereby replicates a kind of quarantining practice. A household and funerary Christianity is limited to clearly designated sites, avoiding the exposure of Japanese subjects to contamination" (86).

53 Thank you to Leo Van Arragon for this refinement.

54 David Martin (2000) writes: "in Canada there are identifiable, though modest, hegemonies that have a link to distinct institutional churches rather than to an overall Protestant tone ... the culture most strongly attached to a distinct church is the Catholic one, but

The entanglement of the state, social institutions and religion produces a particular social and political reality, of which Elizabeth Povinelli (2011) asks "what if Christianity were not a thing but part and parcel of a set of social maneuvers within liberal democracies?" (175). The fact that Christianities are so embedded is not surprising given the history of Western democracies: the challenge is to identify the power relations that are constituted from this history. The project is not to turn Christianity into the villain of the story, but rather to ask how existing power relations constitute an impediment to social inclusion, living well together and equality. In *The Invention of Religion in Japan*, Jason Ānanda Josephson (2012) traces the creation of a secular Shinto in late nineteenth-century Japan, which enabled the state to both claim entrance into modernity, complete with official support for religious freedom, and embed Shinto in institutional frameworks. Most important, though, was its infiltration of discourse:

> It embedded an abbreviated Shinto pantheon in the official textbooks read by all Japanese school-children[55]; established a national memorial for the war dead; inserted Shinto in the very constitution of Japan; instituted Shinto as the form of Japanese public ceremonies and official holidays; and reformulated a reading of the emperor in completely Shinto terms. All of this was framed outside of religion. It even succeeded in making the argument that to be Japanese meant to be Shinto. (155)[56]

Positioned outside of religion, Shinto was able to entangle itself in the secular. This occurred while Shinto was seemingly in decline and Christianity and Western science were in ascendance.

Josephson's articulation of the transformation of Shinto is helpful here for two reasons: first, to underscore the point above that Christianity is not uniquely hegemonic and second, to offer a point of comparison and contrast to the current situation, which may be difficult to assess because we are in the midst of it. As pressure mounts both because of declining participation in formerly majoritarian religion and increasing demands by non-Christian religions for equal treatment and public space, survival mode is being invented and, like the creation of secular Shinto, the shift from religion to culture is occurring in a time of intense change, only some of which is captured by my earlier observations about the decline of

that is not initially well placed to combine institutional presence with social dominance, except in Quebec" (26–27). See Seljak (2012; 2016); Bramadat and Seljak (2013); O'Toole (2000). On the English and French contexts respectively, see Davie (2015) and Hervieu-Léger (2000).

55 Christine Cusack (2015) argues that the textbooks used by the Ethics and Religious Culture programme in Quebec schools (ERC) maintain Christianity as the standard against which all other religions and worldviews are measured. Repositioning the study of religion from a confessional to a "secular" framework results in Christianity becoming the "given" or neutral backdrop of culture and heritage.

56 There are other examples of the intertwining of particular worldviews (what some would describe as religion) and the state. See, for example, Litalien (2013) on the construction of Thai citizenship around Buddhism.

institutional religion, the increase in nonreligion and non-Christian religious diversity. There is a great temptation to make simplistic arguments and to veer toward causal links. My purpose here is to identify some of the vectors of change and some of the shifts in state and public discourse related to majoritarian religion. Christianity is not dying, nor is it likely to disappear.[57] However, increased nonreligion, increased visibility of non-Christian religion and human rights promises of equality and freedom of conscience and religion are changing the landscape significantly, prompting a reinvention of religion in western democracies that have historically been characterised by a Christian majority. The conversion of religious symbols and practices to culture and heritage (or what some have described as culturalisation[58]) is one part of that story (Beaman 2012/3).

While Christianity is part of the analysis in the pages that follow, both Josephson and Povinelli gesture to an important qualifier: social context is a key variable. Secular Shinto, as it is described by Josephson (2012), bears an uncanny resemblance to the universal Christianity that is folded into stories of "us" in contemporary cases about symbols and practices and their place in late modern societies. So too does the form of Hinduism circulating as representative of "us" under the current Indian government (Chatterji et al. 2019), or the re-nationalisation of the Russian Orthodox church (Knox 2005; Richardson and Shterin 2008). The dynamic between the nation and its religion requires a site-specific unpacking (Beaman and Sullivan 2013). At the same time, stepping back from those specifics suggests that the configuration of the boundaries of religion and culture is part of a complex social web.

What impact does the shift from religion to culture have? Why does it matter that a prayer is transmuted into a practice that is framed as being universal and inclusive of shared values? Broadly, such a move contributes to exclusionary practices in diverse societies. It does this by fabricating an entrenched vision and version of a history that belongs only to a particular segment of society, which is in turn located at the apex of a hierarchy of citizenship and belonging. At a normative level this translates into the language of "core values". But, it also has significance on another register: symbols generate powerful emotional responses that vary from person to person: one person's comfort is another's pain. Beyond the individual, symbols carry nationalist, colonial and founding people's stories (Riis and Woodhead 2010). They also mark group boundaries, signalling both exclusion and inclusion.

A critical understanding of heritage and culture examines the circumstances under which they are produced,[59] rather than seeing them as fixed entities or "truths" which stand above examination. From this perspective, heritage and

57 Christianity is, however, shrinking. See Abby Day (2017). Further, while Christianity is not dying per se, it is arguably shrinking (by traditional measures of self-identification, church attendance and participation in ritual) in the countries which are the focus of this book.

58 See Kühle et al. (2018, 123) and Ferrari (2010).

59 Drawing on Emma Waterton and Steve Watson (2013), Avi Astor et al. (2017) note the distinction between theories in heritage, focused primarily on the material management of heritage, and theories of heritage, which focus on power.

culture tell a particular narrative of who "we" are. That narrative emphasises "certain time periods, events, and narratives while obscuring others, and are connected to projects of identity formation and nation building" (Astor et al. 2017, 128). These narratives carry a particular weight when they are reproduced in social institutions such as education or law. They shape reality (Amsterdam and Bruner 2000).

The cases discussed in the following chapters trace a pattern of the fabrication of culture and heritage from majoritarian religious practices and symbols and map their shape in public discourse and law.[60] Some of the markers of that pattern include:

1 The constitution of a religious practice or symbol as culture and heritage in need of protection (by the state) and defence (by citizens);
2 An identification of and reliance on shared values to justify the continuation of the practice or presence of the symbol;
3 Pronouncements on the nature of the society in question;
4 An insistence on the universality of the message being conveyed by the symbol or practice;
5 A convoluted interpretation of state neutrality that positions the protection of human rights and culture and heritage against each other: "the state must protect religious freedom, but ... not at the cost of culture and heritage";
6 A subtext of a radical other (who takes the shape of the atheist/heathen or the Muslim) who is a threat to the precious heritage under attack.

These markers appear both within the confines of the legal decisions themselves as well as in the public discussion about the cases. The Saint-Sacrement hospital story that began this chapter acts as an entry point to this discussion of religion and culture. In many ways, there is nothing particularly unique about it; rather, it is simply one of many such stories. The hospital's decision to remove the crucifix, prompted by a patient complaint, was in keeping with the secular function of the hospital. The hospital board discussed the possibility that because no one chooses to spend time in a hospital, they are not there voluntarily and that patients were especially vulnerable.

In his essay, "From Mirroring to World-Making: Research as Future Forming", Kenneth Gergen (2015) argues that social scientists need to "replace the captivating gaze on the world as it is with value based explorations into what it could be" (287). Building on Gergen's insight, I argue that the court decisions (and instances like the Saint-Sacrement hospital controversy), the public discussion about them and the media coverage surrounding them contain two primary narratives: one is the future forming and the other past preserving. The words of

60 By identifying a practice as "religious" I am not endorsing a religious essence or fixed categorisation; rather, it is undeniable that prayer or a crucifix, for example, have been primarily constructed as being associated with religion. It is admittedly difficult to avoid essentialising religion and while I have tried to avoid doing so, I am aware that I have not entirely succeeded nor is it possible to completely move outside of the bounded categories of culture or religion.

judges, citizens and the media contain traces of both of these narratives, integrating a vision of the world as it should be. Following Gergen and moving beyond the "captivating gaze" he criticises, in a world characterised by a new diversity (superdiversity,[61] multiculturalism,[62] the global[63]), it is the future forming narrative that embraces this new reality, and which necessitates a revised power structure and reconfigured social relations that move horizontally rather than vertically. If the goal is to live well together, and the process is a "world of becoming" in which it is "imperative to negotiate new connections between nontheistic constituencies who care about the future of the Earth and numerous devotees of diverse religious traditions who fold positive spiritualties into their creedal practices" (Connolly 2013, 41; Connolly 2011), the future forming narrative holds the most promise for human flourishing.[64]

Living well together is a conceptual move inspired by Jacques Derrida and is intended to speak back to the bare "vivre ensemble" imperative. In his essay "Avowing—The Impossible: 'Returns,' Repentance, and Reconciliation", Derrida (2013) reflects on the idea of living together and transposes it into a more generous conceptualisation that broadens its scope:

> If "living together" then means "living *well* together," this signifies understanding one another in trust, in good faith, in faith, comprehending one another, in a word, being in *accord* with one another. Why then speak of accord? Why this language of the heart [*coeur*], of accord and concord, even of "mercy [*miséricorde*]," and of the compassion that must bring us closer and a bit more quickly to the question of "forgiveness," with or without *teshuvah*? The language of the heart reminds us that this peace of "living together," even if it is a peace of justice and equity, is not necessarily under the law of the

61 Steven Vertovec (2007) argues that contemporary diversity in complex societies requires a new conceptualisation of diversity beyond ethnicity. The new variables include "differential immigration statuses and their concomitant entitlements and restrictions of rights, divergent labour market experiences, discrete gender and age profiles, patterns of spatial distribution, and mixed local area responses by service providers and residents. Rarely are these factors described side by side. The interplay of these factors is what is meant here, in summary fashion, by the notion of 'super-diversity'" (1025). See also Vertovec (2019), Meissner and Vertovec (2015) and Becci et al. (2017). For a discussion and critique of super-diversity, see Crul (2016). Deirdre Meintel (2016) argues that "the long presence of complex diversity makes 'super-diversity' seem not quite so new as it appears in Europe" (25).

62 For a discussion on multiculturalism see Joppke (2004); Vertovec and Wessendorf (2010); and Williams (2009). For information related to interculturalism see Bouchard (2011); and Rocher and White (2014).

63 See Peter Beyer (2013).

64 Though the seeds of this model were planted by Zygmunt Bauman's (2011) *Culture in a Liquid Modern World*, particularly his identification of the horizontal and vertical nature of cultural relations and his articulation of the three phases of contact, assimilation and the new diversity of the present, there is much in my model that he might disagree with, especially my identification of multiculturalism as playing a positive, future forming role.

> law, at least in the sense of legality, of law [*droit*] (national or international) or of the political contract. (25–26; emphasis in original)

Living well together requires a critical engagement with difference and privilege and a remapping of the boundaries of "us". Majoritarian religious symbols and practices present an important site of negotiation for that remapping in the context of a new diversity that sees institutional Christian religion declining, increased presence of migrant religions, strengthened indigenous voices in many contexts and nonreligious populations increasing at unprecedented rates.

As with any ideal type, the conceptualisations of the narratives must be understood as conceptual maps rather than facts. On the ground, everyday life is much more textured. Nonetheless, the narratives are helpful guides in sorting through the story lines and normative assumptions that weave through the cases, the media and the public conversations.[65] I have summarised the elements of these two narratives in Table 1.1.

The narratives do not exist in pure form in day-to-day life, nor can they be attributed to any one group. Members of majorities embrace the future forming narrative and minorities sometimes implement or support vertical strategies. Moreover, social

Table 1.1

Narratives	*Past preserving*	*Future forming*
Social relations	Vertical	Horizontal
Conceptualisation of religion	Culture and heritage; tradition	New diversity; one among many worldviews
Rhetoric	Foundational	Emergent; becoming
Future	Pluralism; intercultural; clear boundaries; us/them	Diversity; multicultural; superdiverse
Equality	Formal; accommodation; tolerance	Substantive; deep; textured; context-specific
Key words	Our values; universal; immigrants fit in	Respect; context; welcome
Impact	Minimised (trivial), particularised (one individual), no complaint	Significant harm to self and others
Other	Radical; draconian; hypersensitive; different	Belonging, similarity
State	Benevolent neutrality	Neutrality
Strategy	Assimilation, social cohesion	Inclusion

65 On the importance of narrative in law, see Berger (2015), Cover (1983), and Ewick and Silbey (1998). Benjamin Berger (2015) notes: "Like an individual's life story, the historical narrative that frames law's perception and reception of all events is the entirety of its past" (58).

actors are complex: interests, values, commitments make for varied approaches and strategies. Taken together, though, the decisions, media coverage and public conversations reveal patterns in expectations about the role of the state, citizens and a vision of how society should function. Traces of the narratives manifest through the submissions to the courts and tribunals, in the decisions themselves, in media coverage and in public discussions and debates. Elements of the narratives are linked and build on each other—the future cannot cleanly break from the past and the past is only constructed from the future.[66] For instance, the success of the preservation narrative is dependent on the reconfiguration of religion as culture and heritage, which serves as the foundation for state action, justifies continued vertical cultural relations and configures a rationalised hierarchy in which freedom of religion is one of many rights but from which culture is exempt. How are prayer, a crucifix and a sacred heart statue constituted as culture and heritage?

A brief methodological note is necessary: different kinds of information or evidence are available through the cases, public discussion and media. In the following pages, I draw from various levels of proceedings, including administrative tribunals, appeal processes and high court decisions. The fact of losing or winning the case is largely irrelevant for my purposes, though certainly not for the parties involved. I am interested in the discursive framing of the prayer and artefacts, not the law's logic. The cases are drawn upon to illustrate the different ways that the parties understand and frame what is at stake. Each quotation indicates the source of the information (*Tribunal, Court of Appeal–CA*, or *Supreme Court of Canada–SCC*, for example). The three cases are not meant to be fully comparable: one is about symbols and prayer, one about a symbol and the third about prayer. I could have chosen any number of cases, particularly in the United States where these issues over symbols have repeatedly arisen as "establishment" cases. Rather, I use the cases as heuristic devices to consider the ways that majoritarian religion retains privilege in the context of a new diversity.

The decision to remove the crucifix in the Saint-Sacrement hospital and to return it to the Sisters of Charity triggered a public debate that characterises the tension between two narratives of living together. One is characterised by the retention of a majoritarian vision that folds in religious practices as tradition and heritage, accords a special place to groups who are mythologised as foundational and maintains a vision of the future as pluralism into which those who are not part of those foundational groups must fit. In this narrative, the state has a duty to protect minorities, but only to the extent that that protection does not threaten the foundational myth and the groups accorded credit for its creation. Culture and heritage thus trump minority religious expression. At the citizen level, reasonable accommodation has become the guiding principle for sorting out difference. Within this narrative, relationships retain their vertical character. An alternative

66 Thank you to Christian Polke for this insight offered during his comments at the *Religious Freedom and the Varieties of Religious Establishment* workshop held at the Göttingen Institute for Advanced Study in the Humanities and Social Sciences in Göttingen, Germany in 2017.

narrative responds differently to the new diversity, which includes both immigrant newcomers, previously excluded groups (in Canada this highlights Indigenous peoples) and the nonreligious. The state in this narrative has a duty to implement a strategy of neutrality that opens space for the presence of minority groups, which sometimes means shifting practices and the organisation of the public sphere. Citizens practise deep equality in their everyday lives, and relationships are horizontal rather than vertical (Beaman 2014; 2017).[67] Though these narratives are ideal types, they can be traced through the cases and the public discussion surrounding them. It is to those that we now turn.

67 Bauman's (2011) vertical and horizontal analogy is developed by a number of authors. For example, Richard Park (2016) refers to a vertical and horizontal dimension of civility; Whitney Bauman (2015) suggests a vertical and horizontal way of charting theology where the vertical focuses on God and the horizontal on nature; Hans Peter Hansen et al. (2016) refer to horizontal and vertical aspects of democracy; John Urry (2010) understands mobility as horizontal rather than vertical; and Maggie O'Neill (2010) frames success as horizontal rather than vertical.

2 Praying for good governance

> The story of the suddenly vocal Saint-Sacrement crucifix, it turns out, cannot be understood without some knowledge of its surroundings. Someone, an unidentified patient of unnamed religious or nonreligious pedigree, had complained about the crucifix. After discussing the matter thoroughly, taking into account the diversity of its patients, the fact that people do not choose to be in a hospital, and consulting the province's human rights code, the hospital board decided to remove the crucifix. It was following this removal that the crucifix began to speak, or perhaps more accurately, to shout ... loudly. Though speaking in a different register, once one was attuned to it, the crucifix had lots to say. And it was not alone. A chorus of like-minded voices was contributing to the cacophony—not only in Canada, but in Germany, Italy, France ... Some had even made court appearances, subjecting themselves to assessments of their pedigree, quality and conformity to the dictates of religious fashion. In a crushingly humiliating moment, one crucifix, thanks to a complaint by an atheist named Alain Simoneau, was found to fall short of canonical standards for a proper crucifix.

Though part of a broader trend related to majoritarian religious symbols mentioned in Chapter 1, the Saint-Sacrement crucifix incident is encased in the specificities of the Canadian province of Quebec's historical narrative. The decision of the hospital board and the public reactions to it reference ongoing debates about nationalism, diversity, citizenship, racism, multiculturalism and religion in that province that are too numerous and complex to fully describe here. These currents are rendered more complicated by the fact that scholarship is contradictory and history, as always, partial.

Religion in Quebec

Of particular note is the historical dominance of the Catholic Church in Quebec society and social institutions.[1] Quebec had what was arguably the strongest

1 Quebec is unique in that "unlike many European countries, it never had an established church paid for directly through taxes; unlike the rest of North America, it never developed a pattern of voluntary denominationalism" (Kaell 2017, 9).

religious establishment of any Canadian province.[2] This is often told as a story of oppression in contemporary accounts, described as the *Grande Noirceur*, which ended with the Quiet Revolution in the 1960s and 1970s.[3] However, there are more nuanced renderings of this history that point, among other things, to the progressive role the church played in many instances.[4] Ultimately, though, in either account, the Catholic Church remains a persistent presence in Quebec society. Though few attend church regularly, 75 per cent of the total population of Quebec's 7.7 million residents identify as Catholic (6.3 million identify as Christian).[5] Catholic symbols are ubiquitous in public institutions: until July 9, 2019, a crucifix was displayed in the main legislative house and chamber (the Salon Bleu in the National Assembly).[6] The crucifix is also displayed in many hospitals, city halls and universities. The famous cross on Mont Royal, the Frederick law Olmstead designed public park, looms over the city of Montreal.[7] Geneviève Zubrzycki (2016) observes that despite its fall from grace in the Quiet Revolution, religious heritage is now being "enshrined as a collective good, and resacralized through the notion of cultural patrimony" (168). In an attempt to inform and educate a public that no longer practises religion, the state launched awareness campaigns, posting large banners on religious sites whose preservation was funded and justified by the state under the slogan, "Our cultural patrimony, it's sacred!" (168). This resacralized religion (which, as we will see shortly is not limited to Catholicism or Quebec) and renewed Christian identity is especially embraced by the radical right, which, as Joppke (2018) observes, is not evidence of religious fervour, but is inspired by anti-Muslim sentiment (237).

2 For more detailed discussions of this, see, for example, Baum (2000), Gauvreau (2005), Seljak (1996, 2000) and Simpson (2000). Hillary Kaell (2015) notes: "Though never an established church, Catholicism (especially in rural areas) was fully imbricated in civil society—in healthcare, education, and local politics—providing an institutional counterpoint to the Anglo-Protestant control of macro affairs such as the federal parliament, army, and economy" (104).

3 For an excellent overview of Quebec history that takes a multidimensional approach see John Dickinson and Brian Young (2008).

4 Lefebvre and Breton (2011) and Gauvreau (2005). See especially Meunier (2016).

5 See Statistics Canada's (2011) National Household Survey. Sarah Wilkins-Laflamme (2017) notes "Catholic identity, not to be mistaken for actual ties with the Catholic Church, is still seen as the 'default' affiliation option among many Quebecois: an important aspect of group identity that maintains a link with culture and family tradition" (169). As Kaell (2017) points out, "weekly church attendance [in Quebec] went from 88 per cent in the 1960s to less than 15 per cent today—by far the lowest in North America" (13).

6 *The Star* (Valiante 2019). Out of 125 Members of the National Assembly, 103 voted to remove the crucifix from the National Assembly, which had been in place since 1936 (CTV News Montreal 2019). This is in odd contrast to the unanimous vote, 10 years previously, to keep it. The crucifix will apparently be displayed in another part of the legislature.

7 The presence of such symbols, though, is not without debate and controversy. See Radio-Canada (2017a) and *HuffPost* (Levesque 2019).

Paradoxically, Quebec remains a leader in Canada for access to reproductive services including abortion[8] and the "morning after" pill,[9] its birth rate one of the lowest in the world (Kaell 2017, 11) and cohabitation rather than marriage rates are the second highest in the country.[10] Further, official and public discourse persistently describes Quebec as a "laïque" society.[11] Though slower to move in the nonreligion direction, Brian Clarke and Stuart Macdonald's (2017) analysis of census data suggest that Quebec too will soon have a significant proportion of the population abandon Roman Catholicism as an identity.[12]

Immigration, which is debated in the context of nationalism and identity contests (Barker 2010, 12) adds another dimension to the picture of Quebec and the shape of diversity there. Most immigrants who arrived in Quebec between 2005 and 2014 came from Algeria and France as well as other French speaking countries (Ministère de l'Immigration, de la Diversité et de l'Inclusion 2016a, 26). Data from 2011 shows that only 37.3 per cent of these immigrants were Catholic; 17.1 per cent were Muslim and 14.7 per cent had no religion (Ministère de l'Immigration, de la Diversité et de l'Inclusion 2015, 9). Most recently, Quebec has assumed an important role in Canada's commitment to accelerating receipt of Syrian refugees: Quebec has received the second highest number of Syrians in Canada overall, and Montreal has received the most non-government sponsored refugees.[13]

8 Quebec has the second highest abortion rates in Canada, behind only Ontario. In 2017, there were 22,966 abortions in Quebec (Abortion Rights Coalition of Canada 2019). Quebec has "the greatest overall access to abortion providers and care" (Reid n.d.). Kozlowska et al. (2016) note that this liberal approach "is the product of a long political struggle, which took place after decades of highly restrictive and punitive abortion policies backed by the Catholic Church" (835).

9 British Columbia was the first province to grant independent prescriptive authority to pharmacists in 2000, followed by Quebec in 2001 (Soon et al. 2004, 23).

10 Benoît Laplante (2014) reported in 2006 that over half of children born in Quebec were from unmarried parents: "Cohabitation is more widespread in Quebec than in the rest of Canada since at least the middle of the 1980s and more common as a way to enter the first union" (261). Approximately 39 per cent of Quebec couples live in common-law (Statistics Canada 2017). The only province or territory to have more common-law families is Nunavut (48 per cent) (Statistics Canada 2017).

11 For information regarding the unique aspects of Quebec laïcité, see Baubérot (2008), Koussens (2013; 2015a) and Milot (2002, 2005, 2013). Interestingly, there is very little research on nonreligion in Quebec: see Johnston (2012), LeDrew (2013) and Wilkins-Laflamme (2016).

12 Clarke and Macdonald's (2017) thorough analysis of religious participation in Quebec suggests that, while lagging behind in terms of nonreligious identity, Quebec will soon catch up with the rest of Canada: "Of the 937,545 Quebecers with No Religion, one-third of them (some 336,110 in all) are between the ages of twenty-five and forty-four. These Quebecers are in the prime age group for raising children, and it is very likely that their children will be raised without religion. So those Catholics who have switched to become Nones will be joined by those who never had religion" (205).

13 Quebec has received 5,674 Syrian Refugees (from November 4, 2015 to July 31, 2016), second in number only to Ontario (Government of Canada 2016; 2017; Ministère de l'Immigration, de la Diversité et de l'Inclusion 2016b).

Three related developments are especially pertinent to understanding the context in which the crucifix and prayers are transformed into culture and heritage: First, in order to appear to be adequately publically managing the newcomers, the state has initiated a series of bills that purport to regulate especially the wearing of religious symbols in the public sphere. Though the bills do not ostensibly target specific religious groups, there is a disproportionate impact on Muslims, Sikhs and Jews. Bill 94 was introduced in March 2010,[14] Bill 60 in November, 2013[15] and Bill 62[16] in 2015. The latter was enacted into law on October 18, 2017, and states that "[p]ersonnel members of a [public] body must exercise their functions with their face uncovered. Similarly, persons who request a service from a personnel member of a [public] body [...] must have their face uncovered when the service is provided".[17] Discussion of the bills has occupied a great deal of public space in the past decade and have generated not only debate, but also open hostility toward religious minorities.[18] These bills have served to function as an ongoing reminder of religious difference and to keep alive divisive public debates.[19] Rarely is the religious character of the host

14 Bill 94 was entitled "An Act to establish guidelines governing accommodation requests within the Administration and certain institutions." This bill called for the ban on the wearing of the niqab and emphasised "un visage découvert" or "naked face" when public service was provided or received in Quebec. See Pascale Fournier and Erica See (2014) for their argument that the bill effectively extended the public sphere and disproportionately impacted Muslim women.

15 The full title of Bill 60 was the "Charter affirming the values of State secularism and religious neutrality and of equality between women and men, and providing a framework for accommodation requests." This bill proposed to ban civil servants from wearing religious symbols—turbans, kippas, head scarves, burkas, and large crosses—while at work. For a critical analysis of the so-called "Charter of Values", see Amiraux et al. (2014) and Beaman and Smith (2016).

16 Bill 62 is known as "An Act to foster adherence to State religious neutrality and, in particular, to provide a framework for requests for accommodations on religious grounds in certain bodies." The bill seeks to "foster adherence to State religious neutrality" (p. 2).

17 See R-26.2.01, Section 10. The purpose of the Act is, among other things to impose "a duty of religious neutrality, in particular on personnel members of public bodies in the exercise of the functions of office [...] A further purpose of the Act is to recognize the importance of having one's face uncovered when public services are provided and received so as to ensure quality communication between persons and allow their identity to be verified, and for security purposes [...] The Act also sets out criteria to be taken into consideration when dealing with requests for accommodations on religious grounds resulting from the application of the Charter of human rights and freedoms (chapter C-12)" (R-26.2.01 2018).

18 Incidents include the reinforcement of negative stereotypes of Muslims (*Montreal Gazette*, Solyom 2015); verbal harassment (*National Post*, Hamilton 2013); and physical violence (*Global News*, Adam 2014). In addition, the murder of six Muslims at a Quebec mosque in January, 2017 (*Montreal Gazette*, Riga 2017).

19 During the same time as Quebec was vetting various bills related to religious clothing, the federal government was engaging in parallel actions: it issued a directive that banned people from taking the oath of citizenship while wearing a face covering on December 12, 2011 (Immigration, Refugees and Citizenship Canada Operational Bulletin 359). This directive was struck down in *Ishaq v. Canada (Citizenship and Immigration)*, 2015 FC 156, aff'd in 2015 FCA 151. The federal government also

society discussed, and when it is it takes the shape of culture and heritage, as we see in the "exemption" provided for in Bill 62, which is now law. Immediately after it became law, Bill 62 was the subject of a legal challenge on the basis of its violation of the equality guarantees of both the Quebec and Canadian Charters of Rights and Freedoms. Consequently, the Superior Court of Quebec suspended the face covering law[20] until proper guidelines[21] had been developed to address requests for accommodation. In more recent developments, the Premier of Quebec, François Legault, introduced Bill 21, *An Act Respecting the Laicity of the State*, on March 28, 2019, in another attempt to ban religious face coverings. Bill 21 was passed into law on June 16, 2019 (The Canadian Press 2019).[22]

The second contextualising factor that shapes the understanding of current discussions of religion and culture is the Bouchard-Taylor Commission. In 2007, the government formed a commission to:

> a) take stock of accommodation practices in Québec; b) analyse the attendant issues bearing in mind the experience of other societies; c) conduct an extensive consultation on this topic; and d) formulate recommendations to the government to ensure that accommodation practices conform to Québec's values as a pluralistic, democratic, egalitarian society. (Bouchard and Taylor 2008, 17)

introduced Bill C-75, the "Oath of Citizenship Act", on June 19, 2015. This bill would have banned the wearing of the niqab in citizenship ceremonies, but did not successfully pass through the House of Commons.

20 The Superior Court of Quebec suspended the law for a second time before it came into effect on July 1, 2018 (*CBC News*, Shingler 2018). In its decision, the Court concluded "[i]rreparable harm will be caused to Muslim women as of July 1st, 2018, if the stay is not granted [...]" (*National Council of Canadian Muslims (NCCM) c. Attorney General of Québec*, 2018 QCCS 2766, at para 80).

21 The guidelines have since been released by the Quebec Government and state: For a request for an accommodation to be granted, the body must ensure that each of the following criteria is met: "1. The request results from the application of section 10 of the Charter (discrimination) [...]; 2. The request is serious (sincerely held belief) [...]; 3. The accommodation requested is consistent with the right to equality of women and men and the right of every person to be treated without discrimination [...]; 4. The accommodation requested is consistent with the principle of State religious neutrality [...]; 5. The accommodation is reasonable [...]; 6. The person making the request has cooperated in seeking a solution that meets the criterion of reasonableness." (Government of Quebec 2018, 9–13).

22 Compliance with the ban on religious symbols introduced by Bill 21 is not, however, guaranteed. The Mayor of Côte Saint-Luc, Mitchell Brownstein, said the city would "stand against" the ban on the public display of religious symbols (CBC News 2019a). Similarly, the city of Montreal voted unanimously to oppose Bill 21 (*Montreal Gazette*, Scott 2019). According to a recent Leger poll, approximately 66 per cent of Quebecers are either "somewhat in favour" or "strongly in favour" of "a ban on wearing obvious religious symbols for civil servants in a position of authority" (Leger 2019, 13). However, more than 60 per cent of Anglophones in Quebec say people in positions of authority in Quebec should be permitted to wear religious symbols (The Association for Canadian Studies 2019).

Co-led by well-known nationalist and Quebec sociologist Gérard Bouchard, and internationally influential philosopher Charles Taylor, the commission held public meetings in 15 regions in Quebec and eventually received some 900 submissions. Though the mandate was broader than a focus on religion, it was ultimately religion and religious minorities that became the central topic of discussion. Quebec was not unique in this exercise: Europeans were also engrossed in political debates about national identity, values and social cohesion.[23]

The final report of the commission, entitled *Building the Future: A Time for Reconciliation*, offered recommendations designed to address the issue of how to "*vivre ensemble*" in an era of diversity. One of the recommendations (found in the section on "secularism"), suggested the removal of the crucifix on the wall of the main legislative body of the province, the National Assembly, in the "name of both the separation of the State and churches and State neutrality" (Bouchard and Taylor 2008, 260). The same recommendation suggested that the practice of saying prayers at municipal council meetings should also stop for the same reasons.[24]

When the report was released on May 22, 2008, the National Assembly made the following unanimous resolution to keep the crucifix:

> THAT the National Assembly reiterate its desire to promote the language, history, culture and values of the Québec nation, foster the integration of each person into our nation in a spirit of openness and reciprocity, and express its attachment to our religious and historic heritage represented particularly by the crucifix in our Blue Room and our coat of arms adorning our institutions.[25]

The resolution, it is notable, contains the language of culture and history and quite clearly links these to the project of "the nation".[26] As Solange Lefebvre and Guillaume St-Laurent (2018) note in their remarks on the occasion of the tenth anniversary of the Commission, debates that were central to the report continue to be live issues in Quebec today. For example, in an opinion piece on the a recent round of public debate about the crucifix, Toula Drimonis (2018) wrote: "I'm not sure what kind of cognitive dissonance is required to claim, as incoming Quebec premier François Legault recently did, that the crucifix represents Christian values without being a religious symbol, but I'm guessing an ungodly amount."

23 See Barker (2010, 12) and Lefebvre and Brodeur (2017).
24 For academic discussions related to the Bouchard-Taylor commission, see: Adelman and Anctil (2011), Bosset (2009), Côté (2008), Gauderault-DesBiens (2016), Lefebvre (2008; 2017) and Rousseau (2012).
25 This motion was later used by the Court of Appeal of Quebec in justifying the retention of religious symbols in public spaces.
26 Though public hearings were also conducted in relation to Bill 60, the Bouchard-Taylor Commission hearings and report were far more extensive and have had lasting reverberations in Quebec, including solidifying the language of reasonable accommodation as the framework within which to assess disputes about minority requests for equality. See Barras (2016) for a discussion of the impact of the discourse of request.

A third development that shapes the discussion about religious symbols in the public sphere is the transformation of the education system to end confessional schools and to implement a mandatory course on ethics and values. In 1997 the Quebec government ended the confessional system that had been in place since 1887 and struck a commission headed by Jean-Pierre Proulx to reconfigure the new non-confessional system. In 1999 a new linguistically based system was implemented and eventually the Protestant, Catholic and "general" moral education courses were replaced by a mandatory Ethics and Religious Culture course[27] that was to be taken by all students at all levels in both private and public schools.[28] The course begins with the premise that Catholicism and Protestantism are foundational:

> This program devotes special attention to the religious heritage of our society. The historical and cultural importance of Catholicism and Protestantism in Quebec is especially highlighted, while Judaism and native spirituality, which have also marked this heritage, are also covered, along with other religious and spiritual traditions that contribute to present-day Quebec culture and that inspire different ways of thinking, being and acting. (Ministère de l'Éducation et de l'Enseignement supérieur n.d.)

Recalling Josephson's genealogy of the creation of secular Shinto and its integration and naturalisation into Japanese culture, the education system is key in reconstituting religion as culture, heritage and foundational.[29]

Perhaps, though, the greatest shadow cast over the Saint-Sacrement incident was the *Saguenay* case, which, though it originated in Quebec, resonated across all of Canada.

The decision

> It was a hot July evening in 2009 and Alain Simoneau returned to his newly cleaned truck at the local car wash to go home and pick up his kids to take them for an ice cream. As he opened the door to get in he noticed something on the passenger side seat. On closer examination he realized that someone had left several small wooden crosses emblazoned with "Simoneau, the converted one," "Simoneau, the Catholic," "the citizen first" on them.[30] He sighed. It was one more incident in a series of harassing phone calls and shunning behaviour he had experienced since he had complained about the crucifix and the sacred heart statue in the council chamber of the city hall. He had also been vocal about his objection to the prayer the mayor insisted

27 See Berger (2013a) for a discussion of the role of education in the religion–law relationship. For a discussion on religion and education, see also Estivalèzes and Lefebvre (2012), Bouchard and Daniel (2010), Bouchard and Pierre (2006), Caron (2010) and Gravel and Lefebvre (2012).
28 See Boudreau (2011) for a detailed discussion of this history.
29 See Lefebvre (2009).
30 *Simoneau v. Tremblay* [2011] *QCTDP 1*, at para 53. Hereinafter "*Saguenay Tribunal*".

> on saying at the beginning of each meeting. An avowed atheist, Alain didn't think it was appropriate to have such religious symbols and rituals associated with a governing body like a municipal council. His complaints, which were now before the Quebec Human Rights Tribunal, had unleashed a maelstrom of public debate, some of which had not been particularly pleasant.
>
> As is the case with such legal battles, Alain's personal history became part of the evidence. His sincerity as an atheist, or "sincerity of non-belief" was uncontested. Though he had been a member of the Catholic Church, he left at age 14 and had actively taken steps to renounce his membership by sending a declaration of apostasy to his local diocese. He refused to have his first child baptized, relented when his second child was born and, in his words, had since regretted that decision. He ensured that his children were exempted from religion class at school.

The case of Alain Simoneau and his complaint against the City of Saguenay began when he asked the mayor to stop reciting the prayer in December 2006. Prior to reciting the prayer, the mayor[31] made the sign of the cross and said, "In the name of the Father, the Son and the Holy Spirit." Mayor Tremblay refused Alain Simoneau's request and continued his practice of saying the prayer at each council meeting. In March 2007—one month after the Quebec government established the Bouchard-Taylor Commission—the Mouvement Laïque Québécois (Quebec Secular Movement), an atheist activist group in Quebec, filed a complaint on his behalf with the Quebec Human Rights Commission.[32] The complaint also mentioned the presence of a crucifix and a sacred heart statue in the council chambers.

Ignoring the complaint about the crucifix and the statue, the Commission affirmed the validity of objection to the prayer, but declined to proceed further. Legally, Mr Simoneau had the right to continue with the complaint on his own, which he did. In the meantime, the City Council changed the wording of the prayer to make it more "neutral".[33] At the 2011 Tribunal hearing the City took the position that the prayer and the crucifix were not religious, but part of the heritage and culture of the City (and of Quebec). The City also claimed that the crucifix, statue and the prayer embodied universal values. The state, they claimed, had a duty to protect the practice of prayer and the artefacts. Numerous witnesses were called to support this position. Ultimately, the Tribunal rejected the City's

31 At the time the complaint was filed the prayer read: *O God, eternal and almighty, from Whom all power and wisdom flow, we are assembled here in Your presence to ensure the good of our city and its prosperity. We beseech You to grant us the enlightenment and energy necessary for our deliberations to promote the honour and glory of Your holy name and the spiritual and material happiness of our city. Amen.*

32 Commission des droits de la personne et des droits de la jeunesse (or the "CDPDJ").

33 The more "neutral" prayer read as follows: *Almighty God, we thank You for the many favours that You have granted Saguenay and its citizens, including freedom, opportunities for development and peace. Guide us in our deliberations as members of the municipal council and help us to be well aware of our duties and responsibilities. Grant us the wisdom, knowledge and understanding that will enable us to preserve the advantages that our city enjoys, so that everyone can benefit from them and we can make wise decisions. Amen.*

argument and held that the prayer and artefacts had religious meaning and Mr Simoneau had been discriminated against:

> The reciting of a prayer and the exhibiting of religious symbols in the state-controlled space constituted by the meetings of the municipal council, where representatives of the people discuss questions of public interest, also have a non-trivial exclusionary effect that substantially stigmatizes people who do not share those values. (*Saguenay Tribunal*, at para 251)

The City appealed to the Court of Appeal of Quebec, which agreed that the prayer and artefacts should be protected under a principle of benevolent neutrality.[34] The Court of Appeal cited the *Lautsi* decision from Italy with approval and the decision mirrors it in tone and approach. The matter was further appealed to the Supreme Court of Canada, in what became the *Saguenay* decision,[35] which agreed with the Tribunal and found that the recitation of the prayer violated Mr Simoneau's rights. Though the Court pointedly noted that the state cannot hide behind "the guise" of culture and heritage to justify privileging religion, it also preserved the possibility that some religious practices and symbols could be protected as culturally important. The Court itself seemed to be caught between the two narratives of living together. The characterisation of the prayer and symbols as culture captures the tension between these visions of who "we" are and by extension who we are not.

Our culture

When I presented a version of this work at a conference in the spring of 2017, an audience member put up her hand to ask me a question. She began by identifying herself as being from Quebec and then said in a somewhat insistent tone "this *is* my culture and heritage, so how do I fit into your research?"[36] At the end of that same month, I was again presenting on another aspect of the research and in the question period that followed an audience member identifying herself as a theologian, insisted "but the crucifix *is* a symbol of love and compassion". Her point was that those who thought otherwise were simply misinterpreting it. Both of these people were resistant to an interpretation of the crucifix as multi-dimensional, as potentially symbolic of religion, oppression, pain, hurt, or, perhaps even worse for both of them, as a meaningless and unnecessary decoration that has no place in a hospital or a council chamber. Each insisted that she had the truth about

34 For a discussion of various state approaches to religion, including benevolent neutrality, see Durham (2013).

35 *Mouvement laïque québécois v. Saguenay (City)*, 2015 SCC 16, [2015] 2 S.C.R. 3. Hereinafter "*Saguenay SCC*".

36 "Economic protectionism and political independence are no longer powerful mobilizers of Quebec identity. But cultural autonomy is. In a 2013 survey, 86 per cent of Quebecers stated that 'Quebec culture needs protection'" (Peker 2017).

the crucifix and both visions clung to a tradition-preserving narrative that asserts a hierarchy to which attaches privilege.[37]

In *Saguenay*, the mayor, members of the public and the Court of Appeal reproduced a construction of the crucifix as a crucial element of a shared history that is virtually uncontested and incontestable. Inextricably tied up with identity, a "we" who is foundational, the crucifix and prayer became part of a story of nation and peoples, reminiscent of the role of Shinto in Japan identified by Josephson in the last chapter.[38] A media statement by the mayor, Jean Tremblay, illustrates this point: "For me, a Tremblay from Saguenay-Lac-St-Jean, a French-Canadian Catholic, a Quebecer—for me, it's the basis of our culture here"; and "If we let go of everything that distinguishes us, where will French-Canadians be in a few years?"[39] We hear the anxiety in Tremblay's voice, one which directly relates to identity and its preservation in a perceived sea of diversity. Geneviève Zubrzycki (2016) argues that Quebec is undergoing a crisis of pluralism, which Astor et al. (2017) identify as creating the possibility of "special traction" for religion as heritage: "Under such circumstances, religion is often recast as culture, facilitating the appeal of religiously inflected identitarian discourses among both religiously observant and nonobservant segments of the populace" (129).[40] Marian Burchardt (2017) elaborates, observing that: "religious diversity has engendered numerous institutional challenges for nation-states: inherited church-state regimes need to be

37 Geneviève Zubrzycki (2016) identifies the range of possibilities for meaning related to icons "as collective representations, as embodiments of ideals and narratives to which the icon gives material form, and as clusters of materials with their own manifold attributes, each of which affords (or constrains) social actors' repertories of potential actions" (22).

38 On the intersections of Quebecois identity and national ideology, the Larochelle Report stated: "L'Eglise Catholique, comme institution social et religieuse, a été rapidement marginalisée après la Deuxième Guerre mondiale; le processus s'est accéléré avec les années 1960. En peu de temps, au regard de l'histoire, l'Église catholique a perdu une bonne partie de son statut et de sa crédibilité. Pourtant, c'est elle qui, a partir du milieu du 19e siècle jusqu'aux années 1940, avait édifié et maintenu l'idéologie du people candien-français et en avait fait une société avec une identité spécifique et profondément religieuse. À ce point qu'on peut dire qu'elle a été une Église nationale et une religion ethnique" (Langevin 1992, 79). The Report is a comprehensive account of the status of Catholicism in Quebec.

39 Canadian Press (2011).

40 "The radical conclusion of the Larochelle Report is that the Catholic Church in Quebec is dying. The report documents the continuing decline of membership in the parishes, the ageing of these communities, the almost complete disaffection of the young, the shrinking numbers of priests, the gradual disappearance of religious congregations, and the shattered self-image of the parishes overwhelmed by a feeling of powerlessness (Larochelle Commission 1992, 17–23). There is evidence that even the Catholics who continue to go to church have only a vague idea of what being a Catholic means and that they are unable to put into words what they really believe. The report concludes that unless the Quebec Church introduces a new pastoral approach, it will disappear altogether. With its back against the wall, the Church must 'risquer l'avenir,' risk its future by embarking upon a radically new path" (Baum 2000, 159).

revisited and reformed so as to enable the incorporation of religious minorities into institutional fabrics" (599). Burchardt notes that reform efforts are often met with resistance when they are perceived to undermine dominant religious traditions, national cultures or identities (599–600).

The City of Saguenay argued that the religious artefacts and practice of prayer were part of tradition and culture. What constitutes tradition is not entirely clear, though. The evidence suggested that the crucifix had been commissioned and placed in the chambers in the early 1980s. The crucifix was over 2 feet high, 1 foot wide and 5 inches thick. The sacred heart statue was placed in the front corner of the Chicoutimi town hall in the late 1970s and measured 2 feet high by 1 foot wide and 12 inches thick. It was placed more than 9 feet from the floor, occupying a prominent place where municipal business is conducted. There was vague evidence about when the practice of prayer commenced.[41] Though the "fact" of tradition is interesting, rather than quibble over whether tradition is triggered at 100 years or 50, following Josephson's approach to the genealogy of Shinto in Japan, it is more fruitful to ask about the implications of particular practices.

In Quebec, the crucifix in the Salon Bleu was installed by the then premier Maurice Duplessis in 1936, 50 years after the National Assembly was created, and was referred to by Duplessis as "La salon de la race".[42] As the Bouchard-Taylor Commission reported noted, the effect of this is to suggest that "a very special closeness exists between legislative power and the religion of the majority" (Bouchard and Taylor 2008, 152). Micheline Milot (2010) succinctly identifies the problem:

> For decades, Quebecers have referred to the Duplessis years as, from a political and religious standpoint, the 'Great Darkness.' What an ironic twist to suddenly make "Duplessis' crucifix" a symbol of Quebec's heritage to which all citizens should show their attachment! (86)

When unravelled, the notion that prayer or the presence of Christian religious symbols in state spaces is representative of what most people imagine to be linked to long-standing traditions is sometimes (though not always) patently false. And, even when they can be legitimately characterised as also having a long history,

41 In 2002, seven municipalities merged to form the City of Saguenay. In some of these municipalities, prayers had been recited as early as 1925 through the 1960s. The crucifix was made by a local sculptor in the 1980s at the request of the La Baie municipality's recreation and culture commission. The sacred heart statue was given to the Chicoutimi council in the late 1970s and was relocated from the town hall basement to the municipal council room (*Saguenay Tribunal*, at paras 97, 112, 117–118).

42 How long does something have to be in place until it becomes heritage? We also see this question arise in discussions around *Vendée*. Construction of the National Assembly was completed in 1886, with Duplessis adding the cross in 1936, during a time of deep enmeshment of church and state. See Assemblée Nationale du Québec (n.d.). According to a Global News article by Raquel Fletcher (2018), Duplessis' crucifix was replaced by the current crucifix hanging in the National Assembly in 1982.

they are inevitably entangled in the politics of the time.[43] Further, as Milot's comment suggests, such symbols do not positively resonate for many people.

The City of Saguenay argued not only on the basis of tradition, but also emphasised the cultural rather than religious nature of the crucifix and the statue, framing them as secular. The Court of Appeal of Quebec reiterated the story of secularisation, positioning the religious symbols as "passive" innocents who are being caught up in a "draconian" interpretation of state neutrality.

> Indeed, things that were once closely linked to specific religious dogma have since become secularized. Given this new context, they cannot, in my view, be removed in the name of a draconian conception of State neutrality. What would be the point of such a result if these things, despite their original meaning, were merely passive witnesses to history? In short, the exercise would involve only drawbacks because it would add nothing more to the concept of neutrality. (*Saguenay CA*, at para. 70)

A local sculptor, Victor Dallaire, made the Sageunay crucifix in the 1980s at the request of the council. The Tribunal cited his evidence to understand the meaning of the crucifix. Mr Dallaire, it was noted, had been a sculptor for 50 years and described his creation as a work of art. He explained to the Tribunal that:

> He did not put nails in the hands, which are instead open toward the room: "Christ is speaking to the mayor and the councillors". Mr. Dallaire believes that the crucifix was blessed at the time. Mr. Dallaire sculpted more crucifixes formerly, for schools and churches, when "religion was stronger". He said he never sculpted exactly the same Christ. He uses the same creative approach for all the crucifixes he sculpts. (*Saguenay Tribunal*, at paras. 114–115)

Despite relying on the same evidence, the Court of Appeal concluded that "Dallaire testified that his sculpture did not have a religious purpose. Indeed, he explained that the work does not represent the dead Christ and does not show the character nailed to the cross" (*Saguenay CA*, at para. 122). An expert who gave evidence about the religious significance of the cross rejected the religious pedigree of the crucifix. The Court of Appeal agreed with the expert, who had said "that this work does not meet the canonical standards for a crucifix" and that "it is a form of art with a certain aesthetic value pertaining to a religious past" (*Saguenay CA*, at para. 124). The crucifix, in the view of the Court of Appeal, was simply a work of art and

43 Roger O'Toole (2000) claims the religious aspect of Canadian Confederation is demonstrated by "the choice of the term 'dominion' and the motto *A Mari usque ad Mare* (both drawn from Psalm 72) in the official symbolization of the body politic" (42). See also Egerton (2000) and Miedema (2005).

a "passive witness to history" (*Saguenay CA*, at para. 70). The characterisation of the crucifix as passive is an important part of the narrative that is constructed to render symbols "harmless", even benevolent, presences in public spaces.

Part and parcel of the construction of the crucifix and the prayer as culture and heritage is a paradoxical mix of both its specificity—"our heritage and culture" which is foundational and thus unassailable—as well as its universal applicability.[44] Robert Yelle (2013) argues that "universalism is a political strategy for the marginalization and replacement of competing systems designated as tribal, parochial or limited" (161). The claim to be universal has a uniquely paralysing effect: the complainant is denied traction for the assertion that he is not included through the deployment of the "fact" or "truth" of universalism, which takes the shape of values, ethical frameworks or a statement of inclusivity. In other words, everyone is included whether she feels that way or not.

Mayor Tremblay maintained that the prayer was inclusive and that "the municipal council decided to pursue the tradition of reciting the prayer, which was considered an important one 'underpinning the foundation of the city', the values to be upheld and the development of families" (*Saguenay Tribunal*, at para. 84). One expert testified that the statue embodied an ethical framework (*Saguenay CA*, at para. 124). These foundational, ethical aspects of the prayer and statue were seen to be universally applicable.

The Tribunal did not accept the expert denial of religious content or the claim that the prayer was a universally applicable statement of common values. In contrast, the Court of Appeal drew on expert testimony that the prayer was part of a theistic modernity that was not just for Christians. That expert also stated that "in the present context, interpreting attachment to a prayer as evidence of the submission of those in authority to a higher power is abusive and does not take into account so-called religious modernity" (*Saguenay CA*, at para. 85). Another expert said, "the prayer recited is appropriate for a large number of religions" and this is an example of "where the values of tolerance and openness to diversity that are necessary for life in a society like ours should prevail" (*Saguenay CA*, at para. 87).

Describing the prayer as an identity ritual, the expert said it was "not an organized action that would give the deliberations a religious connotation" (*Saguenay Tribunal*, at para. 174). He noted "the prayer places the councillors in the serious part of their work" (*Saguenay Tribunal*, at para. 174). The Court of Appeal concluded: "I take from the opinions of these experts that the values expressed by the prayer at issue are universal and cannot be identified with any particular religion" (*Saguenay CA*, at para. 88).

44 In this regard, *Saguenay* resonates with the Italian case of *Lautsi*, which also included a claim to universality: "Moreover, with the benefit of hindsight, it is easy to identify in the constant central core of Christian faith, despite the inquisition, despite anti-Semitism and despite the crusades, the principles of human dignity, tolerance and freedom, including religious freedom, and therefore, in the last analysis, the foundations of the secular State" (*Lautsi and others v. Italy* 2011 [Eur. Ct. H. R. 2012] E.H.R.R. 3).

One of the (non-binding) legal authorities used by the Court of Appeal was *Allen v. Renfrew* (County),[45] a decision from Ontario's Superior Court of Justice, in which a prayer characterised as non-sectarian but religious was acceptable in a pluralistic society. The court there noted that "the current prayer is broadly inclusive and is non-denominational, even though the reference to God is not consistent with the beliefs of some minority groups" (*Renfrew*, at para. 19). The court added that not everyone will be satisfied with "values" expressed in the state contexts: "In a pluralistic society, religious, moral or cultural values put forward in a public governmental context cannot always be expected to meet with universal acceptance." (*Renfrew*, at para. 19). There was no consideration of power relations, privilege or the need to protect minorities.

In interesting contrast with the Court of Appeal of Quebec's conclusion that the prayer and symbols were nonreligious and universal, was the continued public declarations of faith by the City's Mayor Tremblay, who said:

> I'm in this battle because I worship Christ. When I get to the hereafter, I'm going to be able to be a little proud. I'll be able to say to Him: "I fought for You; I even went to trial for You". There's no better argument. It's extraordinary.
>
> I'm in this fight because I worship Christ. I want to go to heaven and it is the most noble fight of my entire life. (*Saguenay Tribunal*, at para. 88)

The fluidity with which religion and culture are constructed in this context is nicely illustrated by the contrast between the legal arguments which insisted that there was no religious content in the prayers or the symbols and the statements of the mayor which are quite clearly positioned as a defence of Christianity for which there may be a heavenly acknowledgment if not reward.

Universalisation erects a protective shield around the symbols and practices in question: even when challenged as being exclusionary they are represented as being inclusive, effectively neutralising anyone who wishes to challenge them. Implicated in this tension is a narrative of goodness: the symbol represents the community, time honoured tradition and culture. It represents a consensus and social cohesion. It carries the mark of collective identity. The challenger is consequently marked as unreasonable, radical or draconian, outside of the imagined community and nation and outside of "us". Traces of these marks of difference are woven through the cases and the public conversations that surrounded the case.

The Court of Appeal concluded that no reasonable person would claim that the artefacts and practices were detrimental. The Mouvement Laïque was described by one of the experts as being "too radical in a western democracy" (*Saguenay Tribunal*, at para. 135). Mr Simoneau was characterised as being "motivated by the defence of a militant ideological vision rather than by a problem of individual discrimination" (*Saguenay Tribunal*, at para. 154). One of the city's expert witnesses stated that:

45 *Allen v. Renfrew (County)* [2004] 69 O.R. (3d) 742 (Ont. Sup. Ct. J.). Hereinafter "*Renfrew*".

> He [the expert] could not see how the reciting of the prayer could have a negative cognitive impact other than minimal inconvenience on a non-believer. Rather, to claim that the municipal council prayer prejudices a non-believer would be indicative of a problem of a "neuropsychological or psychiatric" kind. (*Saguenay Tribunal*, at para. 174)

Alain Simoneau was thus, in this interpretation, not only ideologically radical, but psychologically disturbed.

In its judgment, the Court of Appeal minimised the impact of the prayer and symbols on Mr Simoneau by repeatedly mentioning that the length of the prayer was approximately 20 seconds (*Saguenay CA*, at paras. 17 and 110). The Court also noted that the presence of the symbols is an insubstantial infringement "insofar as Simoneau alleges only mere discomfort at the sight of these objects, a discomfort that is in all probability based more on ideological divergence than on an actual violation" (*Saguenay CA*, at para. 127). "According to her [the expert], his [Alain Simoneau's] testimony showed that he sustained no cognitive interference" (*Saguenay Tribunal*, at para. 154). The theme of minimal harm was also present in the public discussion of the case, which arose most frequently in the context of communities who defended their own practice of saying prayers and displaying the crucifix or cross:

> Mayor Landry does not see how prayer could upset some citizens. "We make the sign of the cross and that's right," he says. "We ask for help in our decisions." Even if he intends to comply with the judgment of the court, the desire to change the wording of the prayer is preoccupying him. "I think I'm going to do another one and nobody can say that it is Catholic." According to him, those who oppose prayer believe in God, but just do not have the same values.[46]

And,

> "The prayer will return to the agenda of the municipal council and council meetings will begin with it, as is done elsewhere," said Marcel Deschênes, the mayor of Grand Falls. "There has always been a prayer in Grand Falls and it will continue to have one." "If a councillor wants to oppose it, all he has to do is not say it," he said.[47]

46 Original French: "Le maire Landry ne voit pas en quoi la prière puisse déranger certains concitoyens. 'On fait notre signe de croix et c'est bien correct comme ça, estime-t-il. On demande de l'aide dans nos décisions.' Même s'il entend se conformer au jugement de la cour, l'envie de modifier le libellé de sa prière le ronge. 'Je pense que je vais en faire une autre et personne ne pourra dire qu'elle est catholique,' songe-t-il. Selon lui, ceux qui s'opposent à la prière croient en Dieu, mais n'ont juste pas les mêmes valeurs" (*Le Soleil*, Fournier 2015).

47 Original French: "La prière sera de retour à l'agenda du conseil municipal et les séances du conseil vont commencer avec celle-ci, comme cela se fait ailleurs', a indiqué Marcel Deschênes, le maire de Grand-Sault. 'Il y a toujours eu une prière à Grand-Sault et il va

The assessment that no harm was done was accompanied in the public conversation by the observation that "no one has complained", which was taken as evidence that there was no real problem:

> The prayer is non-denominational and has been used at Moose Jaw council meetings for about 50 years. "It's pretty generic and pretty neutral. It asks for good governance and decision making and wisdom for us all. It doesn't have a real religion connotation (other) than it being referred to as a prayer," said Higgins. The city's prayer has come into question before. "It's something we look at every time there is a complaint in other cities or the issue is brought up in the media," said Higgins. However, no one in Moose Jaw has ever complained to city hall regarding the prayer.[48]

These silent citizens[49] are cited as evidence of no harm and are (involuntarily) added to those who support continuing the practice or keeping the symbol, the reasoning being that the absence of objection is assent.[50] The result is the amplification of the "unreasonableness" of the objector, who must surely be overreacting, psychotic, radical, especially given that others who are not "believers" do not complain. This reaction constructed as overreaction pushes the objector past citizenship to the status of "other", joining the ranks of the immigrant (most often Muslims in the contemporary imaginary) who is often invoked as part of the threat to the established order.

The issue of harm was mingled with that of coercion: the idea that no one is forced to participate or to believe was articulated as a justification for keeping prayers and symbols. In these discussions and in this instance, Christianity's conceit in its universal applicability is partnered with a rhetoric of voluntary participation and no harm. The City of Saguenay created a bylaw to specify the "optional" nature of the prayer, which included the following preamble:

> WHEREAS the members of Council, unanimously, want this tradition to continue and wish to pursue it on the basis of their individual rights and freedoms, in particular their rights to freedom of expression, conscience and religion; WHEREAS it is important to specify that the Council members and the public are in no way obligated to recite this prayer or attend its recitation;

continuer à en avoir'. 'Si un conseiller veut s'opposer, il n'aura qu'à ne pas faire la prière', a-t-il precise" (*Acadie Nouvelle*, Lachance 2016).

48 *Prince Albert Daily Herald* (2015).

49 I am grateful to Christine Cusack for identifying this theme while she was coding the media coverage of the *Saguenay* case. She observed that (as someone who has sometimes been a silent citizen) her silence is not agreement, but fear of the consequences of speaking out. The cost to be paid for disagreement is very often too high.

50 The higher the stakes (social alienation or even risk of physical harm) the less likely is objection. To be sure, there are those who are quite simply indifferent to the presence of religious symbols and practices. See Quack and Schuh (2017).

> WHEREAS it is important to ensure that members of the Council and of the public who do not wish to attend the recitation of this prayer may nevertheless attend the Council session in its entirety. (*Saguenay CA*, at para 22)

Despite the claim to non-coercion, the body of the non-believer coerced into submission reveals itself through noncompliance. It is, in effect, docile and confessional, caught in the panoptic schema offered by the public meeting.[51] Presence indicates compliance or no real harm, absence a confessional moment of non-belief in the normalcy of believers and their practices. Sitting, standing, leaving or protesting—each produces a particular relation between the non-believer and the state and fellow citizens:

> The City was hoping that this new prayer wording would accommodate the respondents in that all denominational references were removed. As for the procedure surrounding the recitation, it remained the same, except for a two-minute period given to citizens wanting to leave the room during this time and allowing them to return before the opening of the session. (*Saguenay CA*, at para 23)

> The evidence does not show that Simoneau is a person who is particularly vulnerable to any message that is not in harmony with his moral values or that the reported constraint creates disruptive effects in him that are distinct from those caused by the numerous theistic references he is confronted with daily in the public space (Christmas trees, coats of arms, the cross on Mount Royal, and so on). (*Saguenay CA*, at para 112)

> I conclude that in light of the context in which the reported infringement occurs, it is one of those situations where we can say that the constraint, if any, is in any event trivial or insubstantial. (*Saguenay CA*, at para 115)

One of the features of the tradition preserving narrative is the framing of the complainant of a radical individual who is an outlier.[52] The fact that the Mouvement Laïque joins with Alain Simoneau in this complaint is of little consequence: the complaint is individualised and thus interpreted as not being representative of

51 See Foucault (1978).
52 Steven Kettell (2015) argues that in Britain anti-secular discourse has become more common and this discourse is "propagated by leading religious and political figures, this claims that a militant, aggressive and intolerant form of secularism is seeking to drive faith out of the public square, posing a serious threat to religious freedoms and endangering the moral health of the nation" (513).

any broader group or concern.[53] At the same time as the Court of Appeal elevated the protection of culture and heritage, it simultaneously minimised the harm to the "unreasonable" Simoneau:

> The respondents in this case could not simply allege mere references to religious heritage and conclude de facto that the City's duty of neutrality was not respected. A reasonable, well-informed person, aware of the implicit values that underlie this concept could not, in this case, accept the notion that the City's political activities were, because of this prayer, under any particular religious influence. (*Saguenay CA*, at para. 107)

The implication in this wording is that Alain Simoneau is both unreasonable and poorly informed, and ignorant of the complexities of the legal principal of neutrality. The goal of cultural preservation is juxtaposed against Alain Simoneau's moral convictions, rendering the latter insignificant in the shadow of social stability and nation: "the neutrality of the City has not, however, been compromised by these references to its cultural and historical heritage. Overall, objectively, there is no real conflict between Simoneau's moral convictions and the events reported" (*Saguenay CA*, at para. 156). There is no social harm done to the individual, and in fact the individual poses harm to the broader group or to social cohesion. This construction enables the impact to be minimized and the harm to be dismissed. Words like "draconian", "radical" and "no cognitive interference" justify a dismissal of the complaint.

> To conclude on this issue, I do not think a "reasonable person, dispassionate and fully apprised of the circumstances, possessed of similar attributes to, and under similar circumstances as [Simoneau]" would agree that the disputed items have been proven to be detrimental to him or have had [TRANSLATION] "the effect of nullifying or impairing [his] rights." (*Saguenay CA*, at para 136)[54]

Further,

> [E]ven if there had been evidence of some form of coercion exercised against Simoneau's moral convictions, it did not hinder, in a more than trivial or insubstantial manner, his ability to act in accordance with his principles of life. (*Saguenay CA*, at para 129)

53 "On va supposer que la majorité des membres du personnel de l'hôpital sont des musulmans. Ils désirent avoir un local pis, à l'entrée de leur local, ils mettent leur signe, le croissant. J'espère qu'on leur accorderait leur croissant, pis ça serait correct. Ça n'enlève rien à personne." … "Celui qui a arrêté la prière à Saguenay, en passant, ç'a eu une conséquence sur tout le Canada. Ce n'est pas un musulman. Non, non! Ce n'est pas un musulman. Ce n'est pas un juif. Non, c'est un ancien catholique et ça l'a frustré" (*Le Journal de Québec*, Grondin 2017).

54 Here, Justice Gagnon cites *Law v. Canada (Minister of Employment and Immigration)* [1999] 1 S.C.R. 497 at para. 60.

Yet statements from those who have dared to complain would signal the extreme discomfort they feel in being present for such rituals at public meetings. The complainant in the case of *Freitag v. Penetanguishene (Town)* testified that when the council and the attending public rose during the recitation of the Lord's Prayer prior to council meetings in that town it caused him to feel intimidated and uncomfortable. Though he was not forced to participate, he felt great pressure to do so. Moreover, he also reported being deterred from running for office because he could not ethically be a member of a council that used a denominational prayer.[55]

Inclusive generosity sometimes incorporated other religions, but non-belief was expected to be quiet and obedient:

> "The form of prayer is left to the choice of the council member," said Niagara Falls city clerk Dean Iorfida. "If we had a member of a non-Christian faith, they certainly could lead with a prayer based on their particular faith. Council members also do not have to lead in prayer if they do not wish … We have councillors who don't believe and they just don't recite the prayer. They never made it an issue for anyone else."[56]

Experts, public sentiment and judicial opinions collaboratively build a portrait of the complainant, drawing together the story lines to construct a narrative that effectively creates an "other". This narrative is then expanded in its range, drawing in immigrants who are also conceptualised as a threat. Speaking more than a year after the Supreme Court's decision (while expressing his support for another mayor who reinstated the Lord's Prayer before his council's meetings), Mayor Tremblay said: "I am convinced that if it were a Muslim who was in Saguenay, the Supreme Court would never dare to defy the Muslims like this. But when it comes to us Catholics, we are cast aside like it is no big deal."[57] The nonreligious challenge to the presence of a crucifix or a prayer at the beginning of a state meeting is thus transformed into a threat by Muslims to Catholicism. Lest we be tempted to minimise this as a position unique to the speaker, this same sense of threat can be seen in the public outcry that manifested across Canada after the Supreme Court of Canada decision was handed down, as is illustrated in some of the following comments that appeared in various media:

> Personally I am disappointed and I don't support it … Canada was built on a Christian law. We've shown tolerance to all faiths … and I am not about to erode our principles.[58] (Caledon, Ontario Mayor Allan Thompson)

55 See *Freitag v. Penetanguishene (Town)*, 1999 CanLII 3786 (ONCA) at para. 5.

56 *Fort Erie Times* (Spiteri 2014).

57 Original French: "Je suis convaincu que si c'était un musulman qui était installé à Saguenay, la Cour suprême n'aurait jamais osé défier les musulmans comme ça. Mais nous les catholiques, ce n'est pas grave, on se laisse aller" (*Radio-Canada*, Trépanier 2016).

58 *Brampton Guardian* (Criscione 2015).

> The same prayers have been recited in the house since the late 1800s and are part of the daily proceedings. When it comes to saying prayers in the house, MacKay said the legislative assembly regulates its own internal proceedings and claims parliamentary privilege associated with its own business.[59] (Clerk of the Legislative Assembly of Prince Edward Island)

Canadians turned to culture, heritage, custom and our values. Very few defended the prayer as explicitly or solely religious. A forum in the *Toronto Star* (2015) on the ruling[60] illustrates the sorts of ways in which the recitation of prayers were constructed by readers and the drawing in of immigrant others as the threat to culture and heritage:

> We shouldn't feel too upset with the Supreme Court's ruling on prayer before council meetings; we can still engage in private prayer whenever and wherever we choose. But it seems to me that *much of our culture is being slowly stripped away—a culture steep in tradition and passed on to us by our founding forefathers.* It's sad that there are those who feel threatened by these traditions and find it necessary to *deprive the vast majority of Canadians of this precious heritage* so that they themselves can feel comfortable living in Canada. (Donald Cangiano from Oakville; emphasis added)

> Mississauga councillor, C. Parish, agreeing with Supreme Court, said the decision "shows sensitivity to the multireligious nature of Canada today." This is nice, and sounds nice, at least. *Wouldn't it be nice if the same sensitivity were to be shown to "Canada" and its cultures, traditions and religions that the "founding fathers" established and became our heritage and we, as Canadians, have adopted through our parents, grandparents, and great grandparents, who came to Canada to become Canadian citizens.* I can still hear my grandmother say, "Speak English, you are in Canada now, and chose to be a Canadian citizen. Show respect for the culture, laws and religions of this, the country of your choice." (Beverley Griffith from Barrie; emphasis added)

Similarly, the Oshawa, Ontario mayor stated:

> I'm proud to be a Canadian, [and] I intend to continue doing the Lord's Prayer prior to the commencement of the council meetings.[61]

In Fredericton, New Brunswick, the council suspended the saying of the prayer. One councillor made a public statement defending the prayer, arguing that it should be kept:

59 *The Guardian* (Ross 2015).
60 *Toronto Star* (2015).
61 See *The Toronto Star* (Grewal 2015).

> "Are we going to remove prayer from the council agenda, where is this going to stop? Are we next year going to find out that we have to get rid of Volunteer Week or we got to get rid of some of these other proclamations because it is offending someone because they don't do these particular things?" … "In the St. John River Valley, we are the Bible Belt of the province. And where we had no opposition, why would we not have this," she said. "They have taken the prayers out of the school. I guess I kind of wonder what will be next, will it be the Queen's picture on the wall in council chamber?"[62]

One radio interview with two pro-prayer councillors revealed that they worried that if a proposed compromise of a minute of silence were instigated to replace the prayer that people could instead "think about whatever they wanted to, even their grocery lists".

Some explicitly linked being Canadian to prayer:

> "I don't honestly know that somebody would sue us for saying a prayer, I think prayer is part of the Canadian process whether it's the Lord's Prayer or other prayers," said Mr. Anderson. "Praying is not uncommon in this country and I think people can or cannot participate, it's entirely up to them. It's not a mandatory thing."[63]

Though not always naming Muslims, these comments reference a "foreign" other, not a home-grown nonreligious complainant. This move tracks anxiety about Muslims that folds in "nones" and "immigrant others". Contradicting popularly held impressions about stereotypical Canadian *politesse* and openness toward immigrants, results from a 2017 poll revealed a disturbing undercurrent of anxiety towards immigration and in particular, a patent distrust of the religious "other" (e.g., Muslim "other").[64] Results indicated that nearly 40 per cent of Canadians felt there were too many immigrants, putting the "purity" of the country at risk (37 per cent Canada/39 per cent Quebec). The poll also found that Muslims were generally perceived to be the least integrated immigrant group, the wearing of a veil by Muslim women was seen as a sign of submission (48 per cent Canada/62 per cent Quebec), and nearly a quarter of Canadians were in favour of a ban on Muslim immigration (23 per cent Canada/32 per cent Quebec). When asked if current immigration policies threatened "the Christian heritage of our society", 50 per cent of respondents from Quebec and 40 per cent from the rest of Canada agreed (Crop 2017).[65]

62 CBC News (2015a).
63 *Durhamregion.com* (Szekely 2015).
64 The poll, commissioned by CBC Radio-Canada, was conducted by the research and opinion polling organisation CROP, Inc. The final report, *Les Canadiens, le populisme et la Xénophobie* (Canadians, Populism and Xenophobia), was based on interview data from 2,513 Canadian adults (1,024 participants from Quebec and 1,489 from the rest of Canada) (Radio-Canada 2017b).
65 It is noteworthy that the survey was conducted in two separate time frames, from January 27–30 and February 14–20, interrupted not by design, but by tragedy. On January 29,

Interestingly, the religious nature of the prayer was pointed out by a Muslim reader, Abid Khan, from London, ON who wrote:

> I read with interest the recent Canadian Supreme Court judgment that the municipal council in the Quebec town of Saguenay cannot open its meetings with a prayer. The more I read the judgment, the more disappointed I found myself. With this decision the Supreme Court has alienated the majority in order to placate the vocal minority. A simple problem has been given a very complicated answer. Surely, it would have been better for the court to allow the prayer if desired by the majority, whilst permitting anyone with objections to not take part or to withdraw from the room. *I am a Muslim and I have no objection to hearing a Christian prayer*, although it does not mean that I would join in the prayers. In the same way I would never expect a non-Muslim to join me in my prayers. But we each have the right to pray or not to pray. It is as simple as that, or at least it should be. *If the argument is that the feelings of atheists are affected, it could just as easily be argued that through this decision those who are religious are having their feelings affected.* Thus rather than seeking to bridge a gap, the Supreme Court has only failed to increase the divide. How unfortunate. (Toronto Star 2015; emphasis added)

By naming the prayer as religious, this Muslim reader is able to align himself, though he doesn't do so explicitly, as a "person of faith" with the Christian prayer and against the "minority". Given that about one quarter of Canadians identify as nones and another large group is non-practising, it is not clear that the objections came from a "vocal minority".[66]

The phenomenon of the transformation of religion to culture is not unique to Quebec or Canada. Rather, the assertion of Christian heritage and our indebtedness

2017, a 27-year-old man shot and killed six men and injured 19 others in an attack following an evening prayer service at the Islamic Cultural Centre in Quebec City (The Globe and Mail 2017). On the question of Muslim immigrant integration into Canadian society, the poll did show a tempering of anti-Muslim sentiment in the wake of collective grief following the massacre: 38 per cent before and 44 per cent after.

66 The Angus Reid Institute (2015) conducted a survey asking people about their opinions on prayer in public life with reference to the SCC decision: 56 per cent were in favour of the SCC decision while 44 per cent were opposed; 67 per cent of younger Canadians support the ban while, compared with 44 per cent of those 55+, 75 per cent think there shouldn't be any ritual; 73 per cent would be okay with a moment of silence for reflection; 65 per cent were okay with a quick, inspiring, and non-religious "pep talk"; 52 per cent would be okay with a prayer to God without any reference to a specific religion; 41 per cent supported having a Christian prayer that refers to Jesus Christ; 30 per cent were favourable of having a rotating prayer that gives time to a different religion at each meeting. Respondents in BC and Quebec were the most supportive of having a ban while the Maritimes and Saskatchewan were the most against a ban. See also *National Post* (Brean 2015).

to it for the moral foundation of society is used to justify the presence of prayers, symbols and other rituals. Similar rhetoric is appearing in Italy, the United States, Australia, France, Spain and Germany, representing a "new normal" that includes a will to religion[67] applicable to everyone.[68] We are all, to quote Winnifred Sullivan (2009), religious now. In the nineteenth century, the construction of a common Christianity was a key pillar of social cohesion in the project of nation-state building in Europe and North America.[69] The present moment is a discursive transformation of that project.

Traces of the past preserving narrative, which is inherently vertical, move throughout the Saguenay story. A particular version of the past is promulgated as the only plausible one, rendering attempts both to tell other histories and to introduce a new narrative for the future ineffective or illegitimate. While there is some space for inclusion, it is only on the condition that the primacy of the version which places the crucifix at the front of the room and above all else be accepted. Accommodation rather than equality is the guiding motif for diversity, and even it must not be "too much" accommodation. Those who might suggest an alternative narrative which would render relations more horizontal are ridiculed, dismissed or presented as radical and extreme. Playing a key role in this is the state, which is called upon to preserve what is designated as culture and heritage and in so doing, to maintain the boundaries of the nation.[70]

67 The "will to religion" refers to the "idea that we are all religious, that we all have spiritual needs, and that those needs are available for scrutiny, examination, correction, regulation, and addressing both by ourselves and by others. These spiritual needs are assessed in terms of imagined universal criteria that are largely based in Christian understandings of religion" (Beaman 2013b, 145).

68 The US Supreme Court decided in *Lynch v. Donnelly* (1984) that a city's Christmas display featuring a nativity scene did not violate the Establishment Clause and in fact had "legitimate secular purposes" (at p. 680). In Australia, several city councils open meetings with prayer, and in one case a politician spoke in favour of reinstating a city council prayer that had been removed, saying "the total abandonment of prayer in councils and parliaments is the abandonment of an important part of our cultural life that most people find important" (Parliament of New South Wales 2005). In Spain, the Constitutional Court has held that "passive symbols have virtually no influence on people's beliefs and, therefore, the religious freedom of individuals is safe, provided that no one is compelled to participate in rites or ceremonies in honour of those symbols" (Martínez-Torrón 2013, 42–43). In Germany, despite a Federal Constitutional Court ruling that a Bavarian law requiring the presence of crucifixes on public school classroom walls was unconstitutional, the Bavarian government legislated to keep the crucifixes in classrooms (BVerfG, 1 BvR 1087/91 vom 16.05.1995; see Martínez-Torrón 2013, 45–46).

69 In his examination of religious education in public schools, Leo Van Arragon (2015, 34) examines the notion of a common Christianity in the context of Ontario.

70 Though one might be tempted to see this as unique to the story of Quebec and the complex politics of nation there, the fact that the same public rhetoric emerged across Canada suggests that this is too narrow a read of the case. Moreover, from country to country the story is similar, as is illustrated by the *Lautsi* case as well as numerous others in Germany, Spain, France and the United States.

The state

There is no constitutional statement regarding the position of the state vis-à-vis religion in Canada, nor in Quebec's *Charter of Human Rights and Freedoms.* The preamble of the *Canadian Charter of Rights and Freedoms* reads, "Whereas Canada is founded upon principles that recognize the supremacy of God and the rule of law" and there are various other constitutional provisions that have resulted in an entrenched, perhaps even established, position for historically majoritarian religion.[71] Moreover, various practices affirm the traditionally close relationship between state and church in Canada, including the recitation of Christian prayers at various state functions (including the opening of Parliament, provincial legislatures and municipal council meetings), the presence of religious symbols in state buildings and the frequent intervention by religious groups in Supreme Court of Canada cases.

Legal scholars have considered the duty of the state to be neutral, with Bruce Ryder's (2005) article "State Neutrality and Freedom of Conscience and Religion" leading the way. He concluded:

> Canadian jurisprudence does not impose on the state a duty of neutrality about religion. Rather, the Canadian position appears to be that the state can aid religion so long as it does so in a manner that respects the principle of neutrality or even-handedness between religions. (174–175)

Ryder was careful to distinguish the Canadian and American positions, a distinction that will become more obvious in the discussion of the *Town of Greece* case in Chapter 4:

> The relationship between religion and state has never been a simple one in Canada. The metaphor of an impregnable wall between church and state, so often invoked in the United States, is not a plausible description of Canadian constitutional traditions. (174–175)

Ryder summarises the neutrality issue this way:

> The text of the Charter as a whole suggests that the Canadian state should aim to secure a religiously positive pluralism in an even-handed manner. This is best accomplished by a secular state that is neutral between religions but not neutral about religion. (177)

71 The guarantee of funding for some religious schools is an historical anomaly dating to the Constitution Act of 1867. For a more detailed discussion, see Bayefsky and Waldman (2007). The *Adler* case affirmed this constitutional arrangement, although the UN subsequently criticised that decision (*Waldman v. Canada*). For discussions of Ontario's school system in relation to the constitutional privileging of Catholicism, see Gidney (1999).

Jocelyn Maclure and Charles Taylor (2011) also weighed in on the role of the state (both were involved in the Bouchard-Taylor commission and report), stating:

> liberal and democratic state cannot remain indifferent to certain core principles, such as human dignity, basic human rights, and popular sovereignty. These are the constitutive values of liberal and democratic political systems; they provide these systems with their foundations and aims. (11)

Maclure and Taylor capture the core challenge the state faces[72]: even a neutral state, whatever that might mean, must protect its citizens. Benjamin Berger (2013a) comments:

> the state must be neutral in its treatment of religion; it need not, however, be neutral about the nature of a good society. Though its demand for even handedness in the state treatment of various religions—as well as non-religion—is noble and sound, what state neutrality should not be heard to demand is the state's indifference to the conditions necessary for a healthy civic life. (121)

Berger is, of course, correct in his assessment of the state's role, but what constitutes a good society is not self-evident. Robert Bellah et al.'s (1992) idea of the "good society" for example, valorises social cohesion, which rests heavily on culture and tradition, often at the cost of minority and disadvantaged groups.[73] The protection of culture and tradition might be justified as central to identity and the stability of the nation. Richard Moon's (2012) discussion of state neutrality vis-à-vis religion would seem to move in this direction:

> Religious practices have shaped the traditions and rituals of the community and so cannot simply be erased from the civic sphere or ignored in the formulation of public policy. More significantly, the courts have indicated that legislators may draw on their religious values when determining public policy—that they should not be expected to leave their religious values at the doorstep of the legislature. (503)
>
> The consequence of this is that values associated with dominant or mainstream religious traditions will sometimes shape public policy. (511)[74]

72 See Maclure (2016) for a discussion on the ban of religious symbols for public employees in Quebec.

73 Meredith McGuire (2008) offers an especially compelling critique of Robert Bellah et al.'s (1992) characterisation of Sheila, a young nurse who builds her spiritual life outside of organised religion.

74 See also Moon and Berger (2016) for further discussion on state neutrality.

Beyond individual religious values, neutrality is reconciled with the protection of the dominant religion by constructing religion as culture. As Joppke (2018) bluntly observes: "The main strategy for the state to square the circle of principled neutrality and unavoidable majority privileging is to declare religion 'culture'" (238).[75] Referencing the Bavarian and Italian crucifix cases, Susanna Mancini (2010) argues that the entanglement of national identity with Christian heritage frames the conceptualization of tolerance and religious rights and exposes the limits of tolerance (15–16).

The role of the state and the notion of state neutrality was a core theme in the *Saguenay* case, taking many forms, sometimes within the same decision. Citing a foundational post-Charter decision, *Big M Drug Mart*,[76] the Tribunal noted that the state has a duty to be neutral and to protect minorities from majoritarian beliefs and practices: "[w]hat may appear good and true to a majoritarian religious group, or to the state acting at their behest, may not, for religious reasons, be imposed on people who take a contrary view" (*Saguenay Tribunal*, at para. 205). The Tribunal concluded that:

> The applicable law on the subject is clear: pursuant to the principle of the religious neutrality of the state, a municipality cannot validly adopt a bylaw providing for "preference for any one religion at the expense of those of another religious persuasion", or "that might simply have the effect of imposing one particular religion". In the same way, "the state acts as an essentially neutral intermediary in relations between the various denominations and between those denominations and civil society". (*Saguenay Tribunal*, at para. 282)

In contrast, the Court of Appeal emphasised the cultural and heritage character of the prayer and the two artefacts and then linked their protection to a duty of the state to protect such expressions of culture and heritage. Unlike the Tribunal, which followed the Supreme Court of Canada in its reflections on majoritarianism and its dangers, the Court of Appeal speculated on majority opinion to justify the shift from religion to culture:

> I am satisfied that the evidence heard by the Tribunal largely supports the idea that these two religious symbols (the cross and the Sacred Heart statue) are, for a significant portion of the population, deprived of their religious connotation

75 "A model for this has been provided by some German Länder, which in the early 2000s passed laws to prohibit the Islamic headscarf being worn by public school teachers (as in violation of liberal state neutrality), while exempting from the religious dress restriction veiled Catholic nun teachers, on the contorted argument that the nun's garb was merely a performance of 'tradition' or of the 'Christian-Occidental' culture that the state had the license, even the obligation, to support and to identify with" (Joppke 2018, 238).

76 *R v. Big M Drug Mart Ltd* [1985] 1 S.C.R. 295.

> and that their presence is primarily of interest from the viewpoint of a historical cultural heritage and in no way interferes with the neutrality of the City. (*Saguenay CA*, at para. 125)

Absolute state neutrality, the Court concluded, is impossible, stating that the objective of neutrality

> does not require that society be sanitized of all religious reality, including that which forms part of its cultural history. Moreover, in this regard, it should be recognized that some of the historical values of Quebec society remain compatible with current values said to be neutral and universal (*Saguenay CA*, at para. 65)

The protection of what is in essence majoritarian religion thus becomes a combined project of law, the state and society:

> While the history of Quebec society, including its symbolic references, must not impede currents of thought that are different from those that originally animated it, we cannot ignore its heritage without running the risk of cutting off the foundations that shaped its evolution. In this sense, absolute State neutrality does not seem possible from a constitutional point of view. (*Saguenay CA*, at para. 68)
>
> Also, according to a "philosophical" approach advocated by some, the claim that the State should practise abstention in religious matters seems to contradict its duty to preserve its history, characterized here by an interconfessional heritage. (*Saguenay CA*, at para. 69)

Taking a slippery slope alarmist approach that we will see repeated in France and the United States, the Court of Appeal defensively posed the question of whether state neutrality means "that any reference to standards of moral conduct must be void of a society's historical points of reference, including religious traditions? I do not think so. First of all, there are significant guidelines that allow us to dismiss theory of all-out secularism" (*Saguenay CA*, at para. 98). In the "guidelines" the court referenced, the multiculturalism section of the Canadian of *Canadian Charter of Rights and Freedoms*[77]; the supremacy of God in the *Charter*; the constitutional guarantee of denominational schools; the unanimous motion of the National Assembly in Quebec to retain the crucifix on the wall of the Salon Bleu; the theistic elements in the national anthem; the white cross on the Quebec flag; the cross on

77 Much has been written about multiculturalism in Canada and its impact. See, for example, Winter (2011; 2015) for a discussion on the changing meaning of multiculturalism. See also Perry (2015); Mudde (2016); Ng and Bloemraad (2015); Adams (2007); and Ryan (2016).

Mont Royal; and numerous other examples (*Saguenay CA*, at para. 102).[78] These are all justified as forms of religious particularism which are historical manifestations of the religious dimension of Quebec and Canadian society:

> These forms of religious particularism which we find scattered here and there in the public space are only historical manifestations of the religious dimension of Quebec society, which, when viewed with proper perspective, cannot have the effect of undermining the neutrality of the various branches of the State. (*Saguenay CA*, at para. 104)

The litany of religious symbols is minimised as being "scattered" and "only" historical dimensions. That they are all Christian is left unnamed by the Court, which justifies them by converting them to evidence of tolerance and openness to diversity. The court works up preservation of culture and heritage as a paramount duty of the state, which supersedes any protection of freedom of conscience and religion.

> I am convinced by these examples that the principle of the religious neutrality of the State is intended to promote tolerance and openness in regard to diversity and not to exclude from the reality of a society any references to its history, albeit religious. (*Saguenay CA*, at para. 106)

Preserving the past as foundational to the present is upheld as a sacred duty of the state, with the Court of Appeal noting that:

> the will of the Quebec government to protect its heritage seems obvious to me if we refer to the unanimous resolution of May 22, 2008. This is the history and ancient traditions that were at issue in Oakes and which must be taken into account when assessing the very purpose of the freedoms of conscience and religion. (*Saguenay CA*, at para. 137)

The "unanimous resolution" to which the court refers is the resolution to reject the Bouchard-Taylor report's recommendation to remove the crucifix from the provincial legislature. The court deployed the notion of "benevolent neutrality" to circumscribe the state's duty. As Joppke (2018) notes, the protection of the crucifix is precarious because the crucifix is a majoritarian religious symbol its

78 For example, "Other examples can be added to these. One only has to think of the theistic references in the Canadian national anthem or the white cross adorning the Quebec flag, intended to symbolize the loyalty of the first francophone Quebecers to the religion of their ancestors (Catholicism). One could also mention the cross on Mount Royal on the island of Montreal and the various theistic elements found on coats of arms, including the motto 'God and my right' under the shield of the Royal Arms, which date back to the time of Henry V, King of England, and which, today still, adorn some rooms presided by judges of the various courts" (*Saguenay CA*, at para. 103).

protection by the state is precarious if the liberal neutrality principle is not to be undercut. The only way to avoid this is to culturalise the crucifix (242–243). I argue that this move—from religion to culture—compromises state neutrality, which in turn undermines democracy and perceptions of fairness and inclusion.

In his article that highlights the "privilege" of secularism as neutrality, David Brown (2005) draws on a speech by the Chief Justice of the Supreme Court of Canada:

> The Chief Justice contended that "the authority claimed by law touches upon all aspects of human life and citizenship … Voting, taxation, mobility, family organization, and public discourse: the rule of law leaves no aspect of human experience unaffected by its claim to authority." Just as when the Tudor monarchs fused state power with religious authority in the person of the sovereign, leaving dissenters to face the double-barrelled allegations of heretic and traitor, one may ask what place the religious "dissenters" in today's Canada would occupy under a "comprehensive system of belief" of the "rule of law"? (231–232)

Brown is citing the Chief Justice's comments to make a point about religious interventions in public debates and the possible disadvantage they are at given what he argues is an equation of neutrality with the secular, which he frames as separating off religion. Given the ubiquity of religious symbols and (it seems) practices in the Canadian public sphere, as well as the ready intervention of religious voices in Supreme Court cases on all manner of matters—including prostitution,[79] assisted death[80] and same-sex marriage[81]—his point might be more apropos in relation to the nonreligious. As someone who challenged the practice of prayer and the presence of two religious symbols, all of which have been transformed into culture and heritage, Alain Simoneau suffered the "double barrelled allegations of heretic and traitor" associated with the religiously committed above. The Court of Appeal of Quebec also equates "complete secularism" with an inaccurate interpretation of state neutrality:

> I conclude from the foregoing that complete secularism is not part of the fundamental protections enumerated in the *Charter* nor does this idea underlie the negative form of freedom of religion. On the contrary, the principle of State neutrality implies that anything that could be associated with a form of religious expression, without being banned, must remain firmly subordinate to the fundamental values protected by the *Charter*, including freedom of religion and conscience. (*Saguenay CA*, at para. 79)

79 In *Canada (Attorney General) v. Bedford*, 2013 SCC 72 [2013] 3 S.C.R. 1101 one quarter of the 24 interveners were religious.

80 In *Carter v. Canada (Attorney General)*, 2015 SCC 5 [2015] 1 S.C.R. 331 nearly half (12 of 26) of the interveners were religious.

81 In *Reference re Same-Sex Marriage* [2004] 3 S.C.R. 698, 2004 SCC 79 there was a total of 27 interveners, 13 of whom were religious.

The idea of neutrality is a central preoccupation of the Supreme Court of Canada as well, occupying more than 20 paragraphs throughout the decision. The Court affirms that the duty of religious neutrality results from an "evolving interpretation of freedom of conscience and religion" rather than an explicitly stated mandate in either the *Quebec Charter* or the *Canadian* (*Saguenay SCC*, at para. 71).

> When all is said and done, the state's duty to protect every person's freedom of conscience and religion means that it may not use its powers in such a way as to promote the participation of certain believers or non-believers in public life to the detriment of others. It is prohibited from adhering to one religion to the exclusion of all others. (*Saguenay SCC*, at para. 76)

The court and tribunal decisions in *Saguenay* evidence traces of both past preserving and future forming narratives in relation to the role of the state, sometimes within the same decision. For example, the Supreme Court decision includes both a clear statement that the state cannot use the "guise of culture and heritage" (*Saguenay SCC*, at para. 78) to express a religious preference, but:

> This being said, it must be recognized that the Canadian cultural landscape includes many traditional and heritage practices that are religious in nature. Although it is clear that not all of these cultural expressions are in breach of the state's duty of neutrality, there is also no doubt that the state may not consciously make a profession of faith or act so as to adopt or favour one religious view at the expense of all others. (*Saguenay SCC*, at para. 87)

Neutrality is not a straightforward notion, as evidenced by the variable terminology used in the court decisions, including "neutrality", "benevolent neutrality", "religious neutrality", "absolute neutrality", "complete secularity", "all-out secularism", "true neutrality", "duty of neutrality", "duty of religious neutrality", "state neutrality", "strict neutrality" and "open secularism". The duty of neutrality has become part of the legal landscape, with variable meanings, which support the preservation of existing power relations or reshapes them in response to the new diversity.

In public discourse neutrality was commonly seen as being overridden by heritage and the protection of who "we" are. Or, given their universal applicability and generative role in shared values, religious symbols and practices were part of a neutral pubic sphere and state approach.

An alternative discourse

Thus far I have focused primarily on the ways that the past preserving narrative is evidenced in the *Saguenay* incident, though the Supreme Court's decision favours, at least tentatively, a future forming narrative that tried to achieve the "delicate balance"[82] between freedom of conscience and religion and state neutrality. A second set of story lines constructed another narrative that was largely overshadowed in the preoccupation with agnosticism/atheism/unbelief versus religion.

The following summary of Alain Simoneau's position as outlined by the Tribunal creates a different version of the radical, unreasonable, draconian portrait created by the Court of Appeal drawn from the expert evidence:

> Although he respects the religious manifestations of others, saying each person is entitled to believe what he or she wants, Mr. Simoneau testified that he feels isolated and uncomfortable in a municipal or government location where his freedom of conscience and religion is not respected. The reciting of the prayer and the religious symbols make him ill at ease because the council [TRANSLATION] "seems to represent only those who share the convictions of His Worship". He said he had no problem with people wearing religious signs in the council room. But he expects the council sittings to be held in a neutral environment. He testified that [TRANSLATION] "it is not so much hearing the prayer that bothers me the most: I don't pay attention to it; I remain silent out of respect; ... it is the idea that that does not belong in the council room". To his mind, a municipality should not display any religion whatsoever: according to him, even if the majority is Catholic, statistics indicate the presence of Muslims, Jews and Protestants as well. (*Saguenay Tribunal*, para. 39)

Recall the features of the future forming narrative: in this summary the Tribunal recognises Alain Simoneau as respectful of the symbols and practices that are not his own. His objection is not to religion *per se*, but to the intertwining of religion and the state. Religious clothing, in his view, would not be objectionable. His concern is not only for himself, but also for other minorities who do not share this particular religious worldview—he specifically mentions Jews, Muslims and Protestants. Neutrality in his view precludes the recitation of the prayer. In his evidence, as recounted by the Tribunal, Simoneau attempts to navigate the complex world of diversity in which everyone has a stake, and to which everyone belongs. He objects to the authoritarian approach by the mayor which displaces some of his fellow citizens and which he himself finds isolating and uncomfortable.

Simoneau did not argue for the abolition of all religious symbols from the municipal buildings nor did he object to the mayor and or members of council displaying religious symbols in their offices or smaller working rooms, though these could arguably be public spaces as well. His concern was about the public spaces in which state and public gathered together to conduct the business of governance.

82 "The state is required to act in a manner that is respectful of every person's freedom of conscience and religion [...] Its corollary is that the state must remain neutral in matters involving this freedom. The interplay between freedom of conscience and religion, on the one hand, and this duty of neutrality, on the other, is sometimes a delicate one" (*Saguenay SCC*, at para. 1).

> For their part, the plaintiffs insisted on respect for Mr. Tremblay's freedom of religion, but were careful to distinguish that issue from the issue of the religious neutrality of democratic municipal institutions. In that regard, the Tribunal notes that Mr. Simoneau is not asking that the crucifix in the mayor's office and the crucifix in the La Baie committee room be removed. His request concerns the reciting of the prayer at public meetings of the municipal council that citizens can attend, and the presence of religious symbols in the rooms where public meetings are held in the boroughs of Chicoutimi and La Baie. (*Saguenay Tribunal*, at para. 249)

In the process of navigating the complex reality of a world of multiple beliefs and non-beliefs, Simoneau's approach embraced a vision of equality that recognised and created space for difference. This horizontal approach reconfigures power relations, displacing the privilege that comes with foundationalism. Even the Mayor, on hearing Simoneau's testimony, conceded that Simoneau was not simply "hypersensitive" to religion, but that he was sincere in his beliefs.[83]

While respect characterised the approach of Alain Simoneau, he himself was cast as a villain who threatened the work of the council and the very core of society through his challenge to the recitation of a prayer and the presence of the crucifix and statue. Like the Tribunal, he understood the link between freedom of religion and conscience, state neutrality, and equality:

> The purpose of the recognition that freedom of conscience and religion can afford the same protection to all religions and people, including atheists and non-believers, is to prevent the inequality that may stem from the imposition of beliefs or practices that are inconsistent with the beliefs of some religious minorities—or even those of the majority—as well as of non-believers. (*Saguenay Tribunal*, at para. 209)

The Supreme Court judgment too has traces of a future forming narrative, particularly in its discussion of the meaning of neutrality which is sensitive to the isolating effects of "tradition" which discriminate against even a small number of people:

> Thus, it is essential to review the circumstances carefully. If they reveal an intention to profess, adopt or favour one belief to the exclusion of all others, and if the practice at issue interferes with the freedom of conscience and religion of one or more individuals, it must be concluded that the state has breached its duty of religious neutrality. This is true regardless of whether the practice has a traditional character. (*Saguenay SCC*, at para. 88)

83 See *Saguenay Tribunal* at para. 83.

> I concede that the state's duty of neutrality does not require it to abstain from celebrating and preserving its religious heritage. But that cannot justify the state engaging in a discriminatory practice for religious purposes, which is what happened in the case of the City's prayer. (*Saguenay SCC*, at para. 116)

Alain Simoneau was in good company. He is one of many atheists and nonreligious people to legally challenge the presence of religious symbols and practices in public spaces in Canada.[84] The sometimes hostile response to these challenges suggests that the characterisation of Canada as a secular country is an inadequate portrait of the complex relationship between majoritarian religion, minority religions and nonreligion.

How might the story have unfolded differently? What is a future forming narrative in this context? History in this story, even in the Supreme Court narrative, unfolds as a relatively monolithic truth which sets up one story of a Christian past. But closer examination would reveal a much more nuanced story involving Indigenous peoples, multiple religious practices and nonreligious people as part of the "tradition" of Quebec. Writing them back into the story would shift the beginning vantage point. So too would explicitly acknowledging the complicated relationship between language, religion and culture. Mayor Tremblay articulates a deeply felt fear of loss that emerges during discussions about removal of symbols like the crucifix and practices like prayer. Recognising that fear as real and considering the importance of practices and symbols to some people might be an important beginning place in renegotiating them to both better reflect historical diversity and an inclusive future.

Conclusion

For a brief moment following the Quebec City mosque shooting in January 2017 that left six Muslim men dead and 19 injured, it seemed that the dialogue about religion in the public sphere might shift and in particular that a self-reflexive

84 In the 1960s Ernest and Cornelia Bergsma were denied citizenship because they had declared themselves to be atheists and were therefore determined by a judge to be unable to invoke God in their oath of allegiance. They received widespread support in the form of letters, newspaper articles and an offer to pay their legal bills from the federal government. See Tomlins and Bullivant (2017, 83) for a discussion. Recent examples of the challenging of religion include *RC v. District School Board of Niagara* (2013). In this case a parent who self-identified as an atheist filed a complaint with the Ontario Human Rights Tribunal regarding the distribution of bibles by the Gideons. He had proposed to the school board that he be permitted to distribute *Just Pretend: A Freethought Book for Children*. The board declined, arguing schools have the right to sponsor the study of all religions without imposing the view of any particular creed. In its view, according to the ruling, atheism isn't a religion. In another Canadian case, *Zylberberg v. Sudbury Board of Education* (1988), a group of parents challenged the daily reading of the Lord's Prayer in their children's public schools. In *Erazo v. Dufferin-Peel Catholic District School Board* (2014), a parent petitioned the Ontario Superior Court for an exemption to obligatory Catholic liturgies and religious retreats.

pondering about obstacles to inclusion might create a greater openness to inclusion and difference.[85] Within a week, however, Coalition Avenir Québec opposition leader François Legault[86] stated, "It's important to be open to welcoming newcomers, but we must limit the wearing of religious symbols so we can better live together" and called for Bill 62 to go further and ban schoolteachers from wearing religious symbols.[87] In February 2017, the Saint-Sacrement crucifix controversy erupted and on March 14 the results of the Crop poll, referred to above, were released. Questions about immigrants' religious practices, construction of religious buildings and wearing of religious vestments revealed how the religious "other", or (unambiguously the Muslim "other", according to the poll) remains a threat in the minds of many Canadians. Nearly three quarters of participants approved the idea of a Canadian values test for immigrants (Crop 2017). Although some questioned the wording of the poll questions,[88] it nonetheless highlighted the powerful sway of a past preserving narrative that at its most extreme would exclude immigrants, particularly Muslims, from entry into Canada and from full participation in Canadian society.[89] As mentioned above, in October 2017 after a decade of public discussion a law was passed that requires an uncovered face by both public service providers and recipients, all in the name of "state religious neutrality". The "Act to Foster Adherence to State Religious Neutrality and, in Particular, to Provide a Framework for Requests for Requests for Accommodations on Religious Grounds in Certain Bodies" seeks to protect what are described as the "emblematic and toponymic elements of Québec's cultural heritage, in particular its religious cultural heritage, that testify to its history" (R-26.2.01, section 16).

In his analysis of Japan, Josephson (2012) argues that superstition has been overlooked as an important element of the analysis of the construction of religion and the "real". He defines superstition as "beliefs that should not be believed" (254) and his observation that "superstition appears most in discussions of monsters, unlucky numbers, and the beliefs of savages" (253) can be matched with some of the public and political statements reflecting the constitution of, for example, Muslims and non-believers, with a broader category of superstition against which religion and the real are positioned. Josephson found that:

85 Six worshippers were killed while praying at a Quebec City mosque by a right-wing university student (The Globe and Mail 2017).
86 Since October 18, 2018 François Legault has been the Premier of Quebec.
87 *The Globe and Mail* (Peritz 2017).
88 Jack Jedwab, executive vice-president of the Association for Canadian Studies, for example, questioned the wording as being "loaded" and challenged the use of the word "purity" in the finding that "39 per cent of Quebec respondents and 37 per cent of the rest of the country agreed that 'there's too much immigration and it threatens the purity of the country'" (*Montreal Gazette* 2017).
89 "The CROP poll also reveals 25% of Canadians support a ban on Muslim immigration" and "75% of Canadians support some form of anti-Canadian values screenings for new immigrants to Canada" (*Toronto SUN* 2017). In contrast, "32 per cent of Quebecers" were either "strongly" or "somewhat" in favour of a ban on Muslim immigration (*CBC News*, Hinkson and Laframboise 2017).

> strongly held beliefs that did not accord with state mandated reality, and were not channelled into acceptable religious forms, were now often described as signs of irrationality of madness. While inheriting the vestiges of an older conception of evil and the demonic, the new category of superstition was legitimated as being in opposition to science and political reality. (253)[90]

We might interpret the expert statements and Court of Appeal assessment as falling into this new category of superstition identified by Josephson: Simoneau is worked up as being overly sensitive, having suffered no harm, and ultimately as being in opposition to the political reality of the cultural weight of prayer.

Given the unfolding of events in the *Saguenay* case, the Saint-Sacrement incident and similar cases elsewhere, it is appropriate here to reflect on the drivers of the shift from religion to culture.[91] Although the purpose of this analysis is not to offer a causal explanation for the shift, it is fruitful to consider the multiple generators of the discourse of culture and heritage. Perhaps surprisingly, clergy and church officials have seen the strategic advantages of linking the churches that comprise majoritarian religion and whose numbers are in sharp decline to the culture, heritage and patrimony of their respective countries. For example, in the Saint-Sacrement controversy, an official statement released by the Catholic Church from Cardinal Gérald Cyprien Lacroix emphasised the historical and cultural aspects of the crucifix:

> I learned yesterday that the CHU reached its decision without taking into account the historical and religious dimension of this crucifix, as part of our cultural heritage. I sincerely believe that it is a lack of respect towards the population and the history of this care establishment founded in 1927 by the Sisters of Charity of Quebec, in the name of their faith following the message of Jesus Christ. Like many Quebeckers, I express my deep disappointment about this decision, but I find it hard to believe that this is the end of the story. As we speak of tolerance, welcoming, respect for difference and openness, the withdrawal of the crucifix from the Hospital of the Blessed Sacrament expresses the opposite.[92]

90 Josephson-Storm (2017) elaborates on this idea in his book *The Myth of Disenchantment: Magic, Modernity, and the Birth of the Human Sciences*. He argues that superstition is positioned between "religion" and "science". "Religion is negated by science, which is in turn negated by superstition or magic" (14–15).

91 My thanks to Effie Fokas for asking this question and for suggesting that a closer examination of clergy adoption of the language of culture might be fruitful.

92 Original French: "J'ai appris hier que le CHU maintient sa décision sans prendre en compte la dimension historique et religieuse de ce crucifix, en tant qu'élément de notre patrimoine culturel. Je crois sincèrement que c'est un manque de respect envers la population et à l'égard de l'histoire de cet établissement de soins fondé en 1927 par les Sœurs de la Charité de Québec, au nom de leur foi dans le message de Jésus Christ. Comme de très nombreux Québécois et Québécoises, j'exprime ma vive déception au sujet de cette décision, mais j'ai peine à croire que ce soit la fin de l'histoire. Alors que nous parlons de tolérance, d'accueil, de respect de la différence et

The cardinal deployed the language of tolerance, respect for difference and welcoming to criticise the removal of the crucifix, a majoritarian religious symbol. As with the woman in the conference session who insisted that the crucifix *really was* her culture and heritage, there is also a pervasive public discourse of "culture and heritage" that appears in media commentary and everyday conversation.[93] The discursive construction of religion as culture and heritage is also taken up by law and legal language, working in concert with public and religious articulations of crucifixes, prayers, and various types of statues as culture and heritage of historical importance.

Is it possible to understand the language of culture and heritage as a translation of religious language into a commonly accessible discourse, such as that discussed by Habermas (2006), who proposes that religious contributions must be translated in the political public sphere prior to entry into the parliamentary domain (10). Habermas argues that requiring a translation also means that the non-religious must be open to the possible truth of the argument being made by religious actors:

> This requirement of translation must be conceived as a cooperative task in which the non-religious citizens must likewise participate, if their religious fellow citizens are not to be encumbered with an asymmetrical burden. Whereas citizens of faith may make public contributions in their own religious language only subject to the proviso that these get translated, the secular citizens must open their minds to the possible truth content of those presentations and enter into dialogues from which religious reasons then might well emerge in the transformed guise of generally accessible arguments. (11)

It is interesting that Habermas uses the word "guise", which is precisely the language employed by the Supreme Court to suggest that majoritarian religion cannot hide behind the guise of culture and heritage. It is difficult to imagine successfully arguing that crucifixes and other Christian religious symbols are not part of the culture and heritage of many of the countries in which these debates are arising. The question is, however: what are the power relations around those symbols (and practices such as prayer)? How is religion/culture mobilised by social actors to protect privilege or to challenge it?

It is also possible that the claim to religious symbols and practices as culture and heritage can be understood as a moment of transition that accompanies the shift from a participating religious majority to a society in which a few perform religion for the many. This references Grace Davie's (2007) idea of vicarious religion, which she describes as "the notion of religion performed by an active minority but

d'ouverture, le retrait du crucifix de l'Hôpital du Saint-Sacrement exprime tout le contraire" (Lemieux-Lefebvre 2017).

93 Both Christine Cusack, one of the doctoral research assistants on this manuscript, and I live in Quebec and have had occasion to observe the ways in which Quebecers readily adopt the language of culture and heritage to describe the presence and practice of religious symbols in their midst.

on behalf of a much larger number, who (implicitly at least) not only understand, but, quite clearly, approve of what the minority is doing" (22–23).[94] Though the somewhat tense relationship many Quebecers have with Catholicism complicates Davie's theory, it is worth considering her proposition as one explanatory variable in the overall picture of the attachment to, in this instance, Catholicism as culture, heritage and identity. This move may be part of the vicarious vocabulary in societies struggling with the residue of religious majoritarianism. Davie anticipates this possibility when she notes that "vicariousness also prompts us to ask about the many ways in which populations and their religious institutions are related to each other" (25).

Past preserving and future forming narratives weave through public debates about symbols such as the crucifix and practices such as prayer. Although Quebec has a complicated context because of language politics, nationalism and the historical role of the Catholic Church, to single Quebec out as having a unique approach solely because of this is not accurate, as the reaction to the *Saguenay* case across Canada surely demonstrates. Crucifixes such as the one in Saint-Sacrement hang in Catholic hospitals all across Canada, which serve a wide range of religious and nonreligious patients.[95] Prayers of a decidedly Christian nature are said in all manner of public circumstances. Though Quebec recently went further with its law banning face coverings for those giving or receiving public services, survey data suggest that opinion in Quebec and the rest of Canada is similar regarding immigrants and Muslims in particular.[96] The *Saguenay* case represents a case study through which the debates and issues are refracted. They replayed again in Saint-Sacrement, and will continue to do so, drawing on narratives of who "we" are, the nature of Canadian values, the parameters of state neutrality and the shape of the future in the context of a new diversity. But, these narratives are not restricted to Canada and emerge in other contexts as well. In the next chapter, we will turn to a French case to explore how the past and future are imagined in relation to diversity there.

94 Grace Davie (2007) elaborates: "Religion, it seems, can operate vicariously in a wide variety of ways: Churches and church leaders perform ritual on behalf of others; Church leaders and churchgoers believe on behalf of others; Church leaders and churchgoers embody moral codes on behalf of others; Churches can offer space for the vicarious debate of unresolved issues in modern societies" (22–23). See Steve Bruce and David Voas (2010) for a critical commentary, including: "Taken in its narrow sense, vicarious religion is an important element of the religious life of societies in which a common religion pervades the worldview. It is almost entirely absent from largely secular societies, because only a strongly supernaturalistic culture can sustain the magical idea that some people can effectively do religious work on behalf of others" (257).

95 The funding scheme for Catholic hospitals is complicated, but the most important fact to note for the purposes of this discussion is that Catholic hospitals receive public funding in Canada (Palley 2006).

96 Jack Jedwab (2017) observes that 22 per cent of Canadians strongly agree that immigrants to Canada should "set aside their culture and try to adopt Canadian culture" (16).

3 Away in a manger ...

As was the case for its European brethren, the crucifix was heartened by the throngs of supporters its removal attracted. Politicians came to its defence, as did many who had not darkened the door of a church in decades. Though not always encouraged by its relegation to the dustbin of history—"it is our culture and heritage"—the crucifix came to realise that this new designation as "patrimoine" re-inscribed its power under a new name. And, after all, what's in a name?

Religion in France

Like Quebec, France has historically been dominated by Roman Catholicism, and it too has a complicated history related to the negotiation of identity, state and citizenship. The mantra of "*liberté, égalité, fraternité*" has circumscribed the parameters of the conversation about what it means to be French and the values which attach to that.[1] The national myth is that anyone who adopts these values can be French. The reality is much more complicated and tempered by a subtle class order, in part informed by colonialism,[2] that regulates citizen relations in a vertical manner that is endemic to French society. This results in a hierarchical order in which we might say some are more "French" than others.[3] Religion plays an important role in the social fabric of France.

According to a Pew-Templeton (2015a) study, 63 per cent of the French population identify as Christian; the French Institute of Public Opinion Poll found

1 John Bowen (2011) argues that there was a shift in legal reasoning related to women's dress from a harm-based assessment to one which focused on values. For example, he cites the example of a Moroccan woman who was denied French citizenship because the values she held as a result of her religious practices ran "counter to the equality of men and women and that caused her to suffer from insufficient assimilation to become a citizen" (332).

2 For a discussion of colonialism and the ordering of French society see Guénif-Souilamas (2006).

3 Jennifer Selby (2014a) states "If a person or group does not behave or perform properly, they are excluded from the rights and freedoms granted to citizens. Bio-power effectively aligns the moral positions of citizens with the maintenance of state power. The State has a clear interest in shaping 'acceptable' sexuality across public and private spheres as a central component in the production of its citizens" (452).

that two thirds of the French population identified as Catholic,[4] with only 4.6 per cent of those who identify as Catholic attending mass regularly.[5] A 2010 poll found that 57 per cent of those who identify as Catholic in France are "non-practising" Catholics and do not attend mass.[6] Until recently much of the French negotiation of religion was focused on the place of Catholicism: "In the 1800s and early 1900s, this meant a sustained reflection of the influence of the Catholic Church on the religious, political, and economic life of the nation" (Adrian 2015, 372) and consequently sustained attempts to delimit the influence of the Church through the regulation of various social institutions, especially education. There remains, though, a strong institutional residue of majoritarian religion in France: state funerals are organised by the Catholic Church[7]; potential appointees as bishops are vetted by the French state for compatibility with the values of the Republic[8]; the government is responsible for the upkeep of religious buildings constructed before the 1905 law[9]; and the region of Alsace-Mosel[10] receives state

4 See Institut français d'opinion publique (2009).

5 See Institut français d'opinion publique (2010). In France, approximately 46 per cent of the population are non-practising Christians (the largest faith group of individuals in the Country) (Pew Research Center 2018, 7).

6 See Institut français d'opinion publique (2010). In addition, 37 per cent of the population of France identifies as religious; religious being circumscribed by those who responded affirmatively to the following question: Irrespective of whether you attend a place of worship or not, would you say you are a religious person, not a religious person or a convinced atheist? (Gallup International 2012) "The prohibition on state subsidy of religion comes only from the 1905 Law, which the Council of State reaffirmed does not apply in the region. The 1905 Law also abrogated the Concordat of 1801 between Napoleon Bonaparte and Pope Pius VII, as well as the Organic Articles of 1802, by which the French state had exercised the authority of appointing both Catholic and Protestant clergy. But once again, because Alsace-Moselle was not part of France in 1905, the French state continues to play a role in the appointment of Catholic bishops and, to a lesser extent, Protestant clergy in that region" (Gunn 2009, 958). The Paris mosque is often cited as an example of French state support for religion and for the "fact" that it extends beyond Christianity.

7 See, for example, Laborde (2013, 80).

8 See Troper (2016, 327). Michel Troper (2016) notes "a nonprofit private organization was created in 2005, the Conseil Français du Culte Musulman ('French Council of the Muslim Religion'). The intention of the government was to facilitate contacts with the [Muslim] community through a representative body, with the hope that it would favor a version of Islam more in tune with French values, help train new imams with some knowledge of French culture, and enable local authorities to help fund indirectly the construction of mosques, through cultural associations functioning under private law" (321). See also Baubérot (2014) and Gunn (2009).

9 The 1905 law also safeguarded state protection of and funding to certain religious buildings which were to remain public property and used by Catholics, Protestants and Jews (Troper 2016, 319).

10 "In addition, the French state, acting on a case-by-case basis, subsidizes private religious schools, the majority of which are Roman Catholic. Although French public schools are prohibited from teaching sectarian religion courses-Alsace-Moselle being the continuing exception-and although since 2004 public school students are prohibited from wearing 'conspicuous' religious symbols or attire, members of the clergy, wearing clerical robes, are authorized to go on to public school property and provide religious counseling to students who wish to receive" (Gunn 2009, 960). Gunn observes that the "the French state,

funding for religious schools and is largely exempt from the 1905 law. Despite being an officially "laïque" state (a point we will return to shortly), Catholicism[11] is the majoritarian religion in France.[12]

To further complicate matters, France has an extraordinarily high number of people who self-identify as atheists, in fact ranking fourth overall in the world.[13] Fully 29 per cent of the population self-declare as atheist[14] with a further 34 per cent describing themselves as "not a religious person".[15] Religious participation has declined dramatically (by about 21 per cent) between 2005 and 2012, with the overall global average drop, according to Gallup International (2012), being 9 per cent. This might, in theory, mean that Christian religious symbols would have no support in the public sphere. However, as we shall see in the case study in this chapter, public support and the legal interpretation of the presence of a nativity scene as a violation of France's laws related to laïcité do not follow in that direction. Instead, Christian symbols have been more fully synthesised into everyday relations as unassailable components of French society. Recalling the genealogy of Shinto in Japan by Josephson (2012), symbols and practices have been successfully repositioned as cultural rather than religious.

Immigration in France

Immigration in France is another important dimension of social context that shapes the response to religious symbols in the public sphere.[16] As of 2016, 7,902,783

however, has placed greater importance on the 'historical' reasons for granting an exception to the region than it has on the implications of the terms secular and indivisible in the 1958 Constitution" (958). See also Baubérot (2014, 106) for a discussion on this point.

11 The Paris mosque is frequently noted as an exception to the dominant pattern of state support for Catholicism, having been created in 1920 recognition of the 100,000 Muslims who died for France in the First World War (Lavoie 2016, 40).

12 Over a decade ago Pippa Norris and Ronald Inglehart (2004) observed that "overall levels of church disengagement had advanced furthest in France, Britain, and the Netherlands" (86). See also Kuru (2007, 2009) for further discussion of French policy related to religion. Confusingly, a report by the Pew Research Center found that although many Europeans say they are neither religious or spiritual, 71 per cent in Germany and 64 per cent in France identify as Christian (Sahgal, Pew Research Center 2018).

13 France ranks number four in the top ten atheist populations in the world behind only China, Japan and the Czech Republic (Gallup International 2012).

14 Michael Kelly (2017) states that, "Atheism remains an influential strand in several political organisations, particularly on the left, though it is also present in centrist movements in the tradition of the old Radical Party, and in some parts of the right. At the same time, atheism was most visibly promoted by a number of organisations devoted more specifically to arguing the case for non-belief and for its political expression in laïcité. A roll call of these associations signed a protest in 2012 against the resurgence of blasphemy laws in different countries" (114).

15 See Gallup International (2012).

16 Forty-three per cent of the French population is opposed to the building of mosques in France (Institut français d'opinion publique 2012, 20); 43 per cent of individuals in France also view the Muslim community as a threat to the national identity of France (Institut français d'opinion publique 2012, 5). Ironically, 69 per cent of French

people residing in France were born in a country other than France, accounting for approximately 12 per cent of the total population (Eurostat 2017).[17] In 2008, the majority of immigrants to France came from Algeria and Morocco with many also coming from other African countries such as Tunisia and colonies in the Maghreb (Selby 2014b, 26). Between 2009 and 2014, 58 per cent of the total immigrants to France were from continental Africa (INED 2017). [18] France has the largest Muslim population among the European Union member states, with 8.8 per cent of its population identifying as Muslim (Hackett 2017),[19] although given the official prohibition against measuring race, ethnicity and religion in official statistics it is difficult to know with any real precision the numbers, which are estimated to be between three and four million (Lavoie 2016, 41).

The contract of welcome and integration entered into by each immigrant on arrival in France identifies France as a laïque country and democracy and equality as non-negotiable values, which are foundational to the nation (Republican Integration Contract, n.d.).[20] Cécile Laborde (2008) characterises the approach to French immigrants as fully embracing the assimilationist model[21]—newcomers were expected to fit in, developing what she calls a national habitus that was "made up of specific social roles, moral outlook, and cultural dispositions", which was achieved through what Laborde describes as "forcible socialization and benign asset" (184–185). Laborde argues that immigrants are "not seen as altering the profound structures of French culture and society, but merely as yet another dissolvable ingredient into the capacious 'melting pot' that France had been for centuries" (184–185).[22] France,

society feels as though France is open and welcoming toward Muslims (Institut français d'opinion publique 2012, 11).

17 Interestingly, a recent Pew study showed that both practising (35 per cent) and non-practising Christians (36 per cent) believe that immigration levels should be reduced in France (Pew Research Center 2018, 22).

18 In 2012, 7 per cent of African immigrants to France came from Morocco, an additional 7 per cent from Algeria and 3 per cent from Tunisia (INSEE 2014). In addition, 24.5 per cent of the immigrants during this period originated in Asia; 10.5 per cent from continental America; 6.3 per cent from European countries other than EU member states and of the Vatican, Iceland, Liechtenstein, Norway, Andorra, Monaco, San Marino and Switzerland; and only 0.4 per cent from Oceania states (INED 2017).

19 James Beckford et al. (2005) note that "In France, the paradigms of universalism and laïcité prohibit the recognition of any ethnic or religious minorities in the public domain" (37). Consequently, this prohibition makes it difficult for those involved with social institutions (such as prisons) to identify the religious needs of individuals (211).

20 See also Ferrari (2010, 27–28). A recent Pew study points out that 20 per cent of religiously unaffiliated individuals, 41 per cent of non-practising Christians and 45 per cent of Church-attending Christians view Islam as incompatible with French culture and values (Pew Research Center 2018, 21).

21 See also Selby (2014a).

22 "En France, l'organisation de la politique d'immigration se fonde régulièrement sur la présence d'un modèle républicain axé sur la promotion de valeurs communes. Fondé sur la devise 'Liberté, Égalité, Fraternité', ce modèle politique républicain est souvent reconnu comme étant peu enclin à reconnaître l'existence de 'minorités' ou de 'communautés', qu'elles soient religieuses ou ethniques. La place des musulmans dans la

notes Laborde, was not unique from other colonial powers, but it was distinct in its revival and celebration of the assimilationist model in the 1980s and 1990s. Dire warnings of multiculturalism's divisive tendencies quashed a brief period of multicultural potential (185–186).[23]

Several terrorist attacks by Muslim extremists have served to foreground anxieties about immigrants and in particular Muslims.[24] The attacks include: the 2015 Charlie Hebdo massacre[25]; the Bataclan attacks in Paris[26]; and the 2016 Bastille Day attack in Nice.[27] These attacks have translated into an Islamophobia that

> has become the engine sustaining the many ways the larger narrative by which European nationalist societies represent themselves is given ideological and emotional resonance and urgency. Islamophobia provides the immediate rationale for the programs national states undertake to remain unified and coherent and by which they enact the State's role in providing social unity and security. (Amiraux 2016, 39)

It is in this context that the historic response to religion is able to be harnessed and mobilised to respond to contemporary issues. We thus see an entanglement of historical anti-clericalism, which largely prompted the re-crafting of the church–state relationship in France and present-day anxieties about the preservation of French values in face of growing diversity.

République française est souvent associée au passé colonial algérien, ce qui est problématique, selon Franck Fregosi" (Lavoie 2016, 39).

23 For a less stark assessment of multiculturalism in France see Paul May's (2016) media analysis of four national newspapers which found that multiculturalism has in fact infiltrated French public culture and the intellectual elite.

24 "After the January 2015 Charlie Hebdo attacks in Paris, the French government announced new efforts to encourage Imams to take civic lessons in which they would learn about French values and the place of religion in secular France. Manuel Valls, the prime minister at the time, explained: 'We need French chaplains and imams, who speak French, who learn French, who like France. And who believe in its values. And we also need French funding.' These attempts to train French Imams are not new; they have been ongoing since the past two decades. They are part of the efforts by different French governments to create an Islam of France rather than an Islam in France, that is: to regulate the forms and organization of Islam in France. This is also visible in the numerous attempts of successive French governments to facilitate the creation of a body that represents Islam in France, which led to the establishment, in 2003, of the French Council of the Muslim Religion" (Barras 2017, 142–143).

25 Three days of attacks in Paris left 12 people dead (BBC News 2015a).

26 In Paris, 130 people were killed and more than a hundred injured in attacks around the city, including at the Bataclan concert hall, a major stadium and various bars and restaurants (BBC News 2015b).

27 In Nice, France, 84 people were killed and 307 injured when a truck drove into a crowd of Bastille Day fireworks spectators. The driver possibly inspired by ISIS calls to target the citizens of countries who are involved in the fight against the terrorist group (BBC News 2016).

The defining concept in relation to state involvement in religion is laïcité,[28] the interpretation of which is varied and the subject of extensive scholarly and public debate. David Koussens (2015a) persuasively argues that it is more appropriate to talk about "laicites francaises" than "laicite francaise", noting that narratives about laïcité and juridical interpretations of laïcité are often very different. Michel Troper (2016) notes that:

> [laïcité] has meanings so diverse that Catholics and conservatives, who were strongly opposed to it during the Third Republic, nowadays accept it or at least some version of it. Thus, some view laïcité as a complete separation of religion and state; others as a kind of civil religion, sometimes, as at the beginning of the twentieth century, as an antireligious doctrine, criticized by its opponents as laicisme; while still others regard it as a system where the state may or ought to regulate religions provided that all religions are treated equally. Some will claim that the laic state, which puts limits to some public expressions of religious beliefs such as processions or some types of dress, is antiliberal, but others argue on the contrary that the state is liberal because it only limits religious freedom in order to guarantee other liberties and the general interest. (317)

As with other "secular" countries, a closer examination reveals the currents of majoritarian religion that course through the social institutions and practices of the state.[29]

The legal trajectory of the principle of laïcité[30] can be traced from the "*loi concernant la séparation des Églises et de l'État*" of 1905[31] (*Law on the Separation of*

28 See Baubérot (2013) for a historical account of the development of laïcité in France.

29 In her comparative comments, Waheeda Amien (2015) divides regimes with a commitment to secularism into two categories: exclusive secularists seeking to exclude all religion from the public sphere, and inclusive secularists who want to provide a space for all religions to some degree—or at least equally—within the public sphere. Canada and the United States are two inclusive secularist democracies, while France stands, until today, as a paradigmatic example of the exclusive secularist.

30 "Laïcité has been a hotly debated topic in France for the last 20 years. It is often presented as a reassertion of the 1905 principles for defining the place of religion in society, but increasingly it has provided a means of claiming historical legitimacy for a wide range of contemporary political and ideological positions" (Kelly 2017, 111).

31 Article 1 of the Law of December 9, 1905 concerning the separation of church and state reads: "La République assure la liberté de conscience. Elle garantit le libre exercice des cultes sous les seules restrictions édictées ci-après dans l'intérêt de l'ordre public" et aux termes de l'article 28 de la même loi: "Il est interdit, à l'avenir, d'élever ou d'apposer aucun signe ou emblème religieux sur les monuments publics ou en quelque emplacement public que ce soit, à l'exception des édifices servant au culte, des terrains de sépulture dans les cimetières, des monuments funéraires ainsi que des musées ou expositions."

Churches and the State), as well as the 1946[32] and 1958 Constitutions.[33] Two kinds of laïcité, "legal secularism" and "narrative secularism", are identified by Alessandro Ferrari (2009, 2016) with the former being rooted most often in constitutions and the latter in social relations.[34] Jean Baubérot (2014), a well-known theorist of French secularism and a member of the Stasi commission (discussed below), has characterised laïcité as having two types of social representation, one which aims to

> build a secular state through a political and juridical process that respects freedom of conscience. The second one wanted to impose a process of secularization politically. Historically, the first representation prevailed, in particular with the 1905 law. Today, there is great confusion, and the second conception claims to follow the 1905 law as well. (110)[35]

In a subsequent book, Baubérot (2015) identifies seven types of laïcité. Despite its increasingly broad and arguably vacuous meaning rendering it all things to all people, laïcité is passionately defended and promulgated.[36]

There is also a special preoccupation with "cults" in France,[37] which has developed a regime of regulation and law specifically targeted at new religious movements.[38]

32 Bowen (2007a) points out that it is the 1946 Constitution that actually introduces the word "laïcité" (1007).

33 Article 1 of the Constitution of October 4, 1958 reads: "La France est une République indivisible, laïque, démocratique et sociale. Elle assure l'égalité devant la loi de tous les citoyens sans distinction d'origine, de race ou de religion. Elle respecte toutes les croyances."

34 For an insightful empirical comparative analysis of Quebec and France which uses this dual conceptualisation of laïcité, see Lavoie (2016). For a discussion on "legal secularism" and "narrative secularism" see Ferrari (2009, 2016).

35 "The first theoretical definition of French laïcité was given by philosopher Ferdinand Buisson. In 1882 an important secular law was passed, establishing that the state schools had to become religiously neutral. According to Buisson, laïcité is the result of a historical process in which the public institutions freed themselves from the power of religion. In France, the decisive factor in this process was the "Declaration of the Rights of Man and of the Citizen" (Baubérot 2014, 104).

36 See Kelly (2017, 113).

37 "The office within the Interior Ministry with responsibility for religious matters is the Bureau of Religious Affairs (Bureau des Cultes). The Bureau has other important responsibilities for religious matters, including issuing guidelines to Préfets regarding which entities should be recognized officially as 'religious associations.' The ability of a religious group to register under the 1905 Law is of major importance because it provides the entity with an additional protection against being labeled a 'cult.' When it was decided that the Jehovah's Witnesses in France did not qualify as a religion under the 1905 Law, the religious society was ordered to pay millions of dollars in taxes, and was fined for publishing religious tracts without approval" (Gunn 2009, 960). See also Richardson and Introvigne (2004) for a detailed discussion of some of the French initiatives to curb the activities of new religious movements.

38 "French citizens provide overwhelming support for the République's egregious measures of social control of minority faiths—all in the name of 'Liberty, Equality and Fraternity'—and there is very little dissenting opinion" (Palmer 2011, 4).

This regime, also created in the furtherance of laïcité, developed prior to the present-day focus on religious symbols in the public sphere, but has eased somewhat since the early 2000s. Private anti-cult organisations were especially successful in influencing public policy and state responses to minority religious groups and there is sometimes an acceptance of a brainwashing rhetoric that has elsewhere been dismissed as lacking credibility.[39] Overall, however, the focus on minority religions, be they new or old, is one of control and regulation.

The relationship between laïcité and republican values has been considered extensively and is one that has changed as its social context has shifted. As in Quebec, France too has engaged in a public assessment of the state's role in managing the new diversity. In 2003, the French president created The Independent Commission of Reflection on the Application of the Principle of Laïcité in the Republic, most commonly known as the Stasi Commission (headed by Bernard Stasi, who served as France's *Médiateur de la République*, or Ombudsman). The Commission's mandate was framed as "A reflection on the application of the principle of laïcité in the Republic" (Stasi 2003, 2) and has been described as focusing on making "proposals about the practical application of the principles of secularism, or *laïcité*" (Prélot 2017, 69). Describing the context within which it was working, the Commission noted the law as establishing the framework for the church–state relationship, the increased diversity of France, the need to rethink integration and national unity and laïcité as the key to living together in this new diversity.[40]

Under this mandate, the Stasi Commission examined numerous questions of religion and state, including the contentious issue of religious vestments worn by students in French public schools.[41] Bowen summarises the findings of the Stasi Commission and a parliamentary commission: "Their hearings and the media coverage of the issue depicted grave dangers to French society and its tradition of secularism (laïcité) presented by Islamic radicalism, a trend toward 'communalism,'

39 For a discussion on the controversies of brainwashing rhetoric see Beckford and Richardson (2003). In addition, for a discussion on France's approach to cults, see Palmer (2011).

40 "La loi du 9 décembre 1905 a affirmé la séparation de l'Eglise et de l'Etat. La question laïque ne se pose plus aujourd'hui dans les mêmes termes. En un siècle la société française est devenue sous l'effet de l'immigration diverse sur le plan spirituel et religieux. L'enjeu est aujourd'hui de ménager leur place à de nouvelles religions tout en réussissant l'intégration et en luttant contre les instrumentalisations politico-religieuses. Il s'agit de concilier l'unité nationale et le respect de la diversité. La laïcité, parce qu'elle permet d'assurer une vie commune, prend une nouvelle actualité. Le vivre ensemble est désormais au premier plan" (Stasi 2003, 66).

41 Talal Asad suggests "not only that government officials decide what sartorial signs mean, but that they do so by privileged access to the wearer's motive and will—to her subjectivity—and that this is facilitated by resort to a certain kind of semiotics. A governmental commission of inquiry claims to bring private concerns, commitments and sentiments into the public sphere in order to assess their validity for a secular Republic, but it does much more than that. It constitutes meanings by drawing on internal (psychological) or external (social) signs, encourages certain desires and emotions at the expense of others" (Asad 2005, n.p.).

and the oppression of women in the poor suburbs" (Bowen 2007b, 1).[42] Following the recommendations of the Stasi report, the French government enacted a 2004 law that banned "ostentatious" religious symbols in public schools.[43] The law disproportionately impacted Muslim girls, although it also had an effect on Sikh boys.[44] A subsequent law enacted in 2010 placed further restrictions on "religious" clothing in public, effectively banning the burqa or niqab, justifying the restriction on the basis of equality rather than security.[45]

A young Muslim woman, S.A.S., who occasionally wore the burqa in public, challenged the 2010 law, with her case eventually coming before the European Court of Human Rights.[46] The court accepted her sincerity and found that she

42 As David Koussens (2009) points out, as recently as 1989, "[t]he conseil d'État clearly affirmed that 'the wearing of religious symbols by students, symbols which are worn with the intent to manifest belonging to a religion, are not in themselves incompatible with the principle of laicism in the measure that they constitute an exercise in the freedom of expression and the manifestation of religious beliefs'" (207–208). See also Lavoie (2016, 57–60).

43 "The law of 15 March 2004 stipulates that 'in primary and secondary public schools, the wearing of signs or clothes through which pupils ostensibly express a religious allegiance is forbidden'. The law's targets are Muslim headscarves, though Jewish yarmulkes and large Christian crosses are also banned in state schools. The law was intended to put an end to the 15-year long affaire du foulard which started in the Parisian suburb of Creil in the autumn of 1989 when two pupils came to class wearing Muslim scarves. The incident—quickly politicized by all sides—sparked a hotly contested national debate about religious neutrality in republican schools, the dwindling status of public education in a fragmented society, the problematic legitimacy of traditional norms of authority and social integration, the status of women in minority cultures, the protracted liquidation of the colonial legacy, the politicization of race and immigration, the seemingly difficult integration of North African immigrants, fears about a 'conflict of civilizations' pitting the West against Islamic fundamentalism, and a sense of diffuse threat to French national identity" (Laborde 2008, 7). See also Barras (2017).

44 Jessica Fourneret (2006) points out that following the passing of the 2004 ban, by "November 2004, forty such students had been expelled, including thirty-six Muslim girls and four Sikh boys who wore turbans" (240). In France, 63 per cent of the population are opposed to Muslim women wearing a "veil" or "scarf". In contrast, only 7 per cent are accepting of women who wish to do so (Institut français d'opinion publique 2012, 22).

45 Selby (2014a) states that "Unlike other Western European nation states like Spain, Italy, and the Netherlands that have emphasized securitization in their justifications for legislating prohibitions on full-face veils, rationales for the 11 April 2011 law in France and for the proposed Bill 94 in Quebec appeal to a desire to safeguard women's equal rights. That is, Government documents in France and Quebec frame face-covering hijabs as countering hard-fought advancements related to sexual liberation and gender parity" (440). Valérie Amiraux (2016) writes of the ban in France: "The ban has paradoxically contributed to creating a hyper exposure of what veiled women want to keep hidden, without consideration for, or attention to, how this private intimacy has suddenly been exposed to outside gaze. For about twenty-five years now, French public opinion has been chattering about veiled Muslim women in much the same way that tabloid headlines gossip about the latest styles and goings-on of a celebrity" (43). See also Amiraux (2018).

46 *S.A.S. v France [GC]* (CEDH, n. 4385/11) (hereinafter *S.A.S.*).

was not coerced into wearing the niqab (this is a central theme of analysis in the case), but ultimately deferred to the margin of appreciation to allow France the freedom to impose such a law.[47] Melanie Adrian (2015) links the meaning of the niqab to the very ordering of French society: "The act of veiling is seen as being opposed to how the public and private are divided, and how laicite is currently interpreted. Being Muslim (in private) is not the issue, but acting Muslim (in public) is" (376). As Adrian argues, the veil acts as a barometer of the degree to which Muslims fit into French society (376–377). More broadly, Cécile Laborde (2012) notes: "After twenty-two years of anti-Muslim hysteria, prohibitionist fever, and legal paternalism in France, there is little evidence that the republican causes of female emancipation, social integration, and inter-cultural understanding have been in any way promoted or furthered" (410).[48]

It is difficult to underestimate the impact of these debates in terms of shaping the context in which discussions about religious symbols in the public sphere unfold. There was fierce debate about religious symbols in the public sphere, mostly directed at Muslim clothing.[49] This debate translated into the place of Muslims in French society, and the headscarf was the refractor for the question of whether and how Muslims were or could be assimilated.[50] The very nature of French society and French values was perceived to be at stake. As Matthias Koenig (2015b) argues, requests for recognition are conceptualised as "polluting the sacred core of the nation", and transgress a symbolic boundary between the public and the private (51). The debate carried over to the *S.A.S.* case, which is a final key contextualising event in the framework for understanding how a nativity scene came to be characterised as culture, heritage, and part of the "religious fact" of French life.[51]

47 Hussein Agrama (2015) states, "But even as a personal belief and choice, the veil was still construed by the state as an essentially religious, and fundamentally Islamic, sign. For state officials, it indicated a will and a desire to manifest Islam. Some saw it as potentially indexing a rising Islamism, one that degraded women in ways incompatible with the French republic's fundamental values. It was thus a will and a desire that the state sought not to encourage, lest its values become undermined" (305).

48 Cécile Laborde (2008) proposes the notion of critical republicanism through which she seeks to reshape the articulation of French republicanism to match the new diversity of France: "Substantively, critical republicanism strongly criticizes the hijab ban but seeks to retrieve and rehabilitate, in a progressive direction, some of the republican concerns which motivate it. It thus offers its own version of the three ideals of laïcité: equality as secular impartiality, liberty as non-domination, and fraternity as trans-ethnic integration" (8–9).

49 Although architecture too has attracted similar attention: "polls conducted in France have revealed a favorable opinion of the limitation on the construction of mosques" (Göle 2016, 15). See also Koussens (2015b).

50 See Bowen (2007b) for an extensive discussion.

51 Janet Epp Buckingham (2014) argues that state-imposed secularism results in the equal marginalisation of all religions (207). If France can be described as a secular society, it is peculiar that the nativity scene is a cultural symbol with authority to be displayed during Christmas while the burqa is a religious symbol banned from public spaces. Thank you to Cory Steele for this observation.

Away in a manger ...

> A white felt-covered, picnic-sized table sits in a large hallway. Arranged carefully atop it are handmade ceramic figurines, or santons, and miniature sheep, a camel, a donkey, all taking shelter in a wooden barn. An angel—glowing in golden light—watches over the scene. In the centre, drawing the focus of all the figures, is Baby Jesus resting in a hand-crafted manger. Cordoned off as a short-term display, the artisanal crèche in La Roche-Sur-Yon's city hall has a homespun character, much like a nativity scene one might find in front of a home or local church. As he hurried by on his way to conduct some business with officials in the town hall, Jean Regourd noticed the same nativity scene that had been there the previous year. It was impossible not to see and he remembered that the year before he had thought about calling it to the attention of the city officials. As president of La fédération de Vendée de la libre Pensée, he was perhaps especially sensitised to such overt religious displays, which, in his view, were obviously contrary to the principle of laïcité. When he arrived home, he sat down at his desk and wrote a letter to the General Council of Vendée, lodging an official complaint.

Home to a population of over 53,000, the town of La Roche-Sur-Yon is the capital of the Vendée department in the Pays de la Loire region in Western France.[52] In December 2012, the Vendée Federation of Free Thought filed a complaint about the nativity scene, arguing that it was a violation of the law of 1905 and the Constitution of 1958. The president of the general council refused to prohibit the installation of a nativity scene in the Vendée town hall, which typically appeared at the beginning of December each year. The town presented a number of arguments to justify its decision: that the 1905 law did not support a demand that religious symbols be completely absent; that a Christmas nativity scene did not constitute a religious symbol but a traditional celebration that evolved from a "religious fact"; and that a strong religious tradition in Vendée justified tolerating the presence of a nativity scene as a symbol of a local specificity that had never before been challenged by elected opposition officials.[53]

The Administrative Tribunal of Nantes agreed with the Federation and outlined the specifically religious nature of the nativity scene in its decision, finding that the

52 Other cases involving France have been brought before the European Court of Human Rights. Of these cases, two were declared inadmissible. The first of these inadmissible cases involved a turban-wearing Sikh in an airport (*Phull v. France* (Dec), no. 35753/03, ECHR 2005-I) and the other a Muslim woman who was refused entry into French consular offices for not removing her veil (*El Morsli v. France* (Dec.), no. 15585/06, March 4, 2008). In *Palau-Martinez v. France* (no. 64927/01, § 43, ECHR 2003-XII), the Court ruled that the applicant failed to establish that her freedom of religion had been infringed under Article 9 of the Convention for the Protection of Human Rights and Fundamental Freedoms. In *Cha'are Shalom Ve Tsedek v. France* [GC], no. 27417/95, § 73, ECHR 2000-VII the applicants claimed their right to freedom of religion was infringed after being refused access to slaughterhouses to perform ritual slaughter as per ultra-orthodox Jewish religious practices. The court ruled that the applicants' right to freedom of religion had not been violated.

53 Tribunal Administratif de Nantes, 14 novembre 2014, Fédération de Vendée de la Libre Pensée, n° 1211647 [*Crèche AC*] at p. 2.

scene represents the birth of Jesus Christ; that the coinciding of the construction of the display with preparations for a Christian festival and of a specifically religious symbol surpasses the simple traditional familial and popular representation of this period; and that the municipality had not successfully analogised the display, which takes place at the same time each year, with a museum display (which is permissible). The tribunal considered the display "religious", and not culture or heritage (*Crèche AC*, at p. 2).[54]

It was not the end of the matter and in 2015 the Administrative Court of Appeal of Nantes issued a decision reversing that of the Administrative Tribunal. The Appeal Court reasoned that the display, which was made up of Mary, Joseph and accompanying shepherds around the bed of Baby Jesus, was not of a religious nature because it was of such a small and non-ostentatious size, did not have other religious elements, and was part of a tradition of the family Christmas celebration.[55] The nativity scene did not, therefore, enter into the realm of those things prohibited by the 1905 law and violated neither the principles of freedom of conscience, nor the neutrality of the public service.

The case was then considered by the Conseil d'État, France's Administrative Supreme Court, with the Federation reminding the Conseil that "La République n'est ni chrétienne, ni juive, ni musulmane, niathée! La République est laïque! C'est ce que vient de rappeler le Conseil d'Etat!"[56] In November 2016 the Conseil d'État ruled on the *Vendée* case, in addition to another case from the Paris Administrative Court of Appeal.[57] The Conseil d'État held that the Administrative Court of Appeal of Nantes had not taken into account all necessary elements, especially the local context, to determine the lawfulness of the display and so

54 Original French: "une crèche de Noël ne constitue pas un emblème religieux mais un emblème d'une fête traditionnelle issue d'un fait religieux; l'existence d'un particularisme local, issu d'une forte tradition religieuse en Vendée, permet de tolérer la présence d'une crèche de Noël comme un symbole d'une situation locale spécifique qui n'a d'ailleurs jamais été remise en cause par les élus de l'opposition".

55 La cour administrative d'appel de Nantes, October 13, 2015, n° 14NT03400 [*Crèche CA*]. Original French: "que toutefois, compte tenu de sa faible taille, de sa situation non ostentatoire et de l'absence de tout autre élément religieux, elle s'inscrit dans le cadre d'une tradition relative à la préparation de la fête familiale de Noël et ne revêt pas la nature d'un *signe ou emblème religieux*".

56 Fédération nationale de la libre pensée (2016).

57 Fédération nationale de la libre pensée (2016). In 2012, the Fédération départementale des libres penseurs de Seine-et-Marne asked the Mayor of Melun not to install a Christmas crèche at City Hall during the month of December. The crèche was erected despite the request of the Libre Penseurs. The matter was brought before the Administrative Court of Melun and later the Administrative Court of Appeal of Paris (Cour administrative d'appel de Paris, 1ère chambre, October 8, 2015, n° 15PA00814, Inédit au recueil Lebon). The Paris court had ruled nativity scenes could not be displayed in public places under any circumstances. The Conseil d'État overruled the decision of the Court of Appeal of Paris (Conseil d'État, 9 novembre 2016, N° 395122, Publié au recueil Lebon). The judgments of the Conseil d'État in France "are written more in a civilian tradition and tend to be short relative to judgments of the higher courts in England and Wales" as well as Canada and the United States (Arden 2015, 243).

referred the case back to the Court of Appeal for re-examination. The Conseil d'État held that a nativity scene could have religious meaning, but it could also simply be decoration marking the end of year celebration and could therefore have no religious significance. The Conseil d'État highlighted the placement of the nativity scene and considered whether it could be construed as an act of proselytisation or as conforming to the principle of the neutrality of public officials.

On November 10, 2016, the Conseil d'État issued a press release commenting on the display of Nativity scenes in general that essentially reiterated the statement of the rapporteur public.[58] The Conseil d'État (2016) affirmed that the nativity scene could evoke different meanings:

> [Nativity scenes] have a religious meaning but are also a decorative element during the end of the year holidays. Given this plurality of significations, the Conseil d'État rules that the display of the Nativity scenes by a public authority in a public space is lawful, only if it has a cultural, artistic or festive purpose, but not if it expresses a public recognition or a preference for a religion.

The Conseil d'État (2016) offered guidelines for determining the religious content of the display:

> In order to examine whether a Nativity scene display fulfills a cultural, artistic or festive purpose, or on the contrary if it demonstrates a public recognition or preference for a given religion, the Conseil d'État rules that the display needs to be contextualized, taking into account the particular circumstances in which it is done, the existence or the absence of local traditions and the location of the display.

Here the celebration of Christmas as a religious holiday is separated from the notion of a "festive purpose" and the crèche becomes, potentially, simply a marker of a vague marking of the "end of year" festival or an artistic expression. Indeed, it must take one of these other meanings in order to avoid expressing a state recognition of Christianity:

> First of all, it was necessary to determine whether a crèche, which is only the staging of the birth of Jesus as the Gospels tell it, is in itself a religious sign or emblem. Not necessarily, the members of the Conseil replied in a landmark decision, in that, according to them, "a crèche is a representation likely to have a plurality of meanings". It certainly has a "religious character" because it illustrates "a scene that is part of Christian iconography". But it is "also an element that is part of the illustrations that accompany traditionally, without specific religious significance, the holiday season".[59]

58 The *rapporteur public*, Madame Aurélie Bretonneau, is a member of the Conseil d'État that acts as an intervener to help formulate the judgment of the Court (Conseil d'État n.d.). Bretonneau issued her statement on November 9, 2016.

59 Translated from the original French by me. Original French: "Il s'agissait d'abord de déterminer si une crèche de la Nativité, qui n'est que la mise en scène de la naissance de Jésus telle que la relatent les Evangiles, est en soi un signe ou un emblème religieux. Pas

As with the somewhat bizarre assessment of the cross in the *Saguenay* case as failing to meet canonical standards, the crèche is rendered religiously meaningless, or at least harmless, and reconstituted as a collection of figurines. A persistent feature of justifications to maintain the prominent public presence of symbols like the crèche in France and the crucifix and other artefacts is their artistic value. The municipality of Vendée took the position that in fact the display of the crèche was an artistic display, an argument that the Court of Appeal accepted:

> The crèche is only installed temporarily for the Christmas period, and has the character of a temporary artistic and/or cultural exhibition, without religious connotation, in the respect of the republican calendar.[60]

Recall that a similar argument was made by the municipality in the *Saguenay* case (an argument that was accepted by the Court of Appeal of Quebec), which was in all likelihood inspired by the French example. In France, however, artistic renderings are specifically exempt by law from the rules of laïcité, if they have an "artistic or historical value".[61] This exemption may well have produced the crèche as an artistic display when it otherwise would not have been so considered.[62]

nécessairement, ont répondu les conseillers d'Etat dans une décision qui fera date, dans la mesure où, selon eux, « une crèche est une représentation susceptible de revêtir une pluralité de significations ». Elle a certes un « caractère religieux » car elle illustre « une scène qui fait partie de l'iconographie chrétienne ». Mais elle est « aussi un élément faisant partie des illustrations qui accompagnent traditionnellement, sans signification religieuse particulière, les fêtes de fin d'année »." See *Le Monde* (Chambraud 2016).

60 Original French: "la crèche n'est installée, de façon provisoire, que pour la période des fêtes de Noël, et a le caractère d'une exposition provisoire, à vocation culturelle et/ou artistique, sans connotation religieuse, dans le respect du calendrier républicain". See *Cour administrative d'appel de Nantes*, Case N° 14NT03400, at page 2.

61 See Article 16 of *Loi du 9 décembre 1905 concernant la séparation des Eglises et de l'Etat*: "Il sera procédé à un classement complémentaire des édifices servant à l'exercice public du culte (cathédrales, églises, chapelles, temples, synagogues, archevêchés, évêchés, presbytères, séminaires), dans lequel devront être compris tous ceux de ces édifices représentant, dans leur ensemble ou dans leurs parties, une valeur artistique ou historique." https://www.legifrance.gouv.fr/affichTexte.do?cidTexte=JORFTEXT000000508749

62 According to a news article published in *France Today* (Vallois 2014), "It was egalitarian because it represented in miniature the entire spectrum of post-Revolution Provence—commoners all, little people most, aristocrats none, except for the royal Magi. It was counterrevolutionary because it incorporated the Nativity scene into its secular world. Ultimately free-spirited, for a time the crèche antagonized both the Church and the Republic. The Church tolerated it only as trivial entertainment for children; the homogenizing French Republic frowned upon it as a subversive expression of regional identity. But the people loved these little figures, who seem to have made their first official public appearance in 1803, within the framework of the Foire aux Santons, held in Marseille by three vendors. The sale of 180,000 santons, recorded in 1886, illustrates their persistently growing popularity despite the hostility from higher quarters." It is worth mentioning that a lively industry of *santonnier* (figurine) production has existed since the 1800s. These miniature figures were apparently invented by a counterrevolutionary as a symbolic levelling of the pre-French Revolution hierarchies.

Over the course of the various court processes, the public reaction to the decisions made local, national and international news. After the initial Tribunal decision, the former chair of the general council for the municipality declared that the elected officials would not apply the decision, which he described as inequitable. He accused Libre Pensée of trying to do away with the "roots of our [French] culture", which he described as "an old Christian territory. The nativity is part of its heritage, beyond beliefs and sensibilities". Using the same slippery slope lament that the mayor of the city of Saguenay had used in Quebec, he declared "if we give up on this symbol today, we'll have to give up the rest tomorrow".[63] A comment along similar lines wondered if street decorations would also have to be removed: "Respect for secularism is not the abandonment of all our traditions and cutting our cultural roots, argued the Department. Must we ban the stars in the Christmas garlands that decorate our streets, on the pretext that it is a religious symbol?"[64]

These extensions, linked to "our traditions" and "our roots" produce a discourse of loss and threat to "us". While statements of public reaction may not be representative of a dominant sentiment, they do give voice to a particular interpretation of events that certainly has traction in public life. Like the religious symbols and practices being debated, such statements lend a certain credibility, and indeed sometimes inspiration, to those who adhere to a past preserving model.

The discussion of the meaning of the crèche was caught in a vortex of religion and culture, each carrying a rich meaning that linked, simultaneously, to legal rules, institutional hierarchies, nation and citizenship, lived religion and nonreligion. The BBC reported a member of the Federation of Free Thinking as saying, "[i]t's a child in a stable with a cow and a donkey … It is clearly a religious symbol, there's no doubt about it. And these local council buildings were built in the 1980s so there is no local nativity tradition to speak of" (in fact, the nativity scene had been displayed in this way only since 1989).[65] The meaning of the crèche was hotly contested, with religious groups claiming both the religious and cultural meaning of it:

63 Ouest-France (2014). Original French: "La France est une vieille terre chrétienne. La crèche fait partie de son patrimoine, par-delà les croyances et les sensibilités." "Philippe de Villiers, l'ancien président du conseil général, critique avec virulence le jugement du tribunal administratif de Nantes interdisant l'installation de la crèche dans le hall. À l'origine de cette initiative, il appelle « les élus du département à ne pas appliquer cette décision inique. À ne pas plier devant la Libre Pensée, qui n'est pas une pensée libre, et qui prône l'éradication de toutes les racines de notre culture. La France est une vieille terre chrétienne. La crèche fait partie de son patrimoine, par-delà les croyances et les sensibilités. Pourquoi ne pas interdire les cloches? Je récuse ce laïcisme totalitaire, qui est une forme de terreur moderne aux conséquences incalculables. Si on cède aujourd'hui sur ce symbole, alors il faudra céder sur le reste demain »" (Ouest-France 2014).

64 Ouest-France (2014). Original French: "Le respect de la laïcité n'est pas l'abandon de toutes nos traditions et la coupure avec nos racines culturelles, motive le Département. Faudrait-il interdire les étoiles dans les guirlandes de Noël qui décorent nos rues, sous prétexte qu'il s'agit d'un symbole religieux?"

65 *BBC News* (Caulcutt 2014). See also Ouest-France (2014).

> "It's a question of a balanced and open approach," argues Jean-Marc Sauvé, Vice-President of the Council of State, "as opposed to a general and absolute ban, which would have constituted a fundamentalist reading of the law of 1905." The Conference of Bishops of France took note of this decision and recalled that "the Church has always affirmed that the crèche was a religious symbol as well as an aspect of culture." On the other hand, the Union of Lay Families has accused the Conseil d'État of "flouting neutrality in the public sphere."[66]

The French Senator Bruno Retailleau[67] released a statement calling the Tribunal decision inequitable and grotesque. He vowed to appeal the decision all the way to the European Court of Human Rights if necessary. "This decision is unfair. Obviously, there are double standards, where at the same time no one challenges the opening of Ramadan dinner offered every year by the mayor of Paris." He went on to say,

> the symbol of the crèche is beyond a religious symbol. It is part of a common heritage that unites us beyond the beliefs of one another. The outrage that arose spontaneously shows how our fellow compatriots, believers or not, remain attached to their collective history … Our cultural roots and our common traditions are also social bonds that keep us united.[68]

Three themes are of note here: first, Retailleau's positioning of the matter as related to Muslims in France; second, his invocation of the notion of common heritage that transcends individual beliefs; and third, the leveraging of compatriots. The boundary between "compatriots" is constructed by folding in "believers or not" (which was also a theme in the comments of the former mayor), claiming the nonbelievers as also being attached to collective history and as contributing to social cohesion through their acquiescence to the crèche and its agreed upon symbolism for "le nous".

Expressing disagreement is in this way constructed a boundary between us and them, who transform from atheists into Muslims in some of the public discourse:

> The santons had provoked a lively controversy as Christmas 2015 approached, with some mayors going on crusade to defend crèches in a France ravaged by the attacks of 13 November. The debate on secularism or identity has never

66 Original French: "Il s'agit d'une approche équilibrée et ouverte, fait valoir Jean-Marc Sauvé, le vice-président du Conseil d'Etat, à l'opposé d'une interdiction générale et absolue, qui aurait constitué une lecture intégriste de la loi de 1905. 'La Conférence des évêques de France a pris acte de cette décision et rappelé que « l'Eglise a toujours affirmé que la crèche était un symbole religieux ainsi qu'un élément culturel ». L'Union des familles laïques a en revanche accusé le Conseil d'Etat de « bafouer la neutralité dans la sphère publique »." (*Le Monde*, Chambraud 2016).

67 Bruno Retailleau was first elected as a member of the French Senate on September 26, 2004 and re-elected on September 28, 2014. According to his official profile, he is *Senateur de la Vendée (Pays de la loire)*. He also served as *Deputé de la Vendée* and *Président du conseil général de la Vendée*. See https://www.senat.fr/senateur/retailleau_bruno04033b.html

68 *LeFigaro.fr* (Retailleau 2014).

> disappeared, igniting this summer around the "burkini", a case also reported to the Conseil d'État, which invalidated a series of orders taken by some communities to ban Islamic bathing suits.[69]

The statements about Muslims and the juxtaposition of the crèche and a terrorist attack,[70] as well as the controversy over the burquini,[71] serve to associate otherwise unrelated events through authoritative declarations of the truth of their links to each other. As Amiraux (2016) argues, such declarations are "reminiscent of the social function of gossip. It betrays secrets and perpetuates rumours" (44). Gossip, proposes Amiraux, creates a "kind of authority, irregardless of its initial source" (44). The spectre of "the Muslim", a racialised religious other in contrast to the raceless (white) secular model, creates a powerful narrative that takes on truth value to identify the threat to the crèche and by extension French culture and values. This conceptualisation and association becomes, through its circulation, impossible to challenge, taking on the authority of a truth that cannot be displaced by evidence.[72]

Though the actual complainants in the case are from the Federation of Free Thinking, lurking in the background is a racialised other who is imagined as being poised to destroy French values. This other is alluded to in the memoire of the town, which refers to the Federation as the "ayatollahs of free thinking" gesturing to an "Other" who is both a foreigner and a despot. The accusation invokes the characterisation of such others (who are barely disguised Muslims) as undemocratic and controlling dictators. How dare such interlopers challenge French values, culture and heritage? The Court of Appeal noted the "regrettable use" of this phrase, but found that the accusation did not exceed the limits of comments made in the context of a contentious procedure such as the one before it.[73]

69 *Le Télégramme* (2016). Original French: "Les santons avaient provoqué une vive controverse à l'approche de Noël 2015, certains maires partant en croisade pour défendre les crèches, dans une France meurtrie par les attentats du 13 novembre. Le débat sur la laïcité voire l'identité n'est jamais retombé depuis, s'enflammant cet été autour du 'burkini', une affaire également remontée jusqu'au Conseil d'État, lequel a invalidé une série d'arrêtés pris par certaines communes afin d'interdire ces tenues de bain islamiques très couvrantes."

70 On November 13, 2015, 130 people were killed and many more injured in an organised series of bombings at a soccer game, malls and the famous Bataclan concert hall in Paris (BBC News 2015b).

71 Many coastal municipalities in France have banned the burkini on their beaches, considering the clothing incompatible with "good morals and secularism" (*The New York Times*, Rubin 2016).

72 Amiraux (2016) notes, "gossip facilitates the soft imposition of dominant ideas that subsequently become almost impossible to contest" (45).

73 "Considérant que, contrairement à ce que soutient la Fédération de la Libre Pensée de Vendée, les termes du mémoire présenté pour le département de la Vendée, qualifiant ses représentants 'd'ayatollahs de la libre pensée' pour regrettables qu'ils soient, n'excèdent pas les limites de la controverse entre parties dans le cadre d'une procédure contentieuse" (Cour Administrative d'Appel de Nantes, N. 14NT03400, pg. 3–4).

The motivation for the demand for removal of the nativity scene is identified as being a desire to impose multiculturalism by "pseudo-laïcards" who wish to eradicate tradition.[74] This is in turn linked to Islam:

> Oh, how smart they are! They drape themselves in the tinsel of secularism to better impose a multicultural society! They claim to act in the name of the law of 1905, but their personal agenda is to open France to communitarianism, whose creeping rise marks the dilution of our society! They attack a symbol of Christianity (a false symbol in fact) to promote the equality of religions, and to be the propagandists of an Islam that is still far from being majority. And on the other hand, certain elected officials are bent on religious traditions that are in fact only popular traditions: blindness everywhere.[75]

Framed as being outside of comprehension, the contestation of the presence of the crèche renders those who challenge it as also being outside of culture, tradition and even reason. To challenge the crèche is to challenge *la fraternité*, that mantra of cohesion infiltrating the French version of "nous".

> That the manger should first have its place in churches or in the houses, who would dispute it? We now hear that its installation in the hall of a general council, even in land historically Catholic, can arouse reservations and criticism.
>
> But it is doubtful whether its dismantling, here or elsewhere, succeeds in erasing the place taken by this symbol in the public mind for centuries as an announcement of peace. The crèches of Provence with their figurines, which represent all the trades of the earth, are they not a sign of this universality and this fraternity, between those who believe in heaven and those who do not believe in it?
>
> Lastly, it is hard to believe that a crèche in a public place could disturb public order, but on the contrary one can fear that its disassembly will disturb consciences. Our country still has a long way to go in the practice of tolerance.[76]

74 *Le Point* (Brighelli 2014).

75 *Le Point* (Brighelli 2014). Original French: "Oh, comme ils sont malins! Ils se drapent dans les oripeaux de la laïcité pour mieux imposer une société multiculturaliste! Ils prétendent agir au nom de la loi de 1905, quand leur agenda personnel a l'ambition d'ouvrir la France au communautarisme, dont l'avènement rampant marque la dilution de notre société! Ils font mine de s'en prendre à un symbole de la chrétienté (un faux symbole en fait) afin de promouvoir l'égalité des religions, et de se faire les propagandistes d'un islam qui est tout de même très loin d'être majoritaire. Et de l'autre côté, certains élus s'arcboutent sur des traditions religieuses qui ne sont en fait que des traditions populaires: l'aveuglement partout."

76 *Le Croix* (Challand 2014). Original French: "Que la crèche ait d'abord sa place dans les églises ou dans les maisons, qui le contesterait? Que son installation dans le hall d'un conseil général, même en terre historiquement catholique, puisse susciter des réserves et des critiques, on peut l'entendre.

Mais que son démontage, ici ou ailleurs, parvienne à effacer la place prise par ce symbole dans l'esprit public depuis des siècles comme annonce de paix, il est permis d'en douter. Les crèches de Provence avec leurs santons qui représentent tous les

Moreover, "tolerance" becomes something that needs to be learned by those who would dare to challenge the universal symbol that harms no one. The problem is worked up as being about an intolerant minority who has much to learn. The weight of the past pushes onto the present, marshalling "our" values, universal symbols and assimilation in a potent mix of response. A subtle invocation of this appears in the statement by the rapporteur public as reported in *La Croix*:

> In his conclusions, the public rapporteur mentioned the position of the Observatoire de laïcité, which proposes a "case-by-case" assessment, and called for a "pacifying" approach to laicite. "The religious fact gives rise to new tensions. We do not believe that this context requires you to instruct in principle the trial of the crèche, to want to scrupulously track down the religious behind the festive tradition or folklore, to stir up suspicions and controversies", assured the magistrate while suggesting the censoring of political "instrumentalizations" that might be being undertaken.[77]

Denied religious meaning, the crèche shrank to an inconsequential, innocuous size that could not possibly harm, even as it takes on epic proportions in its significance to French identity. In their submission, the Departement de la Vendée argued that the crèche was not by nature a religious symbol in the sense of the 1905 law, that "Noël est fêté par tous les français" and that religious displays that do not upset the public order and that coincide with local and popular traditions do not violate the 1905 law.[78] The municipality circumscribed the boundary of what it means to be French, implying that anyone who does not join in the celebration is not truly French. The universal relevance of Christmas is taken as a matter of fact, rendering it beyond scrutiny except superficially and certainly not reducible to a mere religious symbol or practice. It is a matter of culture and a practice of everyone.

Both the Court and the municipality identified collective belonging through the notion of the "*fait religieux*", which further embedded the crèche in French culture as a fact which cannot be disputed, and rendering any effort to do so all the more heinous. The constitution of the "crèche de Noel" as a cultural symbol emphasizes

métiers de la terre ne sont-elles pas le signe de cette universalité et de cette fraternité, entre ceux qui croient au ciel et ceux qui n'y croient pas?

On peine, enfin, à croire qu'une crèche dans un lieu public puisse troubler l'ordre public, on peut en revanche craindre que son démontage ne trouble bien inutilement les consciences. Notre pays a décidément encore du chemin à faire dans la pratique de la tolerance."

77 *Le Croix* (Gorce 2016). Original French: "Dans ses conclusions, le rapporteur public avait mentionné la position de l'Observatoire de la laïcité, qui propose une appréciation « au cas par cas », et avait plaidé pour une approche « pacificatrice » de la laïcité. « Le fait religieux suscite de nouvelles crispations. Nous ne croyons pas que ce contexte vous impose d'instruire par principe le procès de la crèche au risque, à vouloir trop scrupuleusement traquer le religieux derrière la tradition festive ou le folklore, d'attiser des soupçons et des controversies », assurait la magistrate tout en suggérant de censurer les « instrumentalisations » politiques qui pourraient être faites."

78 *Cour administrative d'appel de Nantes*, N° 14NT03400, at p. 2.

tradition by denying its religious symbolism while at the same time identifying the practice as a mere "fact" of France's Christian religious heritage. Asserting the "religious fact"[79] erases diversity, both of other religious practices and of nonparticipation or nonreligion and constitutes the celebration of Christmas as a national activity in which all French can and should participate. On this point the Municipality of Vendée was adamant: "Christmas is celebrated by all French citizens."[80] Senator Bruno Retailleau positioned participation in this symbolic celebration "*par excellence*" as a social interaction capable of weaving strong familial bonds, forging national unity and fostering social cohesion across humanity.[81]

An op-ed in the Catholic French newspaper *La Croix* describes how the Christmas celebration, though devoid of its former spiritual and religious significance, is a part of French life, foundational to shared social life:

> A lot of noise, a lot of wasted time. To these "affairs", renewed each year in a few places, answers a campaign denouncing the Christianophobia of our country. Reasonably, the episcopate refuses to argue, not wishing to comment on a court decision and feed the media echo. Because there is the risk: to talk about it is to play the game of those—in the minority—who waved the secular flag, without even noting that Christmas—devoid of any spiritual sense, and that which touches Christians—is present in all heads and all families, as a moment of joy and tenderness. And that Advent calendars flourish, also totally stripped of their meaning, supposed to teach patience to the children. Traditions deeply rooted in the minds, experienced by the French as opportunities for sharing and gathering, of which no one thinks of depriving themselves.[82]

The reference to "what we all do" subtly creates a vertical relationship that enforces a particular way of being French that is beyond reproach and beyond Christianity. The universalisation of Christianity is a common theme in the transubstantiation of

79 I am grateful to Frédéric Dejean for his guidance on this notion of "religious fact" whose meaning is not easily translated into English

80 Original French: "Noël est fêté par tous les français" (*Cour administrative d'appel de Nantes*, Case N° 14NT03400).

81 Original French: "Réalité sociale également, avec cette fête du rassemblement par excellence où se tisse, dans l'unité des familles, l'unité nationale et la grande unité de la grande famille humaine" (*LeFigaro.fr*, Retailleau 2014).

82 *Le Croix* (Quinio 2014). Original French: "Beaucoup de bruit, beaucoup de temps gaspillé. À ces « affaires », renouvelées chaque année en quelques lieux, répond une campagne dénonçant la christianophobie de notre pays. Raisonnable, l'épiscopat refuse de polémiquer, ne souhaitant pas commenter une décision de justice et alimenter l'écho médiatique. Car là est bien le risque: en parler, c'est faire le jeu de ceux—très minoritaires—qui agitent le drapeau laïque, sans même noter que Noël—débarrassé de tout sens spirituel, et de cela les chrétiens peuvent s'émouvoir—est présent dans toutes les têtes et toutes les familles, comme un moment de joie et de tendresse. Et que fleurissent des calendriers de l'Avent, là aussi totalement dépouillés de leur signification, censés apprendre la patience aux enfants. Des traditions bien ancrées dans les esprits, vécues par les Français comme des occasions de partage et de rassemblement, dont personne ne pense à se priver."

religion to culture across contexts, though it assumes unique contours in each manifestation. Symbols and practices transcend the religious in this imaginary of a "nous" who is unified by their presence.

> It is undeniably a Christian scene since it represents the birth of Christ. But it is certain that it has long since passed the religious sphere. This is a tradition, a rite of the end of the year for many families, Christian or not.[83]

In a case similar to *Vendée*, the nativity scene in the town of Béziers, in the south of France, was also embroiled in a dispute. Robert Ménard, the mayor of Béziers, despite a written complaint, decided not to take down the nativity scene, noting in a radio interview with RMC Radio on December 5 that the display is part of French culture. He admitted that it also had religious connotations, but that "everything has a religious connotation", claiming that even the date is related to the birth of Christ. He then noted that "we are dealing with a type of ayatollahs of laicite".[84] In this statement, attention is turned back on those who challenge the crèche, who are constructed as being unreasonable and radical. This same tone, including the mixing of disparaging those who brought the claim with a paranoia about Muslims and the erosion of culture and history, is evidenced in the following statement:

> In that context, the agnostics of Libre pensée who fought for the banning of the crèche vendéenne have become, against their will, the useful idiots of a communitarian agenda: the crèche was banned to equalize all religions in a French tradition, which nevertheless remains the legacy of Greco-Latin culture (the Revolution, which broke out in the midst of neoclassicism, benefited from it greatly) as well as of the Judeo-Christian legacy (the Third Republic established the separation of Church and State, but it took charge of the repair and maintenance of thousands of religious buildings in France: the restoration of Mont Saint-Michel has become synonymous with the Republic, although it was done in the name of artistic rather than religious principles). Going forward, however, Islam will have the right to demand the same treatment, claiming that it is the cultural tradition of tomorrow—since we will have eradicated the cultural traditions of yesterday.[85]

83 *Le Journal du Dimanche* (Tabet 2014). Original French: "C'est indéniablement une scène chrétienne puisqu'elle représente la naissance du Christ. Mais il est certain qu'elle a depuis longtemps dépassé la sphère religieuse. Il s'agit d'une tradition, d'un rite de la fin de l'année pour beaucoup de familles, chrétiennes ou non."
84 RMC Radio (2014).
85 *Le Point* (Brighelli 2014). Original French translated by Gofen Bar-On Santor: "Dans ce contexte, les agnostiques de la Libre pensée qui se sont battus pour l'interdiction de la crèche vendéenne sont contre leur gré les idiots utiles d'un agenda communautariste: on interdit une crèche pour égaliser toutes les religions dans une tradition française qui pourtant ne connaissait que l'héritage gréco-latin—la Révolution, qui a éclaté en plein néoclassicisme, en fit ses choux gras—et judéo-chrétien—la IIIe République a instauré la séparation de l'Église et de l'État, mais elle a pris en charge la réfection et l'entretien des milliers d'édifices religieux de France: la restauration du Mont Saint-Michel, c'est la République, et ce n'était certes pas au nom de principes religieux, mais artistiques. Mais

Another strategy of displacement of Christianity, which is one that is sometimes also used in relation to the Christmas tree in North America, is to identify the pre-Christian roots of the practice. In an opinion piece published in the weekly magazine *Le Point*, Paul Brighelli (2014) traces the cultural roots of the crèche, arguing that it is more pagan than Catholic:

> This story of the crèche is much more like a recycling of pagan traditions (just like the Christmas tree, a symbol of persistent greenery and immanent rebirth – must we recall that it is not by chance that Christmas was made to coincide with the winter solstice?) than an authentically Christian veneration.[86]

By diluting the practice in question, it is distanced from Christianity, and thus not a manifestation of a church–state relationship, or, put otherwise, a violation of laïcité. The crèche is not really Christian, not really belonging to any one religion, and in fact a practice that represents "everyone".

Danièle Hervieu-Léger (2000) argues that the appeal to tradition, continuity and authority is a compensator for the "looseness of current social ties" (96). She points out that the actual veracity of the claims to tradition are irrelevant, and that they in fact may be "purely imaginary" (96).[87] Like Amiraux's (2016) observations about gossip, the truth content of the narrative is not important. It is the work it does to produce a sense of meaning and shared values that is important. Reflecting on Hervieu-Léger's focus on religion as a lineage of belief and chain of memory, Laniel (2016) points out "metaphorized religion could be used by whomever dares when institutional control diminishes" (379).

As culture, some French authorities are willing to protect nativity scenes as sacred symbols of what it means to be French: there is no possibility of opting out, or of diversity, a position reinforced by language such as "everyone" and "no one", with those who might object being constructed both as noncitizens and a threat. Vertical, hierarchical relations are inscribed in the crèche, which is "us". The role of the state is to guard laïcité, ensuring that the public sphere remains free of religious symbols.

The state

The reference point for the management of symbols in the public sphere in France is the 1905 law, which affirms freedom of conscience and lays the foundation for a

désormais, l'islam aura le droit de revendiquer un même traitement, en affirmant qu'il est la tradition culturelle de demain—puisque aussi bien on aura éradiqué les traditions culturelles d'hier."

86 *Le Point* (Brighelli 2014). Original French: "Cette histoire de crèche ressemble bien davantage à un recyclage de traditions païennes (tout comme le sapin de Noël, symbole de la verdure persistante et qui renaîtra bientôt—faut-il rappeler que ce n'est pas tout à fait par hasard que l'on a fait coïncider Noël avec le solstice d'hiver?) qu'à une vénération authentiquement chrétienne."

87 Danièle Hervieu-Léger (2000) argues that religious traditions preserve chains of collective memory within modern societies.

laïque state. The 1905 law does not actually use the word "laïque", which comes later in 1946.[88] On the issue of state neutrality, the public authority cannot express a public recognition or a preference for a religion, thus effectively meaning that the state must be neutral. David Koussens (2009) summarises the genesis of state neutrality:

> In France, the state's neutrality has its origins in the classical principles of political liberalism. However, its application, influenced by a strong political will—as in the case of the attitude towards religious symbols—remains guided by a very republican conception of laicism. (210)

In 2004, the law transitioned from the state to users of the public service when the headscarf ban was imposed on students (Barras 2017, 145).

The neutrality of the state was an important point of debate in the *Vendée* case. To dispute the argument that it had violated the requirement of ensuring freedom of conscience, the municipality argued that the nativity scene was symbolic of a traditional celebration which is based on a "religious fact", and that the 1905 law does not require a total absence of religious signs, but instead supports freedom of conscience and religious free exercise, restricted only in the interests of public order. The municipality noted that Article 28 of that law stated that "it is forbidden, in the future, to raise or affix any religious symbols or emblems on public monuments or in any public place, except for religious buildings, burial grounds in cemeteries, funerary monuments and museums or exhibitions" (*Creche Tribunal*, p. 3).[89]

The municipality also argued that the nativity scene was an exhibition, again bringing it within the exemptions of the law. The Tribunal rejected these arguments and found that the Federation was justified in its complaint, and that the council president (as the official responsible for of state neutrality) had misunderstood or misinterpreted the 1905 law. The Tribunal noted that the crèche was displayed each year, that it illustrated the birth of Jesus Christ and that its display coincided with the celebration of Christmas. It also noted that the symbolism of the display surpassed a simple representation of a traditional family or popular celebration. The crèche was displayed every year, it was not in an exhibition hall nor had the municipal hall been transformed as such. The display did not have opening and closing hours, but was instead visible to the public at all times during the Christmas period. It was not, therefore, a "local particularism". All of these factors meant, according

88 "In fact, although the law was entitled Separation of the Churches and the State, these words were not repeated in any of its provisions, nor was the word laïcité mentioned in the text. The separation thus consisted mainly in a general prohibition to fund religions, a proclamation of freedom of religion, and provisions regarding properties used for the practice of religion" (Troper 2016, 327).

89 Original French: "Il est interdit, à l'avenir, d'élever ou d'apposer aucun signe ou emblème religieux sur les monuments publics ou en quelque emplacement public que ce soit, à l'exception des édifices servant au culte, des terrains de sépulture dans les cimetières, des monuments funéraires ainsi que des musées ou expositions."

to the Tribunal, that Article 28 of the law of 1905 had been misinterpreted by the president of the Vendée council.[90]

Although it too did not accept that there were local specificities that exempted the municipality, the Court of Appeal subsequently found that: the crèche was located in the hall of the municipal building; that the display was small and non-ostentatious and that it lacked any other religious element; that it was part of a tradition related to the family celebration of and was not a religious symbol or sign. It did not, in the Court's view, violate the principles of the neutrality of the public service.

The Conseil d'État explained in detail the links between the law, state neutrality and the actions of the municipality, being careful to stress that public servants and agents could not recognise or financially support religious groups. The Conseil d'État noted the exceptions to the general rule, which included displays of an artistic or festive nature that did not have specific religious content. The context of the display, including its place of installation, was also a consideration.

We can see that through the rules, which create a regime of exceptions, and their interpretation, the state has authorised preference for Christianity through the display of symbols. Local areas are able to claim, as was the case in *Vendée*, that the unique nature of the local culture exempts such symbols from restrictions imposed in other jurisdictions. A patchwork of exemptions for "special" local cultures creates an overall pattern of privilege for Christian (now cultural) symbols. It is this convoluted regime of exemptions that the Fédération nationale de la libre pensée is essentially objecting to. For instance, the Fédération nationale de la libre pensée was clear about those elements of the crèche that brought it within prohibitions of the law:

> Free Thought also observes that the presence of Christian crèches in certain buildings of the Republic does not constitute a tradition, for the Conseil d'État. Indeed, as has always been maintained, only the representation of Mary, Joseph and the baby Jesus confers a religious character to a Christian nativity scene, insofar as these characters embody the Nativity, and not the donkey and the ox. A crèche with the figurine of a miller poses no problem to free thinkers.[91]

90 The judgment read as follows: "Considérant qu'il ressort des pièces du dossier que la crèche, dont l'aménagement est renouvelé chaque année dans le hall de l'hôtel du département de la Vendée pour les fêtes de Noël et notamment au titre de l'année 2012, représente, par son contenu qui illustre la naissance de Jésus Christ, et sa concomitance avec les préparatifs de la fête chrétienne de la nativité, un emblème religieux spécifique dont la symbolique dépasse la simple représentation traditionnelle familiale et populaire de cette période de fête; que le département n'établit pas que la présence, renouvelée chaque année et à la même période, de cette crèche participerait d'une exposition ni que le hall de l'hôtel du département serait aménagé en tant que musée; qu'ainsi, en refusant de mettre un terme à l'aménagement d'une telle crèche, dans un lieu dont il est constant qu'il est ouvert au public, le président du conseil général de la Vendée, qui ne démontre pas l'existence d'un particularisme local qui l'autoriserait à maintenir une telle présentation, a méconnu les dispositions précitées de l'article 28 la loi du 9 décembre 1905" (*Creche Tribunal*, p. 4).

91 Fédération nationale de la libre pensée (2016). Original French: "La Libre Pensée observe également que la présence de crèches chrétiennes dans certains bâtiments de la

Going one step further in a representation that would seemingly solidify the link between church and state, the crèche in the city hall of Marseille has santon figurines of the mayor and the priest who comes to bless the crèche. The mayor explained his decision to put his figure in the midst of the nativity action:

> "*En effet, un santonnier du Panier m'a offert ce joli santon à mon effigie, et j'ai décidé de le mettre dans la crèche*," confirme la maire (divers gauche) des 2e-3e arr., qui revendique avec humour sa place dans cette "*crèche républicaine*".[92]

The Fédération nationale de la libre pensée was, not surprisingly, critical of an elected official linking the crèche and the state.

In an especially ironic move, two young hijab wearing Muslim women are marshalled to affirm the innocuousness of the crèche—something that pleases children and is a celebration for everyone:

> Passing through the town hall yesterday morning, two young women in hijab confirm: "It's nice, it appeals to children, and we find all the artisans of the past". No, the representation of a Christian scene does "not bother" them: "Christmas is everyone's celebration, no?"[93]

The tiny, harmless symbols, universal in their meaning through the *fête de tout le monde* circumscribe the boundaries of Frenchness, which, despite its "laïque" nature, is deeply intertwined with its religious heritage. In his exploration of French secularism, Baubérot (2014) notes that

> President Nicolas Sarkozy placed official emphasis on France's old "Catholic roots." During a visit to the Pope, the former president said that religious morality was better than secular morals. He also vetoed bills separating civil laws and religious norms, like those pertaining to euthanasia or same-sex marriage. (106)

Like crosses and crucifixes, nativity scenes in societies with traditionally Christian majorities have been a key site of the negotiation of diversity and important indicators of a society's ability to respond to the push (or pull) toward a model of inclusion that is called for by human rights guarantees and their concomitant

République ne constitue pas une tradition, pour le Conseil d'Etat. En effet, comme elle l'a toujours soutenu, seule la représentation de Marie, Joseph et l'enfant Jésus confère un caractère religieux à une crèche chrétienne, dans la mesure où ces personnages incarnent la Nativité, et non l'âne et le boeuf. Une crèche avec un santon de meunier ne pose aucun problème aux libres penseurs."

92 *La Provence* (Manelli 2014).

93 *La Provence* (Manelli 2014). Original French: "De passage en mairie hier matin, deux jeunes femmes en hijab confirment: 'C'est joli, ça plaît aux enfants, et on retrouve tous les métiers du temps passé'. Non, la représentation d'une scène chrétienne ne les 'dérange pas': 'Noël, c'est la fête de tout le monde non?'"

social currents.[94] The French case, however, is especially interesting because of the context in which it is found—laïcité is conceptualised as a value of the Republic. Freedom from religion would seem to take a higher priority than freedom of religion, and is itself entangled in the core values of liberty, equality and fraternity.[95]

An alternative narrative

Although tempered by the continuous pressure of laïcité which shapes the expression of objections to the crèche, there is evidence that some of the public discourse about the crèche cases is also shaped by a concern for a robust and inclusive notion of *vivre ensemble*, which recognises the impact of the crèche on those who enter into public space.[96] For example, a report prepared by the Mayor's Association of France noted that it was up to those locally elected to take responsibility for a laïcité that is both a condition of living together and a powerful factor in human emancipation. In their view, the crèche was not compatible with

94 The US Supreme Court decided in *Lynch v. Donnelly* [1984] that a city's Christmas display featuring a nativity scene did not violate the Establishment Clause and in fact had "legitimate secular purposes" (at p. 680). Justice O'Connor wrote, in his concurring decision, "The evident purpose of including the creche in the larger display was not promotion of the religious content of the creche but celebration of the public holiday through its traditional symbols. Celebration of public holidays, which have cultural significance even if they also have religious aspects, is a legitimate secular purpose" (at p. 691). "These features combine to make the government's display of the creche in this particular physical setting no more an endorsement of religion than such governmental 'acknowledgements' [465 U.S. 668, 693] of religion as legislative prayers of the type approved in *Marsh v. Chambers*, 463 U.S. 783 (1983), government declaration of Thanksgiving as a public holiday, printing of 'In God We Trust' on coins, and opening court sessions with 'God save the United States and this honorable court.' Those government acknowledgments of religion serve, in the only ways reasonably possible in our culture, the legitimate secular purposes of solemnizing public occasions, expressing confidence in the future, and encouraging the recognition of what is worthy of appreciation in society. For that reason, and because of their history and ubiquity, those practices are not understood as conveying government approval of particular religious beliefs. The display of the creche likewise serves a secular purpose—celebration of a public holiday with traditional symbols. It cannot fairly be understood to convey a message of government endorsement of religion. It is significant in this regard that the creche display apparently caused no political divisiveness prior to the filing of this lawsuit, although Pawtucket had incorporated the creche in its annual Christmas display for some years. For these reasons, I conclude that Pawtucket's display of the creche does not have the effect of communicating endorsement of Christianity" (at pp. 692–693).

95 For more on laïcité in France, see Baubérot (2013), Scott (2007), Willaime (2008), Laborde (2008), Koussens (2015a).

96 In his analysis of multiculturalism in four national newspapers, Paul May (2016) found that there is "a sharp dichotomy between two opposing philosophies that reflect different visions of the political community and the individual" (1336). A narrative of inclusion, equality and a broad vision of national identity is evidenced in the national public discourse examined by May.

this vision of laïcité.[97] This language of living together was also, as previously noted, part of the discourse of diversity management in the *S.A.S.* decision.

Similarly, the secretary general of Libre Pensée, David Gozlan, suggested that while the crèche should not be displayed in a building of the Republic because it is "neither Christian, Muslim or Jewish", there are other ways to represent Christmas—a garland or a tree, for example, and that it was important that anyone who enters into a public building must have a feeling of total neutrality. Striking a compromise that would respect the place of the holiday in French culture but not impose a symbol that was too closely aligned with a particular segment of the population and a specific narrative of "le nous" was clearly on the mind of not only Libre Pensée, but others who struggled to renegotiate the symbolic representation of French-ness.[98]

Creative solutions to the display of the crèche were implemented in some municipalities: in Montiers the crèche was moved to a church cemetery wall—still visible to anyone who passed by, but also associated with the church and not a state property.[99] As with the crucifix in Saint-Sacrement, the negotiation of such symbols is a necessary component of living well together in a new diversity—in some cases this means that the symbols return to spaces more readily associated with religion, such as churches, and in others they may require explanation, adjustment of position or the addition of other symbols or modification of practices.

The erasure of religious symbols from public spaces is not unequivocally linked to a future forming model. Rather, the goal is to create a space for discourses of inclusion and negotiation in which difference is respected rather than ironed flat. A narrative that insists that anyone who is French celebrates Christmas creates a rather exclusive vision of belonging as well as an impossible position for those who do not feel part of this "anyone". To position this as the "religious fact" could be seen as a straightforward recognition of the traditional majoritarian place of Christianity in France; however, it becomes problematic when the "fact" is used to actively construct an other who is placed outside of the imagined community[100] in a democratic society.

In order to move to a place of conversation and compromise, those who insist on the inviolable nature of symbols and practices must first acknowledge their own privilege and the exclusionary effects, both in terms of the history being told about "us" and in relation to building an inclusive diversity.

97 Maries de France (2015).
98 *Libération* (Fofana 2016).
99 *La Croix* (Gorce 2014).
100 "Communities are to be distinguished, not by their falsity/genuineness, but by the style in which they are imagined" (Anderson 2006, 6).

4 A Christian nation and the land of the free

A place of prominence ensured that his message, universally applicable to all, would be heard. It is important to hold power in love and with compassion, especially when one has a monopoly. And everyone is free, in the end, to refuse to be saved.

Religion in the United States

The dominant history of religion in the United States is largely a story of Protestant Christianity.[1] In 2010, 78.3 per cent of Americans identified as Christian, though Pew predicts that that number will continue to decline.[2] The story of American religion has been retold a number of times, perhaps most famously in Will Herberg's (1955[1983]) *Protestant, Catholic, Jew: An Essay in American Religious Sociology*, [3] and again in Robert Bellah et al.'s (1985) *Habits of the Heart: Individualism and Commitment in American Life*, [4] a lament for an imagined time of social cohesion that has been formulated as civil religion,[5] and more recently in Robert Putnam's (2000) *Bowling Alone: The Collapse and Revival of American Community* in which he declares "[f]aith communities in which people worship together are arguably the

1 This of course focuses only on settler religion and leaves aside the rich traditions of Indigenous peoples who are the original owners and inhabitants of the United States. See Johnson (2013) and Dunbar-Ortiz (2014).

2 See Pew-Templeton Global Religious Futures Project (2015). Gallup had a similar finding in 2017 suggesting that 37 per cent of Americans identify as being highly religious, whereas 33 per cent are not religious at all (*Gallup*, Newport 2017).

3 "American religion and American society would seem to be so closely interrelated as to make it virtually impossible to understand either without reference to the other" (Herberg 1983, 3).

4 See Herberg (1983) and Bellah et al. (1985). For a wide-ranging discussion of the impact of this work, see the section titled "Symposium on the 20th anniversary of Habits of the Heart" in *Sociology of Religion* 68(2) (Yamane 2007).

5 Will Herberg (1983) also talked about civil religion: "The American Way of Life as the 'common faith' of American society has coexisted for some centuries with the historic faiths of the American people, and the two have influenced each other in many profound and subtle ways" (81).

single most important repository of social capital in America" (66). The establishment of Christianity as the majoritarian religion has been perpetuated by pervasive myths about America as a Christian nation, which is countered by an equally pervasive myth about the separation of church and state, both being seen as "true" simultaneously.[6] An adamant insistence on the separation of church and state combined with *de facto* permeation of state, social institutions and civil society of a protestant sensibility produces a peculiar tension, not unlike that in France related to laïcité, though with its own specificities.

The myth of the Christian nation is especially important to understanding how religious symbols are cast. It also frames the ways in which many Americans think about themselves in relation to the nation, which is itself a fraught relationship—Americans both love and hate the state and are engaged in a continuous project of its denial and its mobilisation. Religion and the conceptualisation of its role is explicitly linked to governance and the role of the state, with conservatives seeing the nature of the United States as explicitly linked to divine order and the moral foundation flowing from that. The state must use law's force to keep moral order. The liberal vision of the role of the state leaves moral choices to individuals, with the state having no link to divine order. As David Sehat (2011) observes, these contrasting visions have resulted in an acrid climate in present day United States (283).

Interminable debates about the religious affiliations of the "founding fathers", their intentions, and the genesis of the notion of the wall of separation between church and state, with varying approaches to "accommodation" permeate American scholarship. As John Fea (2011) points out, the stakes are high in these discussions with the winner not only able to lay claim to the correct historical narrative, but consequently, to the proper moral direction of the United States.[7] Interestingly, as religious diversity has increased in the United States, the number of people who view the United States as a Christian nation has also increased, rather than decreased.[8]

As we shall see, this commitment to a narrative of a Christian nation and its links to conceptualisations of authentic citizenship impacts the translation of practices such as prayer in state meetings in particular ways, evidencing a more overt hostility

6 As Mary Jo Neitz (2013) points out, "what might be categorized as the dominant religion in the United States is not stable. The Protestant mainline had a certain cultural hegemony through most of the twentieth century—so much so that scholars, denominational leaders, and church members in post-Reagan America were surprised to find the mainline increasingly displaced by 'conservative churches'" (137).

7 "For Christian nationalists there is a lot at stake in getting history—'His story'—correct. The removal of God from public life and the ensuing tragedy associated with the failure to teach children about the Christian roots of America have profound consequences for the social and moral fabric of the nation" (Fea 2011, 74).

8 In the mid-1990s, 60 per cent of respondents to a Pew poll considered the United States a "Christian nation". This rose to 67 per cent and 71 per cent in 2002 and 2005 respectively (Straughn and Feld 2010, 281).

to the nonreligious than in Canada and France.[9] Moreover, its constitutive and productive force is a powerful element in the regulation of diversity.[10]

Figures for the number of people who identify as nonreligious in the United States vary, though Gallup International (2012) suggests that 30 per cent of the American population identify as "not a religious person" with a further 5 per cent referring to themselves as "a convinced atheist".[11] One of the distinctive features of the American context is the peculiar attitude toward nonreligion, particularly atheism. The will to religion is especially high in the United States: Although Christianity is the majoritarian religion, there is a dominant ethos that sees having some religion, no matter what kind, as better than having no religion. For example, Gervais et al. (2011) note that 45 per cent of Americans would not vote for a "qualified atheist presidential candidate" (1189). This prejudice extends into the employment sector where Wallace et al. (2014) conclude that "atheists were second lowest overall in the employer preference scale" for hiring practices in the American south (201).[12] This social pressure may in part account for the tendency to default to a declaration of religious affiliation.[13]

Discrimination against the nonreligious has been documented by Hammer et al. (2012) as well as Edgell et al. (2006; 2016), though their research focuses specifically on atheists and atheist identification. As Cragun et al. (2012) point out, "atheists run

9 "By conditioning recognition as an authentic American on adherence to Christian faith, the idea of a Christian America tacitly reinforces the moral prestige of the religious majority, even as it presents Americans of other faiths, or with no formal religion, with invisible barriers to symbolic inclusion" (Straughn and Feld 2010, 281). In a comparative comment, Barry Kosmin (2014) notes: "American attitudes remain less anticlerical than those of the French [...] Nearly one-third of Americans—proportionately three times as many as the French—believe that the clergy are entitled to try to influence national politics" (39).

10 Steven Green (2015) summarises the myth and its consequences: "One of the more popular and enduring accounts of America's past is that of its religious founding. Belief that the British-American colonies were settled largely by religiously devout people in search of spiritual freedom, that the United States government was founded in part on religious principles, that the Founders intended to create a 'Christian nation,' and that America is a specially chosen nation whose success has been directed by divine providence has resonated in the national psyche for generations. Versions of this account have existed since the founding era and have persisted through times of national distress, trial, and triumph. They represent a leading theme in our nation's historical narrative, frequently intertwined with expressions of patriotism and American exceptionalism" (1).

11 Other studies indicate that figures for the number of people who identify as nonreligious in the United States vary. Pew-Templeton (2015c), for example, estimates 16.4 per cent of the people in the United States are nonreligious.

12 "In the workplace, self-identifying as an atheist or agnostic significantly increases the likelihood of reporting discrimination relative to those who self-identify as religious nones" (Cragun et al. 2012, 119).

13 Much like the religious, understanding nonreligion and the nonreligious is context specific. For example, non-affiliated individuals in the United States are more likely to pray or to believe in God than their European counterparts. See Pew Research Center (2018).

counter to what Americans generally think of as culturally acceptable, because they do not, as a group, endorse religion. As a result, they are one of the most despised people in the US today" (105).[14] A climate of dislike or even hatred is perpetuated by the circulation of anti-atheist sentiments through the media and popular culture.[15] In his 2009 inauguration speech, President Barack Obama stated that the United States was composed of "Christians and Muslims, Jews and Hindus—and nonbelievers". This mention of "nonbelievers" was the "first time that an American president has ever acknowledged the existence of nonbelievers in such a public forum" (Zuckerman 2012, 175). Leigh Eric Schmidt (2016) notes that Obama's inauguration speech had a "Jeffersonian ring" to it, except that Obama used the term "nonbeliever" rather than "infidel" (19).[16] Nonreligious individuals who are not atheists are assumed to have some sort of religious inclination, making them more acceptable, though the characterisation of nonreligious as "seekers" comes with its own prejudices. The idea that many of those who self-describe as nones are quite simply indifferent to religion has little place in a society in which people are expected to have a religion.[17]

Immigration in the United States

The United States has historically defined itself as a country of immigrants, with the Statue of Liberty and its inscription, which beckons the "tired, poor and huddled masses yearning to breathe free",[18] providing the symbolic and rhetorical

14 This prejudice is not only part of American culture. In their analysis of attitudes toward atheists worldwide, Will Gervais et al. (2011) found that even in so-called secular countries anti-atheist prejudice was a powerful force. They speculate that there may be a pervasive belief in the link between religion and morality, and that religion acts as a preventative force against immoral behaviour.

15 For atheists, "slander was a nearly ubiquitous form of perceived discrimination. Only 5% of the sample reported never having witnessed anti-atheist rhetoric in print or television media, suggesting that participants found media messages denigrating atheism to be widespread. It was also relatively common for participants to report that they were told their atheism is an immoral choice, reminiscent of the messages directed at LGB's regarding the 'immorality' of their sexual desires and/or choices" (Hammer et al. 2012, 56).

16 "There is an ebb and flow in political sentiment, and America reverted back into the Lockean form of toleration, which distrusts nonbelievers in certain epochs: for example, at the height of the Cold War in the 1950s, with the incorporation of God into the Pledge of Allegiance and onto banknotes, or in the early 2000s, with the Office of Faith Based and Neighborhood Partnerships" (Kosmin 2014, 40).

17 See Quack and Schuh (2017) and Sullivan (2014).

18 The inscription reads: "Not like the brazen giant of Greek fame, with conquering limbs astride from land to land; Here at our sea-washed, sunset gates shall stand a mighty woman with a torch, whose flame is the imprisoned lightning, and her name Mother of Exiles. From her beacon-hand glows world-wide welcome; her mild eyes command the air-bridged harbor that twin cities frame. 'Keep ancient lands, your storied pomp!' cries she with silent lips. 'Give me your tired, your poor, your huddled masses yearning to breathe free, the wretched refuse of your teeming shore. Send these, the homeless, tempest-tost to me, I lift my lamp beside the golden door!'"

touchstone for that image. In 2015, 1,051,031 people became permanent residents of the United States though their religious affiliation is unknown. In 2016, of the 85,000 refugees who entered the country 38,901 were Muslim. Between 1992 and 2012, roughly 1.7 million Muslims entered the United States as legal permanent residents (Pew Research Center 2013). "Of the 15.5 million legal immigrants who entered the United States between 1989 and 2004, only 1.2 million were from predominantly Muslim countries" (Cesari 2011, 25). About 1 per cent of the population in the United States is Muslim (Mohamed 2016),[19] compared with approximately 3 per cent in Canada (Statistics Canada 2011) and an estimated 8.8 per cent in France (Hackett 2017).

Unlike the Canadian and French contexts, there has been no major commission or report on diversity or religious minorities in the United States. Moreover, there is little scholarship that has focused on multiculturalism,[20] diversity or the regulation of religious minorities in the United States, though there is significant literature on migration, much of which focuses on assimilation.[21] All three countries share a disproportionate preoccupation with Muslims and each evidences the presence of Islamophobia; though as Erik Love (2009) points out, in the United States the target is a broader racialised group that extends beyond Muslims: "The complex, racialized phenomenon now known as 'Islamophobia' has affected the lives of many people across the United States with a 'Muslim-like' appearance" (402). The combination of unique contextual factors, including historical debates and their continued presence in contemporary public discussions, a strong anti-communist sentiment that links socialism and atheism, and a minimal presence of Muslims as the pressing issue related to immigration (despite the rhetorical flourish of the current administration on this issue) means that unlike Canada and France, the defence of religious symbols and practices as culture and heritage is more likely to be positioned against nonbelievers rather than Muslims. The "other", in the American context, is the atheist and the religiously uncommitted. Moreover, there is a qualitatively stronger presence of a validation of religion and especially Christianity as holding a place of privilege. In other words, religion appears more frequently as religion, rather than

19 "The situation in Europe contrasts sharply with that in the United States, where Muslims tend to have more education and a higher income than the non-Muslim population. Because the U.S. Census does not ask about religion and Muslims are too small a proportion of the population to be reliably measured in general national surveys, exact information on their status is not easy to obtain" (Cesari 2011, 31).

20 This may in part be because the United States has never had multiculturalism as an official or formal policy, according to Prema Kurien (2007, 13). See also Ronald Takaki (1993) for a comprehensive examination of ethnic and racial diversity in the United States.

21 "This orientation has a long tradition in American sociology and is a legacy of the assimilationist lens through which early American sociologists examined the impact of the country's large-scale European immigration. This assimilationist orientation in turn is a product of a static model of identity that views national culture as given or already accomplished, usually at origin. According to this view, the cultural essence of a nation is defined at its birth and then needs to be maintained and safeguarded through its history" (Kurien 2007, 5).

culture or heritage, though the justification for its dominance is usually coupled with heritage or history.

Tisa Wenger (2017) situates religious freedom in Christianity, whiteness and national identity, arguing that religious freedom talk in the early twentieth century

> functioned in various ways to shape and to navigate the imperial hierarchies of race, nation, and religion. Americans who could assert the racial status of whiteness claimed this freedom as a racial possession and used it to define a superiority that they tied both to their religion (Protestant) and to the secular modernity that it grounded. (2)

Further, there is some research suggesting that non-Christian religions take a Christian shape in order to participate in American culture.[22] Practices such as prayer and constructing community around church-like events are two examples.

Freedom and establishment

The single most influential aspect of American law in regard to religious symbols and practices in the public sphere has been the "Establishment Clause". This first amendment of the US Constitution reads:

> Congress shall make no law respecting an establishment of religion, or prohibiting the free exercise thereof; or abridging the freedom of speech, or of the press; or the right of the people peaceably to assemble, and to petition the Government for a redress of grievances.[23]

There is ongoing debate about what exactly the Establishment Clause permits in relation to state–church relations. However, "The US establishment is an establishment which pretends to reject establishment."[24] Recalling Josephson's analysis of Shinto in Japan, the United States has likewise integrated Christianity into public life in myriad ways. In his book, *One Nation Under God: How Corporate America Invented Christian America*, Kevin Kruse (2015) attributes some of this to the administration of President Dwight Eisenhower in 1953–1961, who, in

22 See, for example, Kurien (2007) on the reconfiguration of Hinduism in the United States.

23 As Winnifred Sullivan (2005) notes, this clause should be read: "'[Neither Congress nor the states] shall make any law ….' U.S. Supreme Court religion clause jurisprudence begins, in a very real sense, in 1940 with the Cantwell decision and its extension of the prohibitions of the religion clauses to the state governments" (25).

24 Beaman and Sullivan (2013, 4). Janet Jakobsen and Ann Pellegrini (2003) argue: "One of the reasons that there is so little religious freedom in the United States is that we do not have genuine disestablishment; as we have seen, Christianity is the de facto established state religion […] Christianity (specifically Protestantism) has been the religion of the land, enacted through American history in everything from prayer in public schools to the religious identifications of the president" (104).

Kruse's words, sacralised the state through the implementation of a number of religious ceremonies and the installation of religious symbols which effectively merged state and church "into a wholesome 'government under God'" (87).[25] Kruse links the popularisation of public prayer by evangelists like Billy Graham to an anti-communist and anti-socialist lobby on behalf of big business in the United States. The "tradition" of public prayer in that context is thus linked to much broader political forces.

There is a voluminous case law on establishment and related issues, as well as accompanying academic commentary that is too extensive to recount here. There is also a significant body of case law related to religious symbols and practices in the public sphere.[26] A major legal touchstone was the 1971 *Lemon v. Kurtzman* case, which articulated the framework for establishment assessment.[27] That test has been modified by subsequent cases to include additional considerations of whether the government activity under question amounts to an endorsement of religion or as coercive in effect.[28]

Another important narrative is that of freedom, which ironically has an almost stifling presence in the public rhetoric of the United States with little clear sense of its content. Winnifred Sullivan (2005) summarises the ideal of freedom:

> To be free, on the other hand, is today understood to mean to have the ability to choose for oneself in all areas of life, without restraint. To be free is to be faithful only to oneself or to such ideologies and communities outside of oneself that one freely chooses. Freedom can, as many have observed, be profoundly unnerving. (156)

However, as Wenger (2017) argues,

> The principle of religious freedom seems necessarily to define the practices and traditions it defends as religious, placing them in opposition to that which is not so designated. To define religion is to limit religion, to set its boundaries and hence to delineate its other. But the potential shape of such definitions and oppositions are infinite in their possibilities. (239)

25 "Ordinary religion, that is, the disestablished religion of ordinary people, fits uneasily into the spaces allowed for religion in the public square and in the courtroom" (Sullivan 2005, 138).

26 In *Newdow v. United States* (2013), a challenge by a group of atheists, secular humanists and organisations to have the phrase "In God We Trust" removed from US currency was unsuccessful. The motto was held to have a "secular purpose and effect" and therefore was not in violation of the Establishment Clause (at p. 3).

27 The *Lemon* test requires first that "the statute must have a secular legislative purpose; second, its principal or primary effect must be one that neither advances nor inhibits religion, [… and] finally, the statute must not foster 'an excessive government entanglement with religion'" (*Lemon* at p. 613).

28 See Sullivan (2009).

Similarly, Richardson (2015) argues that "religious freedom is a socially constructed and quite contested concept" and that courts are deeply intertwined in the construction of such freedom (1, 14). Religion especially is understood to be part of this matrix of choice, a position that has been theoretically encapsulated in market theories of religion, which dominated American social science of religion for about two decades.[29] Both Wenger and Sullivan have underscored the distinctly protestant character of the "free" market.

The narratives of freedom, secularism and disestablishment are entangled to produce an insistence on the simultaneous freedom to choose and a Christian America. That the latter necessarily involves a coercive collaboration between state and civil society is often ignored:

> The frequent invocation of religious freedom has obscured that in actual practice Christian moral and religious ideas pervaded American law and society and formed critical boundaries circumscribing that freedom. Religious partisans assumed control of law and governance and used those tools to coerce dissenters based on their religiously derived moral convictions. (Sehat 2011, 283–284)

When religion comes too close to violating the establishment prohibition, it retreats to its cloak of heritage and history, and its status as a foundational part of American society such that it forms part of the shared values of all Americans. The foundational status of religion accounts for the pull of the vortex of "founding fathers" and their intentions vis-à-vis the church–state relationship.[30]

Despite the differences in context between the United States, France and Canada, the tension between past preserving and future forming models in each example produces differing narratives about diversity and the path to living well together. Reminiscent of the discourse of interculturalism that can be traced in Quebec, the past preserving model inscribes a particular vision of "Americanness" that is Christian, specifically Protestant, in shape (Sullivan 2005; Sehat 2011), which romanticises a conflict free United States.[31] The future forming model

29 R. Stephen Warner (1993) threw down the gauntlet, as it were, in his article "Work in Progress toward a New Paradigm for the Sociological Study of Religion in the United States", in which he notes that what is critical to market theories of religion is "the idea that religious institutions in the United States operate within an open market" (1045). For the most persistent use of this perspective, see Stark and Finke (2000). For a critique of the theory, see Chaves (1995).

30 Green (2015) suggests that "myths about the role of Christianity in creating the nation's governing institutions fuel the jurisprudential debate over interpreting the Constitution consistently with the 'original intent' of the framers" (ix).

31 David Sehat (2011) offers a pointed criticism of Bellah's vision of civil religion, which he says revels in the fantasy of "the consensual nature of American civil religion—a society gathered around a common religious center whose uniform and voluntary support makes possible a harmonious and socially integrated whole. As Bellah claimed, '[T]he relation between religion and politics in America has been singularly smooth … [T]he civil religion was able to build up without any bitter struggle.' This society

pushes at the boundaries of inclusion to expand to multiple religious possibilities, and, sometimes to include nonreligion. A unique aspect of the US context is the overwhelming dominance of scholarship that supports the past preserving model inspired by Durkheim and Americanised through Parsons, Bellah et al. and Putnam. There is a strong current supporting the past preserving model in law, intellectual conceptualisations of social life, and everyday understandings of how American society should work.

Perhaps the most obvious choice of a case to illustrate the use of culture and history as a past preserving strategy for this chapter, for those familiar with the American context, is *Lynch v. Donnelly* (1984),[32] which involved the display of a crèche in a park owned by a non-profit group in Pawtucket, Rhode Island. Relying specifically on the notion of the "tradition" of the display,[33] noting the "passive" nature of the symbol,[34] the dangers of a slippery slope of removing the harmless symbol[35] and the removal as an overreaction contrary to history and "holdings",[36] the language of the Supreme Court is a now familiar template for such cases. "Celebration of public holidays, which have cultural significance even if they also have religious aspects, is a legitimate secular purpose" (*Lynch*, O' Connor concurring, p. 691).[37] In short, the *Lynch* case resonates strongly with territory covered in the previous chapters.

Another plausible comparative case is the more recent *Van Orden v. Perry* (2005),[38] in which the Supreme Court found that a monument inscribed with the Ten Commandments displayed on the grounds of the Texas State Capitol did not

without conflict is a daydream, a chimera. Though proponents of the moral establishment have historically used the language of consensus, they relied upon coercion. And they never overcame the objections of dissenters, nor were they able to stamp them out" (284–285). It is interesting that Bellah proposed the idea of the American moral establishment as civil religion as the civil rights movement gained momentum, and as women and environmentalists fought for a new vision of society and justice.

32 *Lynch v. Donnelly* (1984) 465 U.S. 668. Hereinafter "*Lynch*".

33 "The city, like the Congresses and Presidents, however, has principally taken note of a significant historical religious event long celebrated in the Western World. The crèche in the display depicts the historical origins of this traditional event long recognized as a National Holiday" (*Lynch*, p. 680).

34 "The crèche, like a painting, is passive; admittedly it is a reminder of the origins of Christmas" (*Lynch*, p. 685).

35 "If the presence of the crèche in this display violates the Establishment Clause, a host of other forms of taking official note of Christmas, and of our religious heritage, are equally offensive to the Constitution" (*Lynch*, p. 686).

36 "To forbid the use of this one passive symbol—the crèche—at the very time people are taking note of the season with Christmas hymns and carols in public schools and other public places, and while the Congress and legislatures open sessions with prayers by paid chaplains, would be a stilted overreaction contrary to our history and to our holdings" (*Lynch*, p. 686).

37 For critical commentary of *Lynch v. Donnelly* (1984), see Myers (1988), Hersman (1985), Grant (1985) and Berg (2004).

38 *Van Orden v. Perry* (2005) 545 U.S. 677. Hereinafter "*Van Orden*". For critical commentary of *Van Orden*, see Carmella (2011), Berg (2006), Chemerinsky (2005), Weins (2007) and Muñoz (2006).

violate the Establishment Clause of the First Amendment. The Court emphasised the role of God in the nation's "heritage",[39] noted the prevalence of such practices and the "historical continuity" of such displays[40] and bolstered the justification with a finding of the "secular" purpose of the monument.[41] Astonishingly, the existence of a Supreme Being is taken as uncontroversial fact: "Our institutions presuppose a Supreme Being, yet these institutions must not press religious observances upon their citizens" (*Van Orden*, Opinion of Rehnquist, p. 683). The "passive" nature of the monument and the failure of the petitioner to bring the lawsuit sooner confirmed the harmless nature of the display.[42]

However, despite the obvious similarities of *Lynch* and *Van Orden* with the *Saguenay* and *Vendée* cases, I have chosen *Town of Greece*[43] as the focus of analysis.[44] As a relatively recent decision, it offers an opportunity for a more nuanced examination of the power of history and heritage as well as another vantage point from which to see a different configuration of religion and culture. Ultimately, *Town of Greece* captures a majoritarian privilege and minority exclusion in a hierarchical freeze frame preserved by historical justification. It is not the only case to do so, and in fact during the writing of this book yet another case emerged—*American Legion* (2019)[45]—which will be discussed briefly in the concluding chapter.

The decision

> Though they had attended the town board meeting in their small community of Greece, New York, because they were interested in contributing to its ongoing well-

39 "Recognition of the role of God in our Nation's heritage has also been reflected in our decisions" (*Van Orden*, Opinion of Rehnquist, p. 687).

40 "Our opinions, like our building, have recognized the role the Decalogue plays in America's heritage" (*Van Orden*, Opinion of Rehnquist, p. 689); and "display of the tablets can also convey a historical message (about a historic relation between those standards and the law)—a fact that helps to explain the display of those tablets in dozens of courthouses throughout the Nation" (*Van Orden*, Concurring opinion of Breyer, p. 701).

41 The Supreme Court affirmed the judgment of the District Court that found that "the State had a valid secular purpose in recognizing and commending the Eagles for their efforts to reduce juvenile delinquency" (*Van Orden*, Opinion of Rehnquist, p. 682).

42 "The placement of the Ten Commandments monument on the Texas State Capitol grounds is a far more passive use of those texts than was the case in *Stone*, where the text confronted elementary school students every day. Indeed, Van Orden, the petitioner here, apparently walked by the monument for a number of years before bringing this lawsuit" (*Van Orden*, Opinion of Rehnquist, p. 691).

43 *Town of Greece v. Galloway* (2014) 572 U.S. ___. Hereinafter "*Town of Greece SC*".

44 Other cases involving the public display of religious symbols include: *County of Allegheny v. American Civil Liberties Union* (1989) 492 U.S. 573, which involved Christmas and Hanukkah holiday displays in Pittsburgh, Pennsylvania; and *Capitol Square Review & Advisory Board v. Pinette* (1995) 515 U.S. 753, which involved a Ku Klux Klan member in Columbus, Ohio who wanted to erect a cross at Capitol Square.

45 *The American Legion v. American Humanist Association* (2019) No. 17-1717, 588 U.S. ___. Hereinafter "*American Legion*".

being, Susan Galloway, a therapeutic recreation specialist, and Linda Stephens, a retired school librarian, felt like they were in church rather than a town board meeting. Opening invocations, though in theory open to all creeds, were dominated by Christian clergy. Increasingly uncomfortable, they decided to open a conversation with the board members about the problematic opening invocations, during which they were often enjoined to stand and pray to Jesus by whichever local clergy had been invited to give the invocation. Stephens, who is an atheist, and Galloway, who is Jewish, experienced the invocation as coercive. Instead of feeling included as engaged members of the community who had valuable insights and experiences to offer, they felt like second-class citizens. It was time to take a stand and speak up not only for themselves, but for others who felt excluded by the overtly Christian tone which framed the meetings.[46]

Rather than open conversation about diversity and inclusion, Galloway and Stephens received an oppositional response that eventually propelled them to use the law as a vehicle for change. At the District Court[47] the prayer practice was found to not violate the Establishment Clause, with the Court holding that it was not demonstrated how the town's prayer practice established Christianity. The District Court noted that the town opened the prayer "program" to everyone and that no creed had been excluded, this despite the fact that from 1999 to2007 all of the clergy to give the invocation were Christian[48] and the prayer took a shape similar to the following:

> Lord we ask you to send your spirit of servanthood upon all of us gathered here this evening to do your work for the benefit of all in our community. We ask you to bless our elected and appointed officials so they may deliberate with wisdom and act with courage. Bless the members of our community who come here to speak before the board so they may state their cause with honesty and humility .... Lord we ask you to bless us all, that everything we do here tonight will move you to welcome us one day into your kingdom as good and faithful servants. We ask this in the name of our brother Jesus. Amen. (*Town of Greece SC*, Opinion of the Court, pp. 2–3)

The Court of Appeals[49] reversed the decision of the District Court, holding that a constellation of factors, including the limited promotion of the inclusive invitation to lead the invocation,[50] its geographic limitation,[51] the actions of the board

46 Lauren Markoe and Cathy Lynn Grossman (*The Washington Post*, Markoe and Grossman 2014); Meaghan McDermott (*Democrat & Chronicle*, McDermott 2013).
47 *Galloway v. Town of Greece* (2010), 732 F. Supp. 2d 195, 241–43 (W.D.N.Y. 2010). Hereinafter "*Town of Greece DC*".
48 In 2008, four prayers were offered by non-Christians following the initial complaints of Susan Galloway and Linda Stephens. All other prayers were delivered by Christians until 2010 (*Town of Greece SC*, Breyer, J., dissenting, p. 2).
49 *Galloway v. Town of Greece* (2012) 681 F.3d 20 (2d Cir. 2012). Hereinafter "*Town of Greece CA*".
50 *Town of Greece CA*, p. 18.
51 *Town of Greece CA*, p. 17.

members (bowing heads or making the sign of the cross)[52] and the continuous use (or, in its words "steady drumbeat") of "often specifically sectarian" Christian prayers[53] would lead a "reasonable observer" to conclude that the town was affiliating itself with Christianity and was thus unconstitutionally establishing religion.[54] The Court of Appeals, however, was careful to state: "We do not hold that the town may not open its public meetings with a prayer or invocation. Such legislative prayers, as *Marsh* holds and as we have repeatedly noted, do not violate the Establishment Clause."[55] The Supreme Court of the United States found that the prayer did not violate the establishment clause.

Interestingly, before 1999, the Town of Greece had begun its monthly town board meetings with a moment of silence. Then a new town supervisor decided to import from the country legislature the practice of inviting local clergy to offer a prayer after roll call and the recitation of the Pledge of Allegiance. Mirroring the practice and reasoning in Saguenay, Quebec, discussed in Chapter 2, the prayer was reportedly to "place town board members in a solemn and deliberative frame of mind" and "invoke divine guidance in town affairs" (*Town of Greece SC*, Opinion of the Court, p. 2).[56] This goal is linked to the historical practice of Congress, which has appointed and paid official chaplains since the framing of the Constitution, a practice that has been maintained "virtually uninterrupted since that time" (*Town of Greece SC*, Opinion of the Court, p. 7). The practice was fully recognised as "religious" but as compatible with the Establishment Clause because of its historical weight.[57] As long as it fit within the tradition followed by Congress, the prayer was constitutional. The possibility of challenging that "tradition" is nonexistent and in a somewhat odd logical progression, the fact of church establishment in the early history of the United States was (and is) used to justify the exception of sectarian prayer to the Establishment clause.[58]

52 *Town of Greece CA*, p. 20.
53 *Town of Greece CA*, p. 19.
54 *Town of Greece CA*, p. 23.
55 *Town of Greece CA*, p. 22.
56 "As practiced by Congress since the framing of the Constitution, legislative prayer lends gravity to public business, reminds lawmakers to transcend petty differences in pursuit of a higher purpose, and expresses a common aspiration to a just and peaceful society" (*Town of Greece SC*, Opinion of the Court, p. 7).
57 "Yet *Marsh* must not be understood as permitting a practice that would amount to a constitutional violation if not for its historical foundation. The case teaches instead that the Establishment Clause must be interpreted 'by reference to historical practices and understandings.' County of Allegheny, 492 U. S., at 670 (Kennedy, J., concurring in judgment in part and dissenting in part)" (*Town of Greece SC*, Opinion of the Court, pp. 7–8).
58 "Construing the Establishment Clause as a federalism provision accords with the variety of church-state arrangements that existed at the Founding. At least six States had established churches in 1789" (*Town of Greece SC*, Opinion of Thomas, J., concurring, p. 2).

Tradition, history and freedom

One of the core arguments of this book is that "religion" is transformed into heritage and culture in law and public discourse in the face of challenges to majoritarian practices and symbols. These challenges are becoming more likely because of a new diversity that forces a critical engagement with the privilege that has attached to Christianity during the past centuries in many western democracies. *Town of Greece* is intriguing in that the prayer practice is given some measure of privilege not as culture and heritage but as religion.[59] Caroline Mala Corbin (2015) notes that "in earlier cases the Court downplayed the religious significance by claiming that the religious display was really about acknowledging our nation's history or celebrating a national holiday" (306). In other words, religion qua religion is not permitted to be "established", but religion as historical and traditional practice is. Though religion as religion may be permitted to have a slightly greater presence in *Town of Greece*, it is nonetheless accompanied by a recurring emphasis on the historical presence of Christianity, a Supreme Being, and prayer as a part of legislative ceremonies, as is illustrated by this statement from the judgment:

> The prayer opportunity in this case must be evaluated against the backdrop of historical practice. As a practice that has long endured, legislative prayer has become part of our heritage and tradition, part of our expressive idiom, similar to the Pledge of Allegiance[60], inaugural prayer, or the recitation of "God save the United States and this honorable Court" at the opening of this Court's sessions. (*Town of Greece SC*, Opinion of Kennedy, J., p. 19)[61]

The constitutionality of "legislative prayer", established as an exception to the prohibition otherwise imposed by the constitution and the case law, is interpreted by the Court to mean that the town has no obligation to attempt a non-sectarian prayer. The possibility that prayer as a restatement of Christian hegemony might be seen as problematic is not something that the Court took up in any serious

59 In contrast to the acknowledgment of religious significance or meaning, Grace Y. Kao and Jerome E. Copulsky (2007) note that "The legal strategy that the Bush Administration and others took to defend the constitutionality of the Pledge of Allegiance's contested phrase was to minimize or even deny its religious import altogether" (129).

60 History is often constructed for convenience. For example, Kao and Copulsky (2007) point out that from 1892 until 1954 the Pledge of Allegiance did not mention "God" (122).

61 "Justice Kennedy conceded that the historical tradition of legislative prayer upheld in Marsh had some substantive limits. The purpose of the legislative prayer was ceremonial-to solemnize the legislative deliberations and inspire legislators to work together for the common good. Prayers that disparaged non-adherents or attempted to proselytize or preach conversion exceeded the permissible scope of these invocations. Even where individual prayers ignored these constraints, however, the Constitution would not be violated. There must be a pattern of disparaging or proselytizing prayers over time to support a viable Establishment Clause claim. No such pattern had been demonstrated by plaintiffs in this case" (Brownstein 2014, 380).

way. In fact, it is seen as a positive good.[62] Yet, as Nancy Blyth Hersman (1985) argues,

> the government actions in both *Marsh* and *Lynch v. Donnelly* should have been found to violate the establishment clause based on the *Lemon* test. However, the Court appeared to be of the opinion that the governmental practices in those cases had been a part of our society for decades and the "status quo" should be preserved. (174–175)

These cases are used subsequently in *Town of Greece* (and other cases) to justify a blurry boundary between church and state based on historical "fact".[63] The flexible boundary is affirmed by Justice Kennedy who said that "it is not necessary to define the precise boundary of the Establishment Clause where history shows that the specific practice is permitted" (*Town of Greece SC*, Opinion of the Court, p. 8).[64]

The distinguishing feature of US rhetoric is the extraordinary emphasis put on history explicitly as history (rather than culture) and the weight it has to justify continuing practices of exclusion. This straightjacket of history, sometimes referred to as the "framers' intention", the intentions of the "founding fathers" or the "originalist position", has occupied an inordinate amount of scholarly and legal energy in the United States.[65] As one commentator has put it,

> Justice Scalia's view of the Establishment Clause, which is itself a reflection of his originalist theory of constitutional interpretation, reflects a certain privileged viewpoint. More particularly, both at a general (originalism) and a specific (the Establishment Clause allows state preference for Judeo-Christianity) level, it is one made possible by white/Christian privilege. (Corbin 2017, 191–192)[66]

62 Horwitz (2015, 262).

63 "*Marsh* stands for the proposition that it is not necessary to define the precise boundary of the Establishment Clause where history shows that the specific practice is permitted. Any test the Court adopts must acknowledge a practice that was accepted by the Framers and has withstood the critical scrutiny of time and political change" (*Town of Greece*, Opinion of the Court, p. 8).

64 "Ceremonial deism is a government invocation of God that the courts have found constitutional on the grounds that the practice is longstanding and its religious impact is minimal and nonsectarian" (Corbin 2010, 1549). Steven B. Epstein (1996) adds that "The implications of ceremonial deism are far-reaching because courts frequently employ this amorphous concept as a springboard from which to hold that other challenged practices do not violate the establishment Clause" (2086).

65 "[L]aw and religion scholarship should ease up on its obsession with Founding-era history or abstract theory, stripped in both cases of geographical context, and take more account of the role played by space and place in American religious pluralism" (Horwitz 2015, 295).

66 "Justice Scalia would have argued that he espoused originalism not because it benefits the privileged but because it curtails judicial discretion. Without it, judges could impose their own personal preferences onto constitutional law. Instead, originalism forces judges to interpret the constitutional by relying on something objective, namely

Moreover, there is a strong argument for the position that "religion was viewed as a privileged public good by *all* of the founders. The pro-religionists argue, then, that the only constitutional issue is the equal treatment of religions and of believers" (Sullivan 1994, 164; emphasis in original).[67] Although "culture" is not often part of the language used in the American context, history steps up to create a justificatory framework that works to preserve the privilege of Christianity in the same way that culture and history do in Canada and France (as well as Italy, Germany and so on).

The quest of the Court is defined as determining whether the prayer holds to tradition "long followed in Congress and the state legislatures" (*Town of Greece SC*, Opinion of the Court, p. 9).[68] History and tradition are seen by the justices as the primary interpretive tool (Horwitz 2015, 261). The fact that sectarian prayers were part of the social landscape of Congress when the First Amendment was drafted is seen as justification for their retention (*Town of Greece SC*, Opinion of the Court, p. 10). The possibility that the prayers might, even then, have been controversial is not considered, nor is the idea that there is something contrary to justice and equality when the tyranny of the majority[69] (a practice reflecting the beliefs of "many Americans" in a "higher power")[70] is permitted to define the practices of public institutions.[71] The idea of both majority rule and Christianity as foundational is also present in public discussion, as evidenced by this statement

the original understanding or original public meaning. It just so happens that in the case of the Establishment Clause, originalism yields a doctrine that countenances government sponsored Judeo-Christianity" (Corbin 2017, 217).

67 This is supported by the following statement: "In the United States, religion and public life have always been entwined. The Establishment Clause was never intended to keep religion out of the public square" (Chapman 2015, 450).

68 The District Court referenced the "long history of legislative prayer in Congress, which is often overtly sectarian" (*Town of Greece DC*, pp. 79–80); and "the long 'unique history' of legislative prayer in the United States, and particularly in the United States Congress" (*Town of Greece DC*, p. 44).

69 The Supreme Court of Canada in *Big M* ruled, "what may appear good and true to a majoritarian religious group, or to the state acting at their behest, may not, for religious reasons, be imposed upon citizens who take a contrary view. The *Charter* safeguards religious minorities from the threat of 'the tyranny of the majority'" (at para. 96).

70 "Ceremonial prayer is but a recognition that, since this Nation was founded and until the present day, many Americans deem that their own existence must be understood by precepts far beyond the authority of government to alter or define and that willing participation in civic affairs can be consistent with a brief acknowledgment of their belief in a higher power, always with due respect for those who adhere to other beliefs. The prayer in this case has a permissible ceremonial purpose. It is not an unconstitutional establishment of religion" (*Town of Greece SC*, Opinion of Kennedy, p. 23).

71 "It is virtually inconceivable that the First Congress, having appointed chaplains whose responsibilities prominently included the delivery of prayers at the beginning of each daily session, thought that this practice was inconsistent with the Establishment Clause. And since this practice was well established and undoubtedly well known, it seems equally clear that the state legislatures that ratified the First Amendment had the same understanding" (*Town of Greece SC*, Alito, J., concurring, p. 12).

from Carrol Mitchem, the Chairman of the Lincoln Country Board of Commissioners, when he commented on the inclusion of non-Christian prayers in government meetings:

> Other religions, or whatever, are in the minority. The U.S. was founded on Christianity [...] I don't believe we need to be bowing to the minorities. The U.S. and the Constitution were founded on Christianity. This is what the majority of people believe in, and it's what I'm standing up for.[72]

Some weeks later when a leader of an interfaith group opened a Lincoln county meeting Mitchem walked out. The commissioners then decided to open their meetings with a moment of silence.[73]

The "post-truth" approach to historical fact is not uniquely American, as we have already seen (recall Hervieu-Léger's [2000] comments about the imagined history that creates social cohesion). Steven Green (2015) notes that "all nations and peoples have myths that help explain their origins, distinguish them as a group, and legitimize their heritage" (15). The myth of religious origins, argues Green, goes to the very heart of American identity: "The idea of America's religious origins is essentially a myth created and retold for the purpose of anointing the founding, and the nation, with a higher, transcendent meaning" (243). Scholars have challenged the monolithic narrative of an agreed upon Christian priority in defining the public life of the nation. There has not, they argue, been a common consent, even if the United States was demographically a majority Christian nation (Sehat 2011, 7–8), and

> the frequent invocation of religious freedom has obscured that in actual practice Christian moral and religious ideas pervaded American law and society and formed critical boundaries circumscribing that freedom. Religious partisans assumed control of law and governance and used those tools to coerce dissenters based on their religiously derived moral convictions. (Sehat 2011, 283–284)

Despite the myth of the Christian nation, there is a tension in the *Town of Greece* decisions: while the *religious* nature of the prayers is admitted, their specifically *Christian* nature is not. To be sure, the courts acknowledge (and justify) their "sectarian" nature, but not the fact that the "sectarian" is explicitly Christian. This may seem to be splitting hairs, but it is an effective tool for displacing the privilege given to one religion in a nation that is theoretically diverse and even multicultural. Similarly, God is cloaked as a "higher power" and the purpose of prayer is about lending "gravity" to the occasion and to "reflect values long part of the Nation's heritage" (*Town of Greece SC*, Opinion of the Court, p. 14).

What is especially intriguing is that the "history" of the prayer in the *Town of Greece* was relatively recent—the prayer practice had not been part of the council

72 *The Charlotte Observer* (Cominsky 2015).
73 *The Charlotte Observer* (Dunn 2015).

proceedings until 1999. As was the case with the symbols and prayers in the *Saguenay* and *Vendée* cases, the limited historical span of the practice is overlooked. Instead, the local practice is linked to a broader narrative of a Christian history and character of the nation that in turn recreates the local history as a truth. The factual length of time becomes irrelevant—an inconvenient truth that is swept aside in the grand narrative of who "we" are.[74] Eric Hobsbawm and Terence Ranger (1983) explore this tenuous relationship between facts and tradition in their edited collection *The Invention of Tradition*. In that volume they examine the relationship between tradition and social cohesion, and in his chapter Hobsbawm explicitly identifies the challenge of integrating heterogeneous masses and the solution of creating rituals and practices, which quickly become tradition identified with the nation. Although Hobsbawm mentions this specifically in the context of the United States, his argument may have relevance for the other contexts I have explored here. The potential loss of majoritarian status and its concomitant loss of power is another factor to be added into the mix. So too are racism, prejudice and fear of the "other".

The *Town of Greece* decision also sparked other attempts to use the straightjacket of an imagined heritage. In Roanoke, Virginia one of the members of the county's board of supervisors initiated a Christian only prayer policy, noting:

> I think America, pretty much from Founding Fathers on, I think we have to say more or less that we're a Christian nation with Christian ideology ... If we're a Christian nation, then I would say that we need to move toward our Christian heritage.[75]

This same member had previously written a letter to the local newspaper arguing that religious freedom should be reserved for Christians.[76]

The narrative of history and its importance is not only woven through decisions of courts, but into the very fabric of American society. It is a story that has powerful resonance and which structures the "we" in a manner that is similar to that of the laïcité-crèche story in France or the neutrality-crucifix/prayer story in Canada. In both instances the legal and public discussion erases the "other", who is folded into the narrative, or dismissed as unreasonable, too radical, or mentally unstable. In a recent decision by the Kentucky state government, public schools will now be able to teach a course on the bible: "The bill's sponsor says students need to understand the role the Bible played in American history."[77] For those who might object, the Governor of Kentucky, Matt Bevin, said: "The idea that we would not

74 Thus, it is not so clear that Nancy Blyth Hersman (1985) is correct in her analysis of the *Lynch* case when she states that: "Because the history of public endorsement of Christmas as a religious holiday is sketchy at best, the City of Pawtucket's inclusion of the crèche in its Christmas display may have been disallowed under the historical analysis as well" (175).

75 *Slate* (Lithwick 2014).

76 *Slate* (Lithwick 2014).

77 WDRB (2017).

want this to be an option for people in school, that would be crazy. I don't know why every state would not embrace this, why we as a nation would not embrace this."[78] The notion that the bible and Christianity are the foundation of human rights and constitutional documents was stated as fact by the then Kentucky Legislature Representative D.J. Johnson: "It really did set the foundation that our founding fathers used to develop documents like the Declaration of Independence, the Constitution, the Bill of Rights [...] All of those came from principles from the Bible."[79]

The folding in of everyone, who surely must appreciate this historical fact and its value, reproduces the universal impetus of Christianity identified by scholars like Jonathan and Daniel Boyarin (see Chapter 1). Governor Matt Bevin, for example, claimed: "You could be an atheist, and you would appreciate there's a lot of wisdom in the Bible."[80]

In the *Town of Greece* District Court and Supreme Court decisions, the universal is taken to override the specific (which, on the reasoning of the courts, is permitted by the weight of history in any event). Thus, despite the mention of Jesus, Heavenly Father and the Holy Spirit in some of the prayers "they also invoked universal themes, as by celebrating the changing of the seasons or calling for a 'spirit of cooperation' among town leaders" (*Town of Greece SC*, Opinion of the Court, p. 16). The idea that the prayers serve the function of drawing together diverse constituencies under the Christian umbrella (which is not specifically articulated by the courts, as mentioned above) is presented as fact. Nowhere is there acknowledgment of those who have objected to this practice, those who dare not object (and the threat to those who speak out) and those who do not participate at all because they do not see themselves in the practices assumed to be uniting and universal:

> From the earliest days of the Nation, these invocations have been addressed to assemblies comprising many different creeds. These ceremonial prayers strive for the idea that people of many faiths may be united in a community of tolerance and devotion. Even those who disagree as to religious doctrine may find common ground in the desire to show respect for the divine in all aspects of their lives and being. Our tradition assumes that adult citizens, firm in their own beliefs, can tolerate and perhaps appreciate a ceremonial prayer delivered by a person of a different faith. (*Town of Greece SC*, Opinion of the Court, p. 16)

Perhaps more disturbing, though, is the following statement:

> Not only is there no historical support for the proposition that only generic prayer is allowed, but as our country has become more diverse, composing a prayer that is acceptable to all members of the community who hold religious

78 WDRB (2017).
79 WDRB (2017).
80 WDRB (2017).

> beliefs has become harder and harder. It was one thing to compose a prayer that is acceptable to both Christians and Jews; it is much harder to compose a prayer that is also acceptable to followers of Eastern religions that are now well represented in this country. Many local clergy may find the project daunting, if not impossible, and some may feel that they cannot in good faith deliver such a vague prayer. (*Town of Greece SC*, Alito, J., concurring, p. 5)

The idea that increasing diversity means that the only way to proceed is to maintain the universalising steamroller of the Christian prayer recast as Judeo-Christian[81] because being inclusive is "hard" is highly problematic. As Paul Horwitz (2015) argues in his analysis of the case, even the dissent and majority decisions offer a "single vision of American religious pluralism" (268).[82]

None of this means that Greece's town hall must be religion- or prayer-free. The "universal" is necessarily religious, as is illustrated by this statement by dissenting Justice Kagan in the Supreme Court decision:

> "[W]e are a religious people," *Marsh* observed, 463 U. S., at 792, and prayer draws some warrant from tradition in a town hall, as well as in Congress or a state legislature[…] What the circumstances here demand is the recognition that we are a pluralistic people too. When citizens of all faiths come to speak to each other and their elected representatives in a legislative session, the government must take especial care to ensure that the prayers they hear will seek to include, rather than serve to divide. No more is required—but that much is crucial—to treat every citizen, of whatever religion, as an equal participant in her government. (*Town of Greece SC*, p. 18)

The Supreme Court's sentiment regarding common ground was echoed in public statements such as the following one from Pastor Vince DiPaola of Greece's Lakeshore Church (and who had delivered invocations at the council meetings):

> [the] majority of people certainly believe in God in our community. The majority of people would believe in Jesus Christ. And so it represents our

81 Jakobsen and Pellegrini (2003) challenge the invocation of "Judeo-Christian", arguing that the "hyphen actually passes off a wished-for assimilation of Jewish difference into Christian tradition as an instance of religious pluralism" (31).

82 "For Justice Kennedy, the vision is one of active, public, but friendly *American* religiosity, an American religiosity that is in equal measure hallowed and hollowed by tradition. That it is public, and that it may be active—full-throated in tone, sectarian in content—is clear from his opinion. He treats legislative prayer with great approval, calling it a 'benign acknowledgment of religion's role in society.' He insists on the value of allowing chaplains at official events 'to express themselves in a religious idiom.' That idiom can be sectarian, not just 'generic.' People are entitled to use public proceedings as an opportunity to 'show respect for the divine in all aspects of their fives and being'" (Horwitz 2015, 262).

> community, and it would be pathetic if our community could not even express itself in that way.[83]

Town of Greece reflects an ongoing narrative about who and what Americans are, encapsulated by Robert Bellah (2005) as civil religion, of which he says "is a genuine apprehension of universal and transcendent religious reality as seen in or, one could almost say, as revealed through the experience of the American people" (49). The recitation of the Christian creation story regarding the American nation is a powerful socialising framework which, among other things, establishes the parameters for the good citizen. What is striking about the prayer discussion is that prayer itself as a part of governance is not seen as an exclusionary practice. The ways that the very practice of prayer structures non-Christian religions is not part of the conversation. Prayer has, in the words of Justice Kennedy, a "permissible ceremonial purpose" (*Town of Greece SC*, p. 23).

The following legal commentary captured some of the problems with the exclusionary conceptualisation of prayer in the *Town of Greece*:

> Before anyone starts arguing that such prayers could cover the vast majority of Americans, so it's all good, I would point out that there are roughly 10 million Hindus and Buddhists in America, when you take them together, and a growing segment of atheists. Those are not small numbers, and such a sizable portion of American society should not be routinely excluded and marginalized by unnecessary government-backed prayer. And, even in little, isolated Greece, NY, these growing sets of believers are present, as the Respondents in this case prove.[84]

The Court of Appeals did, however, find the overwhelmingly Christian nature of the prayer to be problematic as evidenced in comments such as: "a substantial majority of the prayers in the record contained uniquely Christian language. Roughly two-thirds contained references to 'Jesus Christ,' 'Jesus,' 'Your Son,' or the 'Holy Spirit.' Within this subset, almost all concluded with a statement that the prayer had been given in Jesus Christ's name"[85]; "the town's process for selecting prayer-givers virtually ensured a Christian viewpoint"[86]; and that "the town fails to recognize that its residents may hold religious beliefs that are not represented by a place of worship within the town. Such residents may be members of congregations in nearby towns or, indeed, may not be affiliated with any congregation."[87] Though the Court of Appeals came close to recognising the possibility of a nonreligious worldview, it did not explicitly consider this group (despite the fact that one of the plaintiffs is an atheist).

83 *Aljazeera America* (Posner 2013).
84 The commentary published by *Verdict*, a legal analysis and commentary publication from *Justia*, a legal resource website, concerns the non-sectarian nature of the prayer in *Town of Greece*. See *Verdict* (Hamilton 2013).
85 *Town of Greece CA*, p. 6.
86 *Town of Greece CA*, p. 17.
87 *Town of Greece CA*, p. 17.

Competing visions of the past, present and future stream through the case, framing both the story of the nation and the nature of citizenship. On the one hand, the poetically inclusive dissent of Justice Kagan paints a picture of America which unites past and present and that articulates a particular vision of citizens as freely choosing and practising their religions:

> For centuries now, people have come to this country from every corner of the world to share in the blessing of religious freedom. Our Constitution promises that they may worship in their own way, without fear of penalty or danger, and that in itself is a momentous offering. Yet our Constitution makes a commitment still more remarkable—that however those individuals worship, they will count as full and equal American citizens. A Christian, a Jew, a Muslim (and so forth)—each stands in the same relationship with her country, with her state and local communities, and with every level and body of government. So that when each person performs the duties or seeks the benefits of citizenship, she does so not as an adherent to one or another religion, but simply as an American. (*Town of Greece SC*, p. 1)

Yet, the future forming narrative introduced by Justice Kagan, who both recognises the diversity that characterises the United States and the Christian character of the practices of the *Town of Greece*, [88] is dismissed in the same way as were Alain Simoneau in Quebec, Libre Pensée in France, and countless others who have dared to offer an alternative to the past preserving model. For example, Justice Kagan's colleague, Justice Alito, describes her dissent's "rhetoric" as going "far astray", and dismisses her concerns as "highly imaginative hypotheticals", which are troubling to him because they may suggest to readers that the decision leads "to a country in which religious minorities are denied the equal benefits of citizenship".[89] The fact that the decision affirms the Christian character of the invocation and reifies its establishment, in the process contributing to inequality, cannot be erased by legal abracadabra.

The paradoxical nature of the narrative of freedom discussed in the introduction of this chapter is illustrated by an article published in the *Christian Post* where opening public meetings with a prayer is both noted as an established practice and a freedom, lending a rhetoric of choice to something that is characterised as being

88 Justice Kagan claimed: "Still more, Greece's Board did nothing to recognize religious diversity: In arranging for clergy members to open each meeting, the Town never sought (except briefly when this suit was filed) to involve, accommodate, or in any way reach out to adherents of non-Christian religions. So month in and month out for over a decade, prayers steeped in only one faith, addressed toward members of the public, commenced meetings to discuss local affairs and distribute government benefits. In my view, that practice does not square with the First Amendment's promise that every citizen, irrespective of her religion, owns an equal share in her government" (*Town of Greece SC*, Kagan J., dissenting, p. 2).

89 *Town of Greece SC*, Alito, J., Concurring, p. 13.

foundational and necessary. David A. Cortman, Vice President and Senior Counsel for the Alliance Defending Freedom claimed:

> In America, we tolerate a diversity of opinions and beliefs; we don't silence people or try to separate what they say from what they believe [...] Opening public meetings with prayer is a cherished freedom that the authors of the Constitution themselves practiced.[90]

The historical narrative, which weighs so heavily on the present, constructs a barrier between the ideal of freedom and the possibility of it.

The legal developments around religious establishment and religious freedom in the United States have introduced the notion of coercion as an important consideration in the assessment of whether a practice establishes religion. The consequence of this is that the language of coercion and declarations of noncoercion appear rather frequently in legal and public rhetoric. The backstreaming effect of law in this instance creates a necessity to assert noncoercion without actually proving it.[91] There is a limited engagement with the harm caused to individuals through practices that establish one religion as heritage and culture which defines the nation. A very narrow read of coercion minimises the impact of this establishment and concomitantly minimises the harm as well.

The prayers replicate a particular version of American history that excludes a wide range of narratives other than the dominant Protestant Christian one. David Sehat (2011) summarises the problem this way:

> Protestant Christian influence in U.S. history was long-standing, widespread, and, from the perspective of dissenters, coercive. Religious views pervaded law at all levels. Reformers of all kinds, including abolitionists, women's rights activists, labor organizers, and educational reformers often had to contend with Christian—or, more narrowly, Protestant Christian—moral norms that defined and limited their rights. The omission of these stories from the American historical consciousness is a major flaw in our national narrative. (2)

In a complex twist, states and courts are to take a non-interventionist approach to religion, never (in theory) assessing its content or becoming "arbiters of religious dogma". The consequence is that in a society dominated by one religion (in this case Protestant Christianity) such an approach offers immunity from scrutiny to that religion. In *Town of Greece*, the Supreme Court determined that there was no requirement that prayer be non-sectarian and that such a requirement would in any event force the state to supervise, censor and to be involved in "religious

90 *The Christian Post* (Gryboski 2014).

91 Sullivan (2013) notes that the "shaping of life to suit the law has backstream effects as well, beginning long before life enters the courts. One feature of the modern world is the thorough juridification of life in its very subjectivity".

matters". The potentially coercive nature of any prayer is a point missed even to some extent by the complainant, who argues for a non-sectarian inclusive prayer (Galloway admitted that this may not please everyone). Though Galloway is careful to distinguish between prayers that would be sectarian by going further than "Father", "God" or "Lord God" to mention Jesus, "Apollo", "Allah" and so on,[92] the District Court was unable to see the difference between them, calling the distinction "illusory".[93]

Some discussion took place in both the Court of Appeals and the District Court about whether the prayers were "aggressively proselytising", which was the standard used to measure coercion:

> The mere fact that prayers may contain a reference to Jesus or another deity does not make them proselytizing. Instead, limited references such as, "in Jesus's name," are, under the facts of this case, "tolerable acknowledgment[s] of beliefs widely held among the people of this country." *Marsh*, 103 S.Ct. at 3336. (*Town of Greece DC*, p. 79)

And,

> The prayers in the record were not offensive in the way identified as problematic in *Marsh*: they did not preach conversion, threaten damnation to non-believers, downgrade other faiths, or the like. Prayers of this more offensive sort might be sufficient in themselves to give rise to an Establishment Clause violation. (*Town of Greece CA*, pp. 18–19)

The Court of Appeals disagreed, finding that:

> [M]ost prayer-givers appeared to speak on behalf of the town and its residents, rather than only on behalf of themselves. Prayer-givers often requested that the audience participate, and spoke in the first-person plural: let "us" pray, "our" savior, "we" ask, and so on. Town officials, whether intentionally or not, contributed to the impression that these prayer-givers spoke on the town's behalf. (*Town of Greece CA*, p. 20)

In addition to speaking on behalf of the town, audience participation was also solicited by those leading the prayers with requests to bow heads, stand, or join in prayer.

> The invitation to audience members to participate in the prayer, particularly by physical means such as standing or bowing their heads, placed

92 See *Town of Greece DC*, pp. 17–18.
93 See *Town of Greece DC*, p. 82.

> audience members who are nonreligious or adherents of non-Christian religion in the awkward position of either participating in prayers invoking beliefs they did not share or appearing to show disrespect for the invocation, thus further projecting the message that the town endorsed, and expected its residents to endorse, a particular creed. (*Town of Greece CA*, p. 20)

Moreover, when the plaintiffs complained to the town, they were told that if they didn't like the prayer they could leave the meeting.[94] The social consequences of leaving, which amounts to a forced "outing" of sorts, are not considered as coercive or to have potentially harmful consequences.

Revealing oneself to be in disagreement with religious practice in schools, legislatures or municipal meetings is inherently risky and dangerous in the United States.[95] It is well known that complainants in such cases are exposed to emotional and physical harm. For example, in the introduction to their edited collection on organised secularism, Ryan Cragun and Christel Manning (2017) recount the story of a high school senior who complained about the prayer at his graduation ceremony. As they report it "What followed were death threats from community members and fellow students, weeks of harassment, and eventually his parents disowning him and kicking him out of their home" (1).[96] The recognition that complainants who challenge the Christian status quo may be in danger has resulted in the courts allowing people to bring cases under pseudonyms,[97] as they did, for example in a case in which students and parents challenged prayer at football games at a public school.[98]

The complainants in *Town of Greece* did not experience violence, but they did suffer disparaging characterisations similar to those in *Saguenay* and to a lesser extent in *Vendée*. In one instance, a pastor offering a prayer before the council meeting in the town described objectors as a "minority … ignorant of the history of our country" (*Town of Greece CA*, p. 8). The plaintiffs were also called "God

94 *Town of Greece DC*, p. 19.

95 "[C]hurch-state cases are dangerous. They are not outliers. Although the point could be proved by simply continuing to enumerate a litany of examples, it may be more analytically useful to categorize cases by the type of retaliation plaintiffs have faced and the fears that haunt prospective plaintiffs" (Edwards 2013, 463).

96 Benjamin P. Edwards (2013) documents numerous cases in which plaintiffs in church state cases have been threatened, harassed, and intimidated. Moreover, drawing on the research of Frank Ravitch, Edwards points out that there is a long history of such behaviour in American history. See also Ravitch (1999).

97 See Edwards (2013) for a discussion on pseudonymous litigation and Rosenberger (1982) for a discussion on anonymity.

98 See *Santa Fe Independent School Dist. v. Doe* (2000) 530 U.S. 290. A pseudonym was used in *Doe v. Stegall* (1981) in which prayer and Bible reading were challenged in public schools.

haters" and told to "be careful".[99] Corbin (2010) notes that because a practice may not have engendered significant controversy it is assumed to not cause harm: "courts regularly downplay the harm in ceremonial deism and other Establishment Clause claims. Plaintiffs are routinely described as merely 'offended,' 'irritated,' or 'discomforted' by the challenged practice, rather than actually suffering a serious injury" (1588). That the costs may potentially be very high for those who complain is downplayed or ignored.

Although one of the complainants in *Town of Greece* was Jewish, it is important to remember the backdrop of suspicion of atheism that is embedded in American culture and which in part shapes both the legal response and public discourse. Penny Edgell et al. (2016, 631) note the negative coding of the category atheist (and perhaps even "nones") in contrast to the positive coding of cultural categories like "citizen" and "neighbour" which is a moral code entangled with religion. This translates into a minimisation of the coercive impact of a society that justifies majoritarian religious practices as culture or heritage.

The Supreme Court concluded that offence, disrespect and feelings of exclusion did not equal harm:

> In their declarations in the trial court, respondents stated that the prayers gave them offense and made them feel excluded and disrespected. Offense, however, does not equate to coercion. Adults often encounter speech they find disagreeable; and an Establishment Clause violation is not made out any time a person experiences a sense of affront from the expression of contrary religious views in a legislative forum, especially where, as here, any member of the public is welcome in turn to offer an invocation reflecting his or her own convictions. (*Town of Greece SC*, Opinion of Kennedy, J., p. 21)

The choice of wording—"adults often encounter speech they find disagreeable"—implies that the complainants have overreacted, and that they were, in fact, behaving like children.

Through a narrow framing of coercion, law maintains the fiction of freedom and inclusion, using tradition as a prism through which the practices of the town are justified. The Supreme Court held that the Town of Greece did not "violate the First Amendment by opening its meetings with prayer that comports with *our tradition* and does not coerce participation by nonadherents" (*Town of Greece SC*, Opinion of the Court, p. 24; emphasis added). The "our" marks the boundary between those who belong and those who are, at best, tolerated.

As we have seen in the previous chapters, the fear of Muslims is one driver of the accelerated retrenchment of religion as culture and history in law and public discourse. The discourse around *Town of Greece* had limited overt expression of this fear, however, a year after the Supreme Court decision an incident in North

99 Brief for Unitarian Universalist Association et al. as Amici Curiae Supporting Respondents, at p. 12.

Carolina made the news when a county commissioner attempted to exclude all non-Christians from offering prayers. The commissioner stated:

> Changing rules on the way the United States was founded, Constitution was founded (I don't like), […] I don't need no Arab or Muslim or whoever telling me what to do or us here in the county what to do about praying. If they don't like it, stay the hell away.[100]

And,

> "I ain't gonna have no new religion or pray to Allah or nothing like that," [the county commissioner …] added that anyone who doesn't want to hear a Christian prayer can leave and "wait until we're done praying."[101]

Further,

> "We're fighting Muslims every day. I'm not saying they're all bad," Mitchem [the county commissioner] said. "They believe in a different God than I do. If that's what they want to do, that's fine. But, they don't need to be telling us, as Christians, what we need to be doing. They don't need to be rubbing our faces in it."[102]

The matter was eventually settled when the county commissioners ended the practice of reciting prayers before their meetings altogether following an incident where the chairman reportedly left the meeting during an opening prayer by a Muslim.[103]

Anecdotally, when I asked my legal colleagues whether wearing the niqab or the hijab was problematic in the United States they all agreed that such a practice is seen as freedom of expression and confidently asserted that there is no legal contest over this issue.[104] However, both socially and legally this is not entirely accurate: for example, the New York Metropolitan Transit Authority was sued for discriminating against Muslim and Sikh bus and subway drivers for refusing to allow them to wear headscarves and turbans.[105] The case was eventually settled. Similar suits were brought against Essex County, New Jersey, in relation to a Muslim female prison guard[106]; the Washington Metropolitan Transit Authority[107] by two Muslim women and a Pentecostal woman, who had concerns about their uniform requirements; and Abercrombie and Fitch,[108] who refused to hire a Muslim woman who

100 *The Charlotte Observer* (Cominsky 2015).
101 *The Charlotte Observer* (Cominsky 2015).
102 *The Charlotte Observer* (Cominsky 2015).
103 *The Charlotte Observer* (Dunn 2015).
104 See Abdo (2008) for a discussion of the legal status of the hijab in the United States.
105 See *United States v. New York Metropolitan Transit Authority* (2004).
106 See *United States v. Essex County* (2010).
107 See *United States v. Washington Metropolitan Area Transit Authority* (2018).
108 See *E.E.O.C. v. Abercrombie & Fitch Stores* (2015).

wore a headscarf. Legally, there is protection for religious expression.[109] It is, of course, difficult to know how many Muslims suffer discrimination or harassment if they wear the hijab or niqab: legal suits are both expensive and have social consequences, especially in smaller communities, but in this age of social media, harassment can also come from a distance and mobilisation based on hatred is common.[110]

However, considered from another angle, an examination of social survey data suggests that discrimination is common.[111] For example, the Pew Research Center (2017) found that:

> Of those whose appearance is identifiably Muslim, nearly two-thirds (64%) say they have experienced at least one of the specific types of discrimination asked about in the survey. Among Muslims who say they do not have a distinctively Muslim appearance, fewer report these types of experiences (39%).

Gallup (2011) found that Muslims are the group most frequently discriminated against. Both Gallup (2011) and Cooper et al. (2015) found that Americans recognise that Muslims are discriminated against, but also there is a pervasive belief by non-Muslim Americans that Islam contradicts American values and "the" American way of life. Anti-Muslim sentiment may in part drive the defence of Christian prayer as historically validated, but it must be tempered with what is perhaps less a fear of Muslims than a fear of any "other" who also takes the shape of the atheist and other religious minorities.

The state

During the writing of this book I introduced some of the ideas in this chapter at a workshop I attended in the United States. One extremely bright young lawyer earnestly, and with a somewhat irritated tone, assured me that a legislative exemption for prayer existed and authorised the continuing practice of prayer in legislatures. The matter was settled in his view. His inability to step outside of law's authority, even when it supported an alienating practice that was not inclusive, troubled me. The power of law is such that a wave of the legal wand is enough to forestall debate and discussion about the impact of state practices such

109 "The formal legal institutions of the United States' government unequivocally protect Muslim women's right to wear the headscarf in all manner of commercial and public space, helping the headscarf to maintain its status as a symbolic boundary rather than a social boundary. The headscarf has historically been protected at the local and state level" (Welborne et al. 2018, 3–4).

110 For a discussion of motives and contexts in which Muslims wear head and face coverings, see Westfall et al. (2016). Qualitative research suggests that Muslim women experience veiling as both empowering and alienating. See Read and Bartkowski (2000, 406). See also Williams and Vashi (2007).

111 Discrimination takes on many forms. One example is the harassment faced by Abdul El-Sayed when he ran as a Democratic candidate for the governor of Michigan. A Republican senator accused El-Sayed of having ties to the Muslim Brotherhood (*HuffPost*, Marans 2018).

as legislative prayer. The blatant entanglement of the state with religion is acceptable because law says it is. The entanglement is bounded by rules created by law that seem to render prayer harmless. The District Court outlined the rules that legislative prayer is allowed as long as it is not used to proselytise or advance or disparage any belief or faith; that courts should not scrutinise the content of prayers (except if they had violated the first rule); that prayers in the "Judeo-Christian" tradition are acceptable as long as they don't affiliate the state with any particular religion; and that states can't dictate the content of prayers.[112]

The Court of Appeals, however, was less convinced by the historical argument, and we hear echoes of the Supreme Court of Canada's statement that culture and heritage cannot shield practices that blatantly align church and state when it cites the Supreme Court's decision in the 1989 crèche display case of *County of Allegheny v. American Civil Liberties Union Greater Pittsburgh Chapter* (1989), which noted: "history may affect the constitutionality of nonsectarian references to religion by the government, history cannot legitimate practices that demonstrate the government's allegiance to a particular sect or creed."[113] The Court of Appeals, though, adopted a somewhat convoluted position following previous Supreme Court logic that requiring prayers to be non-denominational would be risking imposing an official or civic religion. This attempt to be neutral would pose the danger of producing a "brooding and pervasive devotion to the secular and a passive, or even active, hostility to the religious".[114]

Prayer is neutered by designating it as "ceremonial", as though somehow this declaration changes its very character and function, eviscerating its Christianity and ensuring that the state is not too intimately connected to religion. Justice Kennedy's statement illustrates the sort of reasoning that accompanies this move:

> In the town of Greece, the prayer is delivered during the ceremonial portion of the town's meeting. Board members are not engaged in policymaking at this time, but in more general functions, such as swearing in new police officers, inducting high school athletes into the town hall of fame, and presenting proclamations to volunteers, civic groups, and senior citizens. It is a moment for town leaders to recognize the achievements of their constituents and the aspects of community life that are worth celebrating. By inviting ministers to serve as chaplain for the month, and welcoming them to the front of the

112 *Town of Greece DC*, p. 51.

113 *Town of Greece CA*, p. 12; original quote from *County of Allegheny v. American Civil Liberties Union Greater Pittsburgh Chapter* (1989) 492 U.S. 573, p. 603.

114 In *Sch. Dist. of Abington Twp., Pa., v. Schempp*, Justice Goldberg ruled that: "It is said, and I agree, that the attitude of government toward religion must be one of neutrality. But untutored devotion to the concept of neutrality can lead to invocation or approval of results which partake not simply of that noninterference and noninvolvement with the religious which the Constitution commands, but of a brooding and pervasive devotion to the secular and a passive, or even active, hostility to the religious. Such results are not only not compelled by the Constitution, but, it seems to me, are prohibited by it" (*Sch. Dist. of Abington Twp., Pa., v. Schempp* (1963) 374 U.S. 203, p. 306).

> room alongside civic leaders, the town is acknowledging the central place that religion, and religious institutions, hold in the lives of those present. (*Town of Greece SC*, Opinion of Kennedy, J., p. 23)

The idea that the prayer is placed in the ceremonial part of the meeting is intended to minimise its impact or importance as a religious practice, at the same time as, just a few sentences later, the centrality of religion to those present (erasing the nonreligious or other than Christian in the process) is stated as a fact.[115]

One of the mechanisms for displacing responsibility for the implementation of the programme of practices and symbols associated with Protestantism is the invocation of civil society and tradition as democratically rooted: "we, the people" thus have decided. Stephen Feldman (1997) has written about this especially in relation to Christmas celebrations in public schools and Sunday closing laws, which he points out have been reimagined as uniquely American aspects of civil life which are secular in nature (223). By invoking American civil life, the state is absolved of responsibility and its neutrality remains pure. Moreover, the state, which is always subject to suspicion (at heightened levels in the United States), is kept in its place by "the people".

The Court of Appeals pushed past a simple acceptance of prayer practices as a legitimate expression of heritage,[116] calling for municipalities to assess the context and to "ask itself whether what it does, in context, reasonably can be seen as endorsing a particular faith or creed over others" (*Town of Greece CA*, p. 21). Of course, reasonableness is in the eye of the beholder. In a final twist on the matter, not only does law justify the prayers, it prohibits review of them, holding that to review the content of prayers would be to put state bodies in the untenable position of supervising them. Both the Supreme Court and the Court of Appeals agreed on the hands off approach to prayer:

> To hold that invocations must be nonsectarian would force the legislatures sponsoring prayers and the courts deciding these cases to act as supervisors and censors of religious speech, thus involving government in religious matters to a far greater degree than is the case under the town's current practice of neither editing nor approving prayers in advance nor criticizing their content after the fact. (*Town of Greece SC*, Syllabus, p. 2)

115 "In addition to questioning the factual accuracy of the claim that religious meaning disappears over time, commentators have emphasized the conceptual and theoretical difficulties that arise from this approach. One prevalent argument is that it is denigrating to religion and insulting to religious believers and nonbelievers alike to say that the Christmas holiday, the national motto, and the like have no religious content" (Hill 2010, 724).

116 The Court of Appeals ruled: "a municipality cannot—in our judgment—ensure that its prayer practice complies with the Establishment Clause simply by stating, expressly, that it does not mean to affiliate itself with any particular faith" (*Town of Greece CA*, p. 21).

> A requirement that town officials censor the invocations offered—beyond the limited requirement, recognized in Marsh, that prayer-givers be advised that they may not proselytize for, or disparage, particular religions—is not only not required by the Constitution, but risks establishing a "civic religion" of its own. (*Town of Greece CA*, p. 22)

The complicated matter of state neutrality, which should logically be an effect of the Establishment Clause, is informed by exceptions for Christian prayers with rules about proselytising, content review and too much scripting by the state. Similar to the case studies in the previous chapters, neutrality is full of content. One might intuitively think that a neutral state would engage more carefully with practices and symbols that could have an exclusionary impact. This does not necessarily mean banishing religious symbols and practices, but it would require a more meaningful engagement from a less defensive posture that would carefully consider the alignment of not only state and religion, but the impact of maintaining a place of privilege for Christian prayer. The argument that this is beyond the scope of the law is disingenuous: law engages in this type of analysis all the time, as did the Court of Appeals in *Town of Greece*: "People with the best of intentions may be tempted, in the course of giving a legislative prayer, to convey their views of religious truth, and thereby run the risk of making others feel like outsiders" (*Town of Greece CA*, p. 23). It is the impact of a conceptualisation of neutrality that privileges some that is more concerning about the move from religion to culture.

An alternative narrative

Despite the rather entrenched notion that prayer in some form is acceptable in government activities, and the embedded hierarchical assumptions that come with privileging "foundational" practices and particular histories, traces of future forming narratives are woven through public discussion and indeed the decisions themselves. Though there are blinders to the fact that prayer itself may not be universal or inclusive, there is a sensitivity to the forms of prayer that may be the most harmful. We have already seen the ways that the Court of Appeals considered the practice of prayer and its impact on a wider constituency of citizens. It was not willing to accept Christian prayer as a universally applicable good. Some of the same considerations were voiced in response to the case, including concern about the potential impact of the decision on people who are members of minority religious groups.

Ultimately, as in the *Saguenay* and *Vendée* cases, legal contortion creates a fiction—the nonreligious, harmless and noncoercive religious practice/symbol—that serves the interests of a particular constituency. The harm caused is not just to religious minorities or to the nonreligious, but to society more generally by excluding some people from the narrative of the "we". Beyond this, the administration of justice is also brought into disrepute: by characterising prayer as not really being an alignment of the state with religion, the law diminishes its own credibility. One commentary illustrates some of these concerns:

> The Court must choose one of two paths in deciding Town of Greece. First the Court might obfuscate the facts and contort "nonsectarian" prayer to mean monotheistic prayer, while it fails to acknowledge what makes America great, its peaceful, teeming diversity. That would be intellectually and morally bankrupt. Second, and alternatively, the Court could frankly acknowledge the fact that there is no prayer at this point in American society that is non-sectarian. There are only sectarian prayers and, therefore, the government must get out of the prayer business entirely.[117]

Religious and nonreligious voices expressed dismay, but also sought to find positive aspects in the decision:

> But the losing plaintiffs also have some religious leaders on their side. Rev. Dr. C. Welton Gaddy, president of the Interfaith Alliance, and Rabbi David Saperstein, director of the Religious Action Center of Reform Judaism, stood against Monday's ruling and may be allies for the position as the fight continues. "If there is any positive side in this disturbing decision it is that the court makes clear that if 'the invocations denigrate nonbelievers or religious minorities, threaten damnation, or preach conversion' ... That circumstance would present a different case than the one presently before the Court," Gaddy said.[118]

The case also had the effect of shifting practices in municipalities by drawing attention to the fact that Christian only prayers were likely to come under scrutiny and by prompting a more inclusive approach to prayer:

> After a vocal campaign urging the Jacksonville City Council to observe a landmark decision on public prayer, history of sorts was made last night when the Council allowed its first-ever secular invocation to be delivered [...] Doing the honors was Earl Coggins of the First Coast Freethought Society, an atheist [...] According to the Society, the campaign involved "repeated e-mails to City Council president, council members, and support staff, urging them to obey the law, subsequent to the Town of Greece v Galloway decision, and imploring them to respect the diversity in Jacksonville."[119]

One of the essential elements of creating an inclusive future is the public recitation of narratives about who "we" are that include a wide repertoire of belonging, a vertical notion of relationships and a premise of equality. That "we" extends far beyond the narrow confines of the past preserving story of "us". Self-narratives are, argues Doug Ezzy (2004), a moral tale as much as a self-description (22). In telling the story of the United States as one of a Christian "us", the myriad participants in its history who did not identify that way (and even those who did but imagined a

117 *Verdict* (Hamilton 2013).
118 *Time* (Dias 2014).
119 *Florida Politics* (Ross 2016).

genuinely diverse nation) are erased. Narrative is not only the metaphorical construction of the past, it is also about the present and the future (Ezzy 2000, 608). Justice Kagan was especially adept at telling a future forming narrative that told an alternative version of the story of who "we" are:

> That is not the country we are, because that is not what our Constitution permits. Here, when a citizen stands before her government, whether to perform a service or request a benefit, her religious beliefs do not enter into the picture. … The government she faces favors no particular religion, either by word or by deed. And that government, in its various processes and proceedings, imposes no religious tests on its citizens, sorts none of them by faith, and permits no exclusion based on belief. When a person goes to court, a polling place, or an immigration proceeding—I could go on: to a zoning agency, a parole board hearing, or the DMV—government officials do not engage in sectarian worship, nor do they ask her to do likewise. They all participate in the business of government not as Christians, Jews, Muslims (and more), but only as Americans—none of them different from any other for that civic purpose. Why not, then, at a town meeting? (*Town of Greece SC*, Kagan, J., dissenting, pp. 7–8)

Embedded in the decisions and the public discussion about the *Town of Greece* case is evidence of an alternative narrative constructed around a future forming model of living well together. Traces of a different vision of American society as one which is inclusive and egalitarian are present in both the arguments made by the complainants as well as the dissenting opinion, which celebrated an alternative historical narrative that did not act as a straightjacket of conformity or an originalist mandate. Referring to the "norm of religious equality", Justice Kagan, for example, celebrated the "the breathtakingly generous constitutional idea that our public institutions belong no less to the Buddhist or Hindu than to the Methodist or Episcopalian" (*Town of Greece SC*, pp. 1–2).

In its own fashion, even the majority decision recognised that inclusion was important:

> The town at no point excluded or denied an opportunity to a would-be prayer giver. Its leaders maintained that a minister or layperson of any persuasion, including an atheist, could give the invocation. But nearly all of the congregations in town were Christian; and from 1999 to 2007, all of the participating ministers were too. (*Town of Greece SC*, Opinion of the Court, p. 2)

A commitment to meaningful diversity was the motivation for Galloway and Stephens to complain in the first place.

The town also attempted to respond to the complaints by expanding the repertoire of those offering prayers:

> After respondents complained that Christian themes pervaded the prayers, to the exclusion of citizens who did not share those beliefs, the town invited a Jewish layman and the chairman of the local Baha'i temple to deliver prayers. A Wiccan priestess who had read press reports about the prayer controversy requested, and was granted, an opportunity to give the invocation. (*Town of Greece SC*, Opinion of the Court, pp. 3–4)

The idea of an accessible public square finds full voice in Justice Kagan's America and is thus worth quoting at some length:

> The town hall here is a kind of hybrid. Greece's Board indeed has legislative functions, as Congress and state assemblies do—and that means some opening prayers are allowed there. But much as in my hypotheticals, the Board's meetings are also occasions for ordinary citizens to engage with and petition their government, often on highly individualized matters. That feature calls for Board members to exercise special care to ensure that the prayers offered are inclusive—that they respect each and every member of the community as an equal citizen. But the Board, and the clergy members it selected, made no such effort. (*Town of Greece SC*, Kagan, J., dissenting, pp. 8–9)

> In performing civic functions and seeking civic benefits, each person of this nation must experience a government that belongs to one and all, irrespective of belief. And for its part, each government must ensure that its participatory processes will not classify those citizens by faith, or make relevant their religious differences. (*Town of Greece SC*, Kagan, J., dissenting, pp. 16–17)

Inclusion, constructed in a context specific manner and with a substantive enactment of equality that accounted for but did not reify difference, was foremost in Justice Kagan's version of American society and how it should function. Rather than positioning one group at the apex of a vertical schema of cultural privilege, this vision of society imagines a diverse society in which citizens are horizontally positioned with equal status. Unlike the majority, Justice Kagan also recognised the harm in the prayer as it was practised in the town of Greece:

> But just for that reason, the not-so-implicit message of the majority's opinion—"What's the big deal, anyway?"—is mistaken. The content of Greece's prayers is a big deal, to Christians and non-Christians alike. A person's response to the doctrine, language, and imagery contained in those invocations reveals a core aspect of identity—who that person is and how she faces the world. And the responses of different individuals, in Greece and across this country, of course vary. Contrary to the majority's apparent view, such sectarian prayers are not "part of our expressive idiom" or "part of our heritage and tradition," assuming the word "our" refers to all Americans ... They express beliefs that

> are fundamental to some, foreign to others—and because that is so they carry the ever-present potential to both exclude and divide. (*Town of Greece SC*, Kagan. J., dissenting, p. 23)

Justice Kagan was not alone in imagining a future forming vision of diversity and in acknowledging the harm caused by the prayer practice of the town. Two Christian pastors spoke out about the prayer practices (Krueger is from First Baptist Church of Pendleton, South Carolina, a small town of about 3,000 people and Glaze is from First Baptist Church of Ahoski, a town of about 5,000 people in North Carolina):

> "Sectarian prayers don't serve any positive purpose in official government settings," he [Krueger] said. Not having legislative prayers, he [Krueger] said, "is the way it should be." [...] "The last thing I'd want to do," Glaze said, would be to pray in a manner that suggested to any citizens attending the meeting that their "interests are not as fully represented here" or that they were "not welcome." [...] That, he [Glaze] added, "would really break my heart."[120]

The executive director of the Secular Coalition for America expressed disappointment that the Court had ignored "the very blatant burden sectarian prayer imposes on the conscience of citizens with diverse religious beliefs and those without religious beliefs".[121]

Perhaps counterintuitively, in his analysis of the *Town of Greece v. Galloway* decision, Ethan Quillen (2018) argues that the decision had positive implications for atheists in that it spurred many communities to re-examine their opening invocations to be more inclusive. Quillen documents numerous atheist invocations offered across the United States in the aftermath of the decision. Similarly, Jay Wexler (2019) noted the flurry of activity, some of it generated by Americans United, related to a wave of invocations that significantly deepened the diversity of voices in the aftermath of *Town of Greece*. Not all of these went smoothly, as Wexler notes, but they did open the door to a more inclusive approach. The presence of Atheists, Wiccans, Buddhists and Muslims has a symbolic weight that presses toward a future forming narrative that may shift who "we" are.

It was not difficult to imagine alternative ways of retaining prayer and being more inclusive. Justice Breyer (in dissent) iterated a plan of action:

> The fact that nearly all of the prayers given reflected a single denomination takes on significance. That significance would have been the same had all the prayers been Jewish, or Hindu, or Buddhist, or of any other denomination. The significance is that, in a context where religious minorities exist and where more could easily have been done to include their participation, the town chose to do nothing. It could, for example, have posted its policy of permitting anyone to

120 *Aljazeera America* (Posner 2013).
121 *The Washington Post* (Markoe and Grossman 2014).

> give an invocation on its website, greeceny.gov, which provides dates and times of upcoming town board meetings along with minutes of prior meetings. It could have announced inclusive policies at the beginning of its board meetings, just before introducing the month's prayer giver. It could have provided information to those houses of worship of all faiths that lie just outside its borders and include citizens of Greece among their members. Given that the town could easily have made these or similar efforts but chose not to, the fact that all of the prayers (aside from the 2008 outliers) were given by adherents of a single religion reflects a lack of effort to include others. (*Town of Greece SC*, Breyer, J., dissenting, pp. 3–4)

As noted at the beginning of this chapter, the story of the United States is crafted around the idea that it is a country of immigrants and thus a nation that is characterised by diversity. This is often taken as sufficient proof of its inclusiveness. As is the case in France, however, it is assimilation that characterises the response to diversity and the transmission of that ethos has been highly successful: Galloway and Stephens did not argue for an end to prayer at the beginning of the town board meeting, but rather that it become more inclusive.[122] The idea that particular iterations of the public sphere—a town board meeting—should be without a religious marker was not part of the conversation.

122 "The idea of super-diversity has received very different reactions on both sides of the Atlantic. In Europe, an increasing number of scholars started using the concept in different domains within the larger framework of migration and ethnic studies. In contrast, the concept has hardly been taken up by scholars in the USA, where the framework of assimilation still pretty much kept its dominant position in the analyses of outcomes for migrants and their children" (Crul 2016, 55).

5 Conclusion

Balancing heritage, culture, religion and inclusion

> Her steps echoed on the wooden floor of the empty hallway. It was dark, but she could see by the light that permeated the space of government from the spotlight that shone on this seat of power. In any event she was familiar enough with the building that she had a sense of her destination. She entered the place where decisions are made, but mostly where partisan, often vitriolic, debate that passes as democracy-in-action takes place. She looked up. There He was. "Hurry!" she whispered. "Get down from there and take my hand." She could not stand it any longer: what to her was most sacred had become a political tool, used to score points, create hatred and condone exclusion. All, it seemed to her, exactly the opposite of the whole point of His life, death and resurrection.

During the course of writing this book the debates about Christian symbols in majoritarian Christian countries have intensified. States that routinely describe themselves as secular are implementing protections for the public display of existing symbols and the presence of practices such as the recitation of Christian prayers. There are new initiatives to create mandatory displays where none existed before. In Italy, for example, a bill was introduced to make it mandatory to display a crucifix in public buildings, including schools, universities and prisons.[1] Similarly, in Germany in April 2018, the regional government of Bavaria announced that "Christian crosses [are] to be publicly displayed in all of its official buildings".[2] The Prime

1 "The bill, 'Dispositions concerning the display of the crucifix in schools and in offices of public administration,' proposes crucifixes be visibly hung in places such as schools, universities, prisons, public offices, consulates, embassies, and ports and would fine 'up to $1,169 for non-compliance'" (*Crux*, Brockhaus 2018). The bill was introduced on March 26, 2018 but does not yet appear to have been passed into law (Senato dell Repubblica 2019; *GQ*, Perisse 2018). However, "a close adviser to Pope Francis [Father Antonio Spadaro] criticized legislation proposed by Italy's anti-migrant League party to require ports and other public institutions to display a crucifix, saying [...] that the religious symbol isn't 'a team emblem' to be shown for political ends" (*Crux*, Somekh 2018).

2 *The Telegraph* (Huggler 2018). The head of the German Bishops' Conference, Cardinal Reinhard Marx, objected to Markus Söder's order arguing that such a display of the cross "amounts to 'expropriating the cross in the name of the state'" and that the cross represents more than a cultural symbol (*Deutsche Welle* 2018). Similarly, The Regional Bishop of the Evangelical Lutheran Church in Bavaria and Chairman of the Council of the

Minister of Bavaria, Markus Söder, claimed that "the cross is a fundamental symbol of our Bavarian identity and way of life".[3] In the province of New Brunswick, Canada, the practice of reciting the Lord's prayer at the beginning of each sitting day was recently challenged.[4] Members of the legislative assembly and the premier of the province defended the practice in the name of culture and heritage.[5] An initiative (House Bill 7055) in Florida has commanded that every school and school administrative building in Florida must display the words "In God We Trust".[6] Quebec City and the city of Sherbrooke have insisted that their crucifixes will remain on display, despite the Supreme Court of Canada ruling on prayer in *Saguenay* and the "religious neutrality bill" in Quebec (CBC News 2019b).

These are but a few examples. Each of these governments claims to be secular, raising the question of the utility of that concept, or at least challenging the idea that the secular is neutral territory that can offer an inclusive space for diverse groups and people. Elizabeth Shakman Hurd (2012) argues that secularism is not the absence of religion, but a "presence" that shapes religion (955). Janet Jakobsen and Ann Pellegrini go further (2003), noting that American secularism is decidedly Christian. Their comments are pertinent beyond the United States: in any country in which Christianity has been a dominant religion secularism is intertwined with it.[7] Thus, various forms of Christianity in those contexts inevitably frame what is neutral, secular and religious.

Evangelical Church in Germany, Bishop Heinrich Bedford-Strohm, also opposed Söder's decision (*The Telegraph*, Huggler 2018). In response to those opposed, the mayor of Deggendorf, Christian Moser, said "this is about culture, not religion" (*The New York Times*, Bennhold 2018). Interestingly, in a poll published by the German newspaper *Bild Am Sonntag* shortly after Söder's announcement, 64 per cent of the German population opposed the display of crosses in public buildings (*Bild am Sonntag* 2018; *Evangelical Focus* 2018).

3 *The Telegraph* (Huggler 2018).

4 In Louiseville, Quebec, however, Mayor Yvon Deshaies found a "novel way around" the forbidding of "prayers at municipal council meetings—reading the national anthem. [... Deshaies] opened the monthly council meeting by asking people to stand as he recited an abridged version of the [Canadian national] anthem, which included the lines about the cross and faith as well as a French translation of 'God keep our land glorious and free,' from the English O Canada [... Deshaies] said his actions were in response to news about religious minorities seeking to work as police officers in Quebec while wearing such symbols as the hijab and turban" (*National Post*, Hamilton 2018).

5 Cathy Rogers, Moncton South Liberal MLA, said that "her faith is important to her and 'to not acknowledge that there is a transcendent belief system in our country would be to not accept what is really a part of our culture'" (*CBC News*, Poitras 2019). The Premier of New Brunswick, Blaine Higgs, "said last week he finds it sad that some are attempting to 'pick away' at historical traditions in the province, and he won't change the prayer practices so long as he's premier" (*Global News*, Tutton 2019).

6 WCTV Eyewitness News (2018). The bill was passed by the Governor of Florida on March 11, 2018 (The Florida Senate 2018).

7 "We think it's important for Americans to come to terms with the fact that Christianity, and often conservative Christianity, functions as the yardstick and measure of what counts as 'religion' and 'morality' in America. To be traditionally American is to be Christian in a certain way. Part of our critique of American secularism, then, is that it is

In addition to seeing a remarkable similarity of resilience of majoritarian religion, there are other insights we can glean from thinking through the cases detailed in the previous chapters and those just mentioned. For example, it is curious that the Supreme Court of Canada challenged the characterisation of the prayer as culture and heritage and found that Alain Simoneau's rights had been violated despite the fact that Canada does not have any constitutional provision similar to the Establishment Clause. Similarly, the long history of France related to laïcité failed to produce an ultimate decision to evict the crèche from public property. Instead, somewhat like the United States, in France a series of rules has evolved in law to protect the established status of Christian symbols within the context of non-establishment.[8] To some extent, the historical differences between the countries explain the degree of state endorsement of religion, or, put otherwise, the number of exceptions a state has. The legacy of anti-communist sentiment which associated it with atheism is an important factor in the US blind spot to the widespread state endorsement of Christianity. So too is the contemporary deployment of religion in the game of politics, especially in the perpetuation of a monovision conceptualisation of the good citizen and a static vision of the nation.

The relationship between majoritarian Christianity in Western democracies and nationalism, negative sentiment toward immigrants and religious minorities is a complicated one, as a Pew Research Center report demonstrates. Focusing on Western Europe, that report found that Christian affiliation (regardless of attendance) was correlated with a negative assessment of the compatibility of Islam and "our country's values and culture" and with seeing their culture as superior to others.[9] The report also found a correlation between Christianity and a desire to reduce immigration levels. Nilüfer Göle (2016) notes the use of anti-Muslim sentiment across Europe in the building of populist parties that have used inflammatory rhetoric to claim a past preserving nationalist vision (15).

Despite the findings of increased support for reduced immigration, Christianity too plays a role in creating an inclusive and just society. To return to an earlier point, Christianities are a more apt description of the religious context in the societies

not really secular. When the president takes his oath of office and makes his inaugural address, there are always references to God, and we all know which God is being invoked (after all, every president of the United States has been Christian in some way, and only one has been Catholic). And when the Christian Coalition talks about 'taking back America,' they want to enforce this connection between Americanness and particular Christian commitments" (Jakobsen and Pellegrini 2003, 13). See also Asad (2003) for a discussion of the secular-religion relationship.

8 Donald L. Beschle (2016) suggests that this curious difference between the United States and Canada signals, at the very least, that the Establishment Clause is being under-enforced, particularly given the number of Americans who identify as non-religious (374).

9 "In Germany, as in several other countries, overall public opinion is split on whether Islam is compatible with German values and culture, with 55% of churchgoing Christians saying Islam is incompatible with German values and culture, compared with 45% among non-practicing Christians and 32% among religiously unaffiliated adults" (Pew Research Center, Sahgal 2018).

discussed in the previous pages. "A Christian nation" is mobilised by particular social actors in specific contexts. This is not to deny the power of such rhetorical mobilisation or the damage it does to a vision of society that is diverse and inclusive. But it is also important to draw out those vectors of Christianity that have moved in the direction of inclusion and equality. Moreover, although frequently defined negatively, nationalism may have other aspects worth considering.

Recent events in New Zealand, though, might provide insight into the potential for re-appropriation of nationalism that defies the past preserving tendencies of most nationalist agendas. In her response to the terrorist attack on two mosques which left 51 dead and dozens injured in Christchurch, New Zealand on March 15, 2019,[10] Prime Minister Jacinda Ardern stated that "'You may have chosen us,' [...] referring to the killer, anger in her voice. 'But we utterly reject and condemn you'."[11] In the days following the attack, as New Zealanders struggled to grasp the scope of the murders and the fact that this had occurred in their country, the prime minister continued to articulate a future forming narrative that noted especially that some of those affected might be migrants or refugees who had chosen to make New Zealand their home, "and it is their home", she affirmed "they are us".[12] She talked about "collective memories" in referencing the events of the day of the attacks, and demonstrated inclusivity and memory by insisting that the names of those who had been killed should be spoken but not that of the terrorist.[13] She quickly banned semi-automatic weapons.[14] Her approach engendered numerous other expressions of inclusion, such as a paper chain made by schoolchildren that said "we are one people" and "I am sorry we could not keep you safe".[15] Boundaries of exclusion were clearly drawn at the terrorist and when an Australian senator suggested that Muslims were to blame the prime minister was quick to draw the line, calling him a "disgrace".[16] Non-Muslim women, including the prime minister, wore headscarves to express solidarity.[17]

Prime Minister Ardern articulated a different shape to nationalism, one which left space for pride in a nation that is inclusive, diverse, embraces horizontal relations between people and which nurtures equality. Her words and actions and then those of countless others demonstrated another narrative about nationalism that creates a unity based on respect for difference. It is this model of nationalism, informed by generosity, acts of caring and deep equality that exemplifies a future forming approach to social diversity. This future forming model shifts the goal from teeth gritted tolerance and living together to one that emphasises living well together.

10 *The New York Times* (Graham-McLay 2019).
11 *The Guardian* (Roy 2019).
12 *The Guardian* (2019).
13 *The Guardian* (Wahlquist 2019).
14 BBC News (2019): "The gun reform bill passed 119–1 after the final reading in [New Zealand's] parliament."
15 *The Guardian* (Wahlquist 2019).
16 *The Guardian* (Roy 2019).
17 *Global News* (Westbrook 2019).

What do our three cases tell us about living well together in a complex future, and indeed in the increasingly complex present? The *Saguenay, Vendée* and *Town of Greece* cases are indicative of a resistance to a loss of power by traditional religions. They also reveal fear, anxiety and emotional attachment to a particular status quo. Despite the fact that each of these countries has some legal protection for freedom of religion, state neutrality in relation to religion and a commitment to a pluralistic vision of society, there is a sense that these are tempered by an overarching privilege to be accorded to majoritarian religion. This has become increasingly difficult to sustain as religion and thus constructing practices and symbols as culture is one way to protect "religion" from challenge in a democratic, diverse and inclusive society. The pressure mounts as increasing number of people identify as nonreligious, a fact made more complex by ardent defence of religious symbols by those who self describe as "nones" through an adoption of the language of culture and heritage. That culture and heritage is linked in public discourse and legal decisions to the moral fabric of the nation, conceptualisations of citizenship and "our values". In turn, a challenge to prayer before a council meeting or a crucifix in a hospital becomes extremely difficult: those who dare to do so are bad citizens, radicals, psychologically unsound and, ultimately, not one of "us".

Each of the cases highlights some of the features of the presence of religion in the public sphere—the importance of both global flows and local contexts; the role of national identity and citizenship (the ways in which public space is constituted to belong to particular constituencies); and the policing of the boundaries of the public sphere and its religious and cultural content. But, as I have discussed in each of the chapters, there were counter-narratives that suggest an alternative vision of each of the societies and of religion.

The religion to culture move

The epigraph at the beginning of this chapter suggests that there are costs to religion when it is constructed as culture. It is not simply that construction, but the politics and power relations around it, that give pause for thought. Danièle Hervieu-Léger (2000) analyses the shift to culture by considering what she argues is a broader trend in contemporary society where continuity is devalued and change is valued for itself. In this context,

> tradition plays only an ancillary role in society's production and legitimization of norms, values and symbols proposed for acceptance and credence by the individual or group. What is there for religion to do in modem societies except play a subsidiary cultural and symbolic role? Or, to put it more bluntly, is it not bound to be marginalized as having little real significance except as folklore? (89)

Although Hervieu-Léger may be overstating the rejection of tradition, she captures the potential cost of realigning symbols and practices with culture, heritage and history:

> To say that religion has to do with tradition, namely with continuity and conformity, in a world dominated by pressure for change effectively denies it any active social or cultural role in modern society. It is thereby effectively consigned to a function of nostalgic or exotic remembrance, apart from fulfilling the function of memory and upholding the survival of tradition in the world of modernity. (86)

I have argued that, for the moment, the transformation of religion to culture is a powerful reclaiming of religion's place which is much more difficult to challenge than if it is merely "religion", which, given human rights guarantees, must inevitably cede a place to competing religions and worldviews. By moving into the realm of culture, tradition and history, practices and symbols formerly characterised as religious assume new life. But for how long? And, does religion risk further diminishment of its relevance? Moreover, the discourse of culture deployed in debates about such symbols and practices is decidedly static, ignoring the historically produced, unbounded, contested, practical and lived production of culture in the context of power relations (Merry 2001, 41–42).

My project is not to defend religion, or, specifically, Christianity in countries that are experiencing a rapid decline in participation in church life. But, in naming the strategy and consequences of religion to culture for the nonreligious and minority religions it is worth considering its impact on those for whom Christian symbols and practices are more than relics. What is the impact of describing cherished beliefs and practices on those for whom prayer is a daily practice or the crucifix a beloved symbol of their faith?[18] How is authority to effect social change transformed in such a characterisation?

Some religious voices have expressed concern about the reconstruction of symbols they view as religious to the realm of culture. For example, the American Jewish Congress has spoken out about The Fraternal Order of Eagles erecting monuments of the Ten Commandments throughout cities in the United States, stating that:

> "To treat the Ten Commandments as an adjunct of sociology, community relations or some other of the secular sciences would be to denigrate their

18 Erin Wilson (2014a) has made this point in her Building Bridges lecture "'But that's Culture, not Religion': The Politics of Christianity as Cultural Heritage," at the University of Ottawa, April 3, 2014. Christian Joppke (2018) argues that "the culturalization of religion, by means of which the privileging of the majority is to be achieved, is not much liked by the churches, who plausibly find that the notion of a Christian identity without a Christian faith 'makes no sense' (Pope Benedict XVI, quoted in Roy, 2016: 194). As the head of the Catholic Church realized, culturalized religion marks the ultimate victory of secularization as the religionist's true enemy, the Christian no less than the Muslim's" (240). However, a read of religious leaders' statements in public debates reveals that they frequently characterise symbols and practices as culture and heritage. They are well aware of the traction this strategy has amongst populations that have abandoned religion.

> authentic purpose, to divest them of their transcendental meaning." And more: "To reduce the Ten Commandments to the level of mere moral instruction would be to sever them from their root and core." (as quoted in Joselit 2017, 39)

As far as the American Jewish Congress was concerned, planting a Ten Commandments monument on public land not only weakened the nation. It also undermined the integrity of the Ten Commandments themselves.

Erin Wilson (2014a) has made similar arguments, noting that reconstruction depoliticises and dehistoricises religion. Wilson argues that it also "keeps religion in its place". My position is a bit different: I argue that the configuration of majoritarian symbols and practices as culture expands rather than diminishes religion's influence, releasing it from the confines of legal categories in which it might be contested and bounded (however inadequate those processes may be). Wilson and I agree, however, that the designation of culture contributes to the delineation of "us" and "them", the "us" having a Judeo-Christian heritage (Wilson's descriptor) that will never include the "them". The debates that have occurred over symbols and practices in the Canadian context, for example, have excluded Indigenous worldviews as well as the early settlement in Canada by Jews, Sikhs and Muslims.[19] As Wilson (2014b) asks, "who is being excluded, however subtly, by the celebration of Christianity as culture, rather than religion?"

In the relentless debates about the presence of religious symbols in the public sphere in Quebec, two issues have been persistent. The first is the wearing of religious symbols for public servants.[20] It is widely acknowledged that a ban has a disproportionate impact on non-Christian religions. The second site of contention has been the presence of the crucifix in various public spaces, including in the legislative assembly of the province. Political leaders have declared that the crucifix is not a religious symbol, but "part of Quebec's history and traditional values".[21] The effect of this is surely not a disempowering of religion, but rather a reintegration of it into the social fabric of day to day life. Some hospitals not only have a crucifix in the lobby, but in patient rooms. Municipal councils may recite prayers (despite the ruling in the *Saguenay* case), some in ingenious ways, and have religious symbols in council chambers. The combination of the regulation and erasure of minority religious symbols from the public sphere with the preservation of a Christian symbol as "heritage" is toxic to democracy.

The transitioning of particular practices and symbols as religion or culture and heritage is not new, as Astor et al. (2017) point out:

> discourses on religion as heritage generally emerge when the place of religion as a marker of national unity is in question, whether in situations of strong

19 The first mosque in Canada was built in Edmonton, Alberta in 1938 (*Globe and Mail* 1938).

20 *CBC News* (Rukavina 2018).

21 *CBC News* (Rukavina 2018).

> clerical/anti-clerical cleavages (as in Spain in the 1930s), contestations over the religious secular divide (as in the late 1970s), or migration-driven religious diversity (as during the 1990s). (140)

Each wave and context has its own contours and consequences. In each of the contexts I've considered there have been moments in which the religious salience of symbols and practices have been denied. For example, in Canada the early post-Charter case of *R v. Edwards Books and Art Ltd.*, upheld a Sunday closing law by erasing the links between Sunday closing and Christianity, separating religious origins from religious intent and purpose. The framework of Christian majoritarianism has been described in the United States by Leigh Eric Schmidt (2016) as "Protestant-suffused statecraft" (207). It is not a surprise that Christianity infuses social practices and institutions in countries that have traditionally had Christian majority populations. The question is how to reconcile that past with a present and future that is diverse and inclusive.[22] In asking this question it also becomes salient to ask how to import a more nuanced texture to the story of "our culture".

In this light, is it possible for those who have been excluded to take up the discourse of culture to protect their practices? The answer would seem to be no. Wendy Brown (2006) suggests that "'we' have culture while culture has 'them,' or we have culture while they are a culture. Or, we are a democracy while they are a culture" (151). A Canadian example illustrates. In October, 2015, 29-year-old Zunera Ishaq took the Canadian oath of citizenship. This was no small matter as Ishaq had to take her wish to swear the oath while wearing her niqab before various levels of courts. The then prime minister had made it a political issue, making public statements such as, "Why would Canadians, contrary to our own values, embrace a practice at that time that is not transparent, that is not open and, frankly, is rooted in a culture that is anti-women?"[23] Culture there takes a different sort of tone: in *Saguenay* it becomes an iconic designation that offers a protective hands of shield—our culture and heritage is unassailable. In *Ishaq*, the statement by the then prime minister reduces a practice that is understood as clearly relating to religious commitment to "merely" culture and something that can thus be unlearned. The Federal Court of Appeal upheld Ishaq's right to wear the niqab and stated that "there is no evidence of broad effects upon Muslim women generally or the larger Muslim community" (para. 36). The court dismissed the state's motion to stay the matter. The then prime minister also stated "it is offensive that someone would hide their identity at the very moment where they are committing to join the Canadian family".[24] The Conservative Party's website stated that covering one's face while being sworn in is "not the way we do things here" (Conservative Party of Canada 2015). In addition, the former prime minister made a statement in which he divided

22 I am grateful to Jim Beckford for this observation.
23 CBC News (2015c).
24 *The Star* (Whittington 2015).

"new" and "old stock" Canadians[25] and described the niqab as a "product of a culture that is antiwoman".[26] In September of 2015 during the federal election campaign, the Conservatives promised to create a "Barbaric Cultural Practices" hotline if they were re-elected.[27]

The ability to make such argument is embedded in power relations, which may not so easily facilitate an argument to that end (assuming a person or group wishes to make that move in the first place). Part of the story being told in this book is about Muslims: in reactions to both *Saguenay* and *Vendée* some of the public discourse includes negative mention of Muslims, despite the fact that both cases are instigated by humanist/free thinking individuals or groups. Recalling the French *S.A.S* case discussed in Chapter 3, S.A.S did not make the argument that her niqab is a "cultural" symbol, but she did argue that she wore the niqab freely, and when she was in the mood to wear it. Though *S.A. S* is not mentioned in the *Vendée* case, certainly the spectre of the imperilled Muslim woman haunts the scene of public discourse, in concert with the Federation of Free Thought.[28] Both are imagined as being enmeshed in a non-democratic regime of otherness that calls into question their legitimacy as speakers and their ability to express opinions about and even in the public sphere, which is fully populated with the heritage and culture represented by the nativity scene.

Although theoretically it is possible for minority religious groups and individuals to recraft practices and symbols as cultural, realising this theoretical possibility is complicated by the realities of power relations that shape the ability to effectively implement a reconstruction. As we see in the example of Zunera Ishaq, culture is indeed used, not by Ishaq, but instead by those seeking to force her to remove her niqab. In that example, she is left without the protection of a religious freedom argument and her "culture" is not "our culture": "the wearing of niqab is cultural, not religious, therefore an argument under religious freedom protections is not relevant".[29] Contrasting this with the reconstruction of prayer and the crucifix as culture, there is an undeniably "special" character of these practices that displaces them and elevates them as being radically different from the practices of others. Majorities are better placed to control the nature and meaning of the discourses of religion and culture.

25 CBC News (2015b).
26 *The Globe and Mail* (Chase 2015).
27 *CBC News* (Powers 2015).
28 Selby et al. (2018) argue that "the Imperilled Muslim woman has a large presence in the public imaginary, which often seems to override evidence to the contrary" (32). The Imperilled Muslim Woman is often "imagined to represent the majority of Muslim women" (42).
29 This position is made even more complicated by the fact that it is often religious groups themselves who engage in these sorts of analyses of belonging. This in turn often relates to orthodoxy or fundamentalism as well as the intertwining of culture and religion and the social imaginary of state leaders. In Turkey, and Tunisia, to name two examples, the hijab has been associated with a commitment to orthodoxy and a lack of modernity.

The *Sedlock v. Baird* [30] case offers an interesting twist on this culture–religion construction, for there the culture argument was successful. In *Sedlock* fundamentalist Christian parents challenged the presence of yoga in their children's school. They argued that it is a religious practice and as such violated the Establishment Clause of the California constitution, which mirrors that of the First Amendment. Ultimately, the Court of Appeal found that "contemporary yoga in the United States is ubiquitous in secular culture" (*Sedlock* at p. 895). This finding was only possible by reconstituting yoga as "American as apple pie", including renaming the poses (the lotus position was, for example, now "criss-cross apple sauce").[31] Both the Court of Appeal and the trial court[32] emphasised the American-ness of yoga: "The essential point is that yoga, as it has developed in the United States in the past 150 years, is a distinctly American cultural phenomenon. It is rooted in American culture as much and sometimes more than in Indian culture" (*Sedlock Superior Court*, at p. 25). Social science evidence was marshalled to demonstrate the secular motives of people who do yoga, "the most common motivations that people gave for practicing yoga included increased flexibility (67.9 percent), stress relief (61.8 percent), and improvement in physical health (60.5 percent)" (*Sedlock* at p. 895). Yoga was reinvented to become American, secular and not "other". Through a reconstitution with the help of the teacher, the school board and law, yoga moves into the realm of the cultural and is accepted as "secular" and appropriate for a public school classroom. To demonstrate the importance of context, almost simultaneously the Indian BJP government established the Ministry of AYUSH[33] and lobbied to have the United Nations proclaim June 21 the International Day of Yoga.[34] The government has also developed an accompanying guide on "common yoga protocol" that offers instructions on the correct way to do poses.[35] The *Sedlock* case demonstrates

30 *Sedlock v. Baird* (2015) 235 Cal. App. 4th 874. Hereinafter "*Sedlock*".

31 In writing about the *Sedlock* decision, one journalist reported the judge as saying "yoga is as American as apple pie, or American cheese" and that yoga "is a distinctly American cultural phenomenon" (Schultz 2013). The apple pie comparison has been used by numerous others, including yoga bloggers and authors of self-help books, to emphasize the "Americanness" of yoga. In *My Journey to the Fountain of Youth*, Azahara Carter (2012) says: "Since Swami Vivekananda first introduced yoga to the West more than a hundred years ago, Yoga has become as American as apple pie" (125). Further, in *Diet Simple*, Katherine Tallmadge (2011) writes: "FORGET any lingering impressions of Eastern mysticism. Yoga today is as American as apple pie—and a lot healthier" (39).

32 *Sedlock v. Baird* (2013) No. 37201300035910-CU-MC-CTL (Cal Super Ct CD). Hereinafter "*Sedlock Superior Court*".

33 Full title: Ministry of Ayurveda, Yoga and Naturopathy, Unani, Siddha, and Homoeopathy.

34 Dia Dabby and Amélie Barras (2018) argue that "a theoretical—if not ideological—*glissement* occurs between religion and culture when situating the claims over yoga. While this slippage from religion to culture is not endemic to yoga, we consider that it exemplifies many of the concerns raised in the literature on this point. Perhaps most explicitly, this *glissement* reshapes the discourse from one steeped in belief (i.e. particular religion) to one imbued with culture (i.e. majority tendencies)" (285).

35 See Ministry of AYUSH (2015) and Basu (2015).

the fluidity of boundaries with a practice that is at the same time "religious", "spiritual" and "other". Again, the essence of the practice in question—this time yoga—is not the focus of the case or this discussion. I have argued elsewhere that "What remains outside of this discussion is the very meaning of 'the secular',[36] the imperialist impulse that demands that yoga be 'American' to be acceptable, and the very tenuousness of anti-establishment itself" (Beaman 2016a, 107).[37] On Hinduism more broadly, Kenneth D. Wald and Allison Calhoun-Brown (2011) note the constitutive power of Christianity:

> It is interesting that historically Hinduism on the Indian subcontinent has varied widely by region and practice. It is being "standardized" in the United States by Hindu organizations trying to conform to the requirements of American governmental policies that reflect acceptable (largely Christian, particularly Protestant) ways of practicing religion in order to receive the benefits and recognition of being classified as a tax-exempt "religious group". (306)

Christianity, or a particular version of it, was a powerful force in shaping an acceptable yoga practice in a public school. A similar example is the inclusion of smudging ceremonies in public school (both nonreligious and Catholic) settings in Canada. As Peter Beyer (2019) argues, although these are acknowledged to have an explicitly spiritual or even religious character, they are primarily understood as an expression of Indigenous culture and therefore are acceptable as part of the ongoing project of reconciliation.

Leo Van Arragon points out that symbols or experiences and practices can be read in multiple ways, whether from a psychological, neurological, sociological or political standpoint, or all of these at once. The "read" one chooses can be very strategic and certainly political: symbols can be mobilised one dimensionally with a view to attaining a particular outcome, and to maintain or create a particular order.[38] Acknowledging multiple perspectives and responding to them in a future forming way is much more difficult than simply asserting one's foundational privilege.

The crucifix and the hospital: the end

In Chapter 1, I introduced the story of Saint-Sacrement hospital and the crucifix that hung in its entryway. Although we have no way to know, it is likely that it is representative of hundreds of similar such cases that may make the news and then recede from view. In all of those cases someone has suggested that the entrenched

36 See Jakobsen and Pellegrini (2003; 2008) for a discussion of the ways in which the secular is entangled with religion. See also Connolly (1999).
37 For an elaboration of this, see Beaman and Sullivan (2013).
38 Personal communication, email dated June 28, 2019.

Christian symbol or practice is inappropriate in a diverse society that includes a wide range of beliefs and worldviews. To conclude, we will return to Saint-Sacrement and consider one version of the events as they unfolded. The hospital's statement justifying the removal of the crucifix noted the following:

> Since our primary mission is to provide health care and services, we must first and foremost respect the rights of our patients, who are somehow captive to the institution. In this regard, the Commission on Human Rights and Freedoms has a clear position: [The] presence of a religious symbol, such as a crucifix or a cross, in a public institution does not raise a problem from the point of view of the *Charter*, unless that symbol acquires a coercive character because of the context in which it is inscribed. Thus, when the clientele of the institution is vulnerable, because it is captive, young or more easily influenced, such as in a school, for example, the display of a religious symbol, such as a cross hanging on the wall, may take on a character that is incompatible with the rights and freedoms of the person. (CHU de Québec 2017; translated from the original French by me)

The sense of being under threat and its accompanying anxiety was palpable. A petition was circulated online, which reportedly received 13,000 signatures.[39] The hospital received 600 phone calls. The hospital and its personnel were threatened.[40] An activist group for the return of a "Catholic Quebec", Mouvement Tradition Québec, put up a crucifix in the hospital (which was taken down).[41]- Archbishop Cardinal Gérald Cyprien Lacroix "expressed disappointment over the removal of the crucifix".[42]

Again, an unnamed "other" was identified as the cause of this threat, couched in a public petition in this way:

> In addition, in the present context in which religions that settle in Quebec must be respected, some people feel that the traditions of long-established people are being put into question. All religions must be respected and the Christian religion is one of those. These people have the right to ask for respect for their culture, their traditions and their religion, even if it is purely heritage.[43]

A more pointed statement named the "other":

39 See the petition at: https://secure.avaaz.org/fr/community_petitions/Hopital_SaintSacrement_Retourner_le_crucifix_a_son_endroit_originel/
40 *CBC News* (Shingler 2017).
41 *Vice* (Eff 2017).
42 *CBC News* (Shingler 2017).
43 Translated from the original French by me. See https://secure.avaaz.org/fr/community_petitions/Hopital_SaintSacrement_Retourner_le_crucifix_a_son_endroit_originel/

> In Quebec, a doctor or a nurse can wear the hijab or even the niqab at work, thus imposing their religious signs on patients who have no say, while a single complaint was enough to tear the crucifix from a wall where it had been for 90 years. Why such a double standard?[44]

Public (state) officials entered the fray, weighing in to claim the heritage and culture status of the crucifix. The then premier of the province, Phillippe Couillard, also weighed in: "Being open and tolerant does not mean erasing our heritage and history."[45] Grasping that there might be a dissonance between allowing Christian symbols in public spaces but restricting minority religious symbols, which might seem like a double standard, the Minister of Health, Gaétan Barrette addressed this, saying they'd be mistaken: "'It's not a symbol of authority,' he said of the cross. 'It's heritage'."[46] He compared the decision of the hospital to "'behaviour similar to Russia in 1917'".[47]

The conservative Catholic group, Mouvement Tradition Québec, said, "We are in our country. When in Rome, do as the Romans do."[48] Some comments were less subtle:

> For better or for worse, in our world religious identities are resurging. Reminding of the importance of the crucifix, in these circumstances, is to remind immigrants that they are here in the Occident, and that Christianity is not one religion among others. It is that which formed our civilization. Everyone must accept this.[49]

The majority of the commentary focused on the culture and heritage value of the crucifix. Few considered the exclusionary power of this symbol, however some comments attempted to articulate a different vision.

Another commentator, though, named the "real" issue:

> The truth is that it is not really the withdrawal of the crucifix that bothers you (it has already been done in schools for a while). It is because you have persuaded yourself that it is the fault of "them" if it is removed. You know who I am talking about, those people you have cleverly and progressively demonized over the past decade, to the extent that it has become normal to despise them publicly or to consider that by shooting at them you do not really become a terrorist, but only unbalanced or a "twit."[50]

44 *The Rebel* (Duhaime n.d.; translated from the original French by me).
45 The Chronicle Journal (2017).
46 *National Post* (Hamilton 2017).
47 *National Post* (Hamilton 2017).
48 *National Post* (Hamilton 2017).
49 *Le Journal de Montréal* (Bock-Côté 2017; translated by Christine L. Cusack).
50 *Le Soleil* (Laprise 2017; translated from the original French by me).

A commentator on the *Friendly Atheist* blog noted that:

> There is precedent for what the hospital did. In fact, there's a cross atop Mount Royal and in the legislature—both are considered historical relics of a more religious time, not endorsements of the faith.
>
> If there are merely symbols, then so be it. My concern is that these symbols are allowed to remain in place because government officials are willing to let Christianity get away with things no other religion ever can. That said, the patients are better off in a secular hospital with a Catholic symbol than a Catholic hospital that doesn't provide a full range of services.
>
> [...] Now, just before they go in for surgery, patients will be able to see a dead man with bloody appendages. I'm sure they'll appreciate it.[51]

Sometime during the night on March 1 the crucifix was returned to the hospital wall. The Cardinal offered his blessing to the "decision", stating: "This is a wise decision that respects the heritage, the historic and the religious aspects of the crucifix."[52] A spokesperson for Mouvement Tradition Québec stated "I don't think they'll faint over this."[53] The instigator of the Facebook campaign thanked those who signed the petition and said "we've achieved our objective and the cross will be put back Wednesday evening."[54] But the crucifix was now accompanied by a plaque that read as follows:

> In the years following the First World War, the only hospital, L'Hôtel-Dieu, in Quebec City was no longer sufficient for the demand. A new hospital was needed. Dr. Arthur Rousseau wanted an establishment for both private patients and poor patients. He obtained the support of the government and the archdiocese and founded a large general hospital equipped with all the modern services needed to treat the sick as well as a school to train future doctors.
>
> Indeed, l'Hôpital du Saint-Sacrement was first conceived to be a university hospital and this was its vocation. It was the nuns of l'Hôtel-Dieu de Québec who took charge of it, and then were succeeded in June 1927 by les Soeurs de la Charité de Québec. Seven departments, governed by eminent physicians, were officially inaugurated on December 15, 1927.
>
> Health care institutions in Quebec have been secular for many years. This crucifix recalls the importance of the contribution of religious communities to the construction of this hospital.[55]

51 *Friendly Atheist* (Mehta 2017).
52 *CBC News* (Shingler 2017).
53 *National Post* (Hamilton 2017).
54 Translated from the original French by me. See the petition at: https://secure.avaaz.org/fr/community_petitions/Hopital_SaintSacrement_Retourner_le_crucifix_a_son_endroit_originel/
55 Radio-Canada (2017a).

The Saint-Sacrement hospital example, like the cases considered in previous chapters, illustrates what is at stake in these battles over symbols and practices. While the public debate often invokes a loss of culture as the core issue, I suggest that what is at stake is the credibility of the claims of liberal democracies about human rights, equality, and universal access to those. Freedom of religion, for example, cannot be only freedom to be religious exactly like "us". And, freedom of religion includes the freedom not to be religious at all—or to be a "none".

Also at stake in cases that come before the courts or human rights tribunals is the credibility of the administration of justice—when law takes the exit route of the "margin of appreciation" in Europe it leaves countries free to discriminate against religious minorities as well as to impose so-called cultural (formerly religious) practices and symbols on those who are not religious; similarly, when the Supreme Court of Canada leaves open the possibility that some majoritarian religious practices might be able to pass the requirement of state neutrality, it too risks the perception that religious minorities and the nonreligious are not really protected and that religious content is being erased in order to protect majoritarian religion. As discussed in Chapter 1, although it found that prayer at municipal council meetings violated human rights protections, the Supreme Court of Canada recognised that "the Canadian cultural landscape includes many traditional and heritage practices that are religious in nature" and that not all of these "cultural expressions" breach the duty of state neutrality. Relying on exceptions or exemptions that have "always" been allowed locks a society in a static pattern of privilege for one group. In the cases I have considered, law contorts itself into peculiar shapes to excuse the very close relationship with majoritarian religion. A Christian prayer at the beginning of a council meeting is the intertwining of state and church. There is no amount of legal reasoning that can change that.

I have already discussed the risk to religion, particularly from the perspective of adherents. For those for whom religious identity is important, dissolving that identity into culture is distressing and diminishes or disrespects what is important to them. It is also important to ask whether there is a lack of authenticity when religious leaders strategically and politically position symbols and practices as "culture and heritage". Such a positioning may contribute to a negative perception and risk to the credibility of religion and religious leaders, despite it being a perhaps clever strategic move.

The shift from religion to culture also tends to create binaries that are not conducive to living well together. "Our culture and heritage" tells one narrative of who we are that, in the cases on symbols and practices, tends to exclude non-Christian experiences and stories of nation building. It also erases the colonial history of countries like Canada and the United States and the much longer "our culture and heritage" of Indigenous peoples. What is at stake here is the ability to define the contents of "our culture and heritage". Who gets to tell the story of who "we" are? This is a critical issue that is often overlooked when "us" and "our culture" are deployed in defence of maintaining the status quo.

There is a potential that open, frank and productive conversation about majoritarian culture, power and inclusion will be shut down or subverted by simply converting Christianity to culture, heritage and universal values. There is a fundamental disconnect, and disrespect, when people say they do not feel included or that they feel alienated, and the response is that the practice or symbols is universal. When they say they are hurt and the response is that that hurt is trivial or they are being overly sensitive, the possibility of an inclusive society becomes less attainable. Or, when the response is to say "they" can just leave, either the country or the room, the desire is to divert attention to the supposed transgression of the other rather than to ask hard questions about power and privilege.

The decision to take down the crucifix at Saint-Sacrement hospital was a future forming act. The hospital board was attempting to create a welcoming atmosphere that was inclusive of everyone. In reinstating the crucifix with the accompanying information the hospital board was acknowledging a very important element of the hospital's history and the nuns who had undoubtedly given much in the service of public health. The solution may not be perfect: the crucifix may still be in a position of prominence that causes stress or anxiety to some. The recognition of the nuns is arguably not accomplished by the crucifix or the plaque. The addition of the plaque may diminish the religious authority of the crucifix for others.

However, such an approach creates space for respect, compromise and recognition of the needs of others. To be blunt, for some nonreligious people the cross may be repulsive and for some religious people it is very precious. Each, though perhaps regretting the position of the other, must work to find solutions to include the other. A moment of silence, for example, before a council meeting may mean a minute of meditation, a minute of prayer, or a minute of making one's grocery list. The comment from one of the councillors in Fredericton, New Brunswick following the *Saguenay* decision and in response to the suggestion that a minute of silence was an appropriate solution was that "well, people could just make their grocery lists then" was revealing. To insist that everyone should be attentive to a prayer reveals a particular desire to impose a religious practice on others. This is contrary to freedom of, and freedom from, religion.

The hospital had made its decision to remove the crucifix in part in response to the guidelines proposed for the display of religious symbols in public places. The elephant in the room was the *Saguenay* decision from the Supreme Court of Canada, which explicitly noted that prayer before council meetings was a religious practice and

> constituted an invocation to God, attributing benefits enjoyed by the City and its citizens to him, and asking him to guide the council's deliberations [...] the prayer was intended as support by the City for the religion professed by individual councillors. (*Saguenay SCC*, at para. 100)

Law can provide inspiration and guidelines for living well together, but as we have seen in the previous chapters, it can also contort itself to justify continuing vertical relationships in which one group is privileged. Such privilege is pervasive and resistant to challenge.

In its recent study, the BC Humanist Association analysed 873 prayers delivered in the BC Legislature between October 6, 2003 and February 12, 2019. The study found that prayers not only favoured "Christianity over other faiths", but also favoured "religious belief over irreligious belief", that they were getting longer and more religious and that both Sikhs, who make up 5 per cent of British Columbia's population, and the nonreligious, who make up 64 per cent, were excluded (Phelps Bondaroff et al. 2019, 10). In their recommendations the BC Humanist Association suggested that the prayers be abolished and replaced by either "nothing, a First Nations territorial acknowledgement, or a time for silent reflection" (Phelps Bondaroff et al. 2019, 10). Perhaps both a First Nations territorial acknowledgment and a moment for reflection might offer a way forward.

How do we achieve what I have called elsewhere "deep equality", or how do we live well together (Beaman 2014; 2017)? Does the hospital's solution achieve that? If the goal is to in fact recognise the contribution of the Catholic sisters whose labour has sustained the hospital over many years, the plaque may accomplish that. By putting a crucifix without explanation on the wall there is an assumption everyone knows what it is and shares in its message. It is a statement of ownership and territory marking. Such an approach buys into the universalism that Christianity often (mistakenly) assumes. Linking the crucifix to the Sisters, to culture and to heritage, and affirming the diverse populations served by hospitals and their mandate to be inclusive may achieve the balance necessary to accomplish inclusion.

Does a future forming approach require the removal of crucifixes and a shift in practices such as prayers? The answer is both yes and no. Most important is the possibility for respectful engagement. The consistent denigration of those who challenge practices and symbols reveals more about power than about commitment to any religious position. I tend to think that social life is much richer when it contains texture and that we are better for it. Erasure can alienate, hurt and create irreparable divisions. So too can the inhabiting of public space by symbols that serve as a reminder of exclusion and nonbelonging.

Despite its shifting shape and status, majoritarian religion remains an influential and *de facto* part of the cultural landscape in Western democracies.[56] Grace Davie (2015) argues this in her second edition of *Religion in Britain*. The challenge, then, is to acknowledge and even celebrate heritage and culture without "misusing it to exclude, shut down, and discriminate or to preserve a particular kind of religion at

56 The Spanish the Constitutional Court has held that "passive symbols have virtually no influence on people's beliefs and, therefore, the religious freedom of individuals is safe, provided that no one is compelled to participate in rites or ceremonies in honour of those symbols" (see Martínez-Torrón 2013, 42–43). Despite a German Federal Constitutional Court ruling that a Bavarian law requiring the presence of crucifixes on public school classroom walls was unconstitutional, the Bavarian government legislated to keep the crucifixes in classrooms (BVerfG, 1 BvR 1087/91 vom 16.05.1995; see Martínez-Torrón 2013, 45–46). Some municipal councils in Australia still open their meetings with prayers and politicians occasionally defend this practice, saying things like "the total abandonment of prayer in councils and parliaments is the abandonment of an important part of our cultural life that most people find important" (Parliament of New South Wales 2005).

a cost to others in increasingly diverse social landscapes" (Beaman 2016b, 32–33). Opening the space for dialogue about privilege, inclusion and new forms of shared social imaginary is one approach. Local solutions may be a more viable solution than broad principles or directives. But this can lapse into a romaticisation of "community" that ignores the potentially abusive and toxic forms of local negotiation.[57]

Symbols and ritual practices such as prayer are powerful mechanisms to tell stories about who "we" are. That "we", though, is potentially fluid and, depending on the path taken, can be inclusive and productive of a society in which people live well together. An expansive approach requires an acceptance that one's own position is not the only position and an engagement with difference characterised by agonistic respect. Social institutions such as law provide a vital space in which to facilitate such engagement. What is at stake in this is not only the ability of individuals to live well together, but the very credibility of liberal democracies in states characterised by a new diversity.

Postscript

On June 20, 2019 the Supreme Court of the United States released its decision in its *American Legion* case. The Court found that a 40-foot tall Latin cross, established in memory of soldiers who died in World War I, and maintained by a local government on public property, did not violate the Establishment Clause. The Court reasoned that "retaining established, religiously expressive monuments, symbols, and practices is quite different from erecting or adopting new ones. The passage of time gives rise to a strong presumption of constitutionality" (*American Legion*, Opinion of the Court, p. 21). The Court also found that the religious meaning of the cross had faded:

> The cross came into widespread use as a symbol of Christianity by the fourth century, and it retains that meaning today. But there are many contexts in which the symbol has also taken on a secular meaning. Indeed, there are instances in which its message is now almost entirely secular. (*American Legion,* Opinion of the Court, p. 3)[58]

Reifying an "us" and "them" approach, which blended religion and heritage, the Court stated: "a campaign to obliterate items with religious associations may evidence hostility to religion even if those religious associations are no longer in the forefront" (*American Legion*, Opinion of the Court, p. 24). In its rendition of

57 Louis Rousseau (2011) argues for the importance of rituals that reflect on the symbolic dimension of political life and thus for re-crafting rituals such as prayers before council meetings anew so that they are both inclusive and acknowledge the contributions of our ancestors.

58 "Even if the original purpose of a monument was infused with religion, the passage of time may obscure that sentiment. As our society becomes more and more religiously diverse, a community may preserve such monuments, symbols, and practices for the sake of their historical significance or their place in a common cultural heritage" (*American Legion*, Opinion of the Court, p. 18).

history, the Court interprets the cross to be a symbol of sacrifice during World War I (*American Legion*, Opinion of the Court, p. 28). Rejecting the idea that the cross is coercive and that it in any way taints the neutrality of the state, the Court interpreted neutrality from the eyes of those who were in favour of keeping it:

> The cross is undoubtedly a Christian symbol, but that fact should not blind us to everything else that the Bladensburg Cross has come to represent. For some, that monument is a symbolic resting place for ancestors who never returned home. For others, it is a place for the community to gather and honor all veterans and their sacrifices for our Nation. For others still, it is a historical landmark. For many of these people, destroying or defacing the Cross that has stood undisturbed for nearly a century would not be neutral and would not further the ideals of respect and tolerance embodied in the First Amendment. For all these reasons, the Cross does not offend the Constitution. (*American Legion,* Opinion of the Court, p. 31)

The concurring judgment of Gorsuch notes that those who are offended can simply avert their eyes (*American Legion*, p. 11). The case reads, in many ways, as a different verse of the *Town of Greece* past preserving song, with its mobilisation of heritage and history, its entanglement of Christianity and neutrality, and its minimisation of harm to those who would oppose the presence of the cross.

But there was also a powerful future forming counterstatement in the decision offered by the judgment of Justice Ruth Ginsburg, who mobilised a different version of history to challenge the narrative of the majority. An important feature of Justice Ginsberg's narrative is her attention to the impact of the cross and the way it is used: "By maintaining the Peace Cross on a public highway, the Commission elevates Christianity over other faiths, and religion over nonreligion" (*American Legion*, Ginsburg dissenting, p. 3). She rejects the characterisation of the cross as a secular symbol, and sees its display on public property as necessarily representing a link between the state and religion. Justice Ginsberg also specifically noted the way that declarations of universality exclude a large number of people from the "us" of American society, insisting that "An exclusively Christian symbol, the Latin cross is not emblematic of any other faith" (*American Legion*, Ginsburg dissenting, p. 7).

Justice Ginsburg then drew on Pew Research Centre data to note that nearly 30 per cent of the population of the United States is not Christian. This means that "the State's choice to display the cross on public buildings or spaces conveys a message of exclusion: It tells them they 'are outsiders, not full members of the political community'" (*American Legion*, Ginsburg dissenting, pp. 5–6). She concludes: "The principal symbol of Christianity around the world should not loom over public thoroughfares, suggesting official recognition of that religion's paramountcy" (*American Legion*, Ginsburg dissenting, pp. 7–8). In contrast to the majority decision, Justice Ginsberg writes from a future forming narrative position, seeking to articulate a vision of an inclusive society that responds positively the new diversity. Her bold counter-narrative invites a re-crafting of the American story to reflect its complexity. In his commentary on the case in the

Washington Post, Paul Waldman (2019) makes a statement that is relevant to all of the cases we've considered in the previous pages:

> When your religion is the *only* religion that has a meaningful place in public life, and then society begins to make more room for other people's beliefs, it can feel like an attack on you. But it isn't. It's a movement in the direction of making everyone feel like they have a legitimate place in our society. (emphasis in original)

On July 9, 2019 the crucifix was removed from the National Assembly in Quebec City. It will, apparently, find a new place within the same building, but will not have a place in the Salon Bleu where state decisions are made.[59]

59 *The Star* (Valiante 2019).

Bibliography

Abdo, Aliah. 2008. "The legal status of hijab in the United States: A look at the sociopolitical influences on the legal right to wear the Muslim headscarf." *Hastings Race and Poverty Law Journal* 5(2): 441–508.

Abortion Rights Coalition of Canada. 2019. "Statistics—Abortion in Canada." *Abortion Rights Coalition of Canada*. January 30, 2019. http://www.arcc-cdac.ca/backrounders/statistics-abortion-in-canada.pdf

Abu Odeh, Lama. 1993. "Post-colonial feminism and the veil: Thinking the difference." *Feminist Review* 43: 26–37.

Adam, Aalia. 2014. "Cases of 'hijabaphobia' increasing in Quebec." *Global News*, February 21, 2014. http://globalnews.ca/news/1165400/cases-of-hijabaphobia-increase-in-quebec/

Adams, Michael. 2007. *Unlikely Utopia: The Surprising Triumph of Canadian Multiculturalism*. Toronto: Viking Canada.

Adelman, Howard, and Pierre Anctil, eds. 2011. *Religion, Culture, and the State: Reflections on the Bouchard-Taylor Report*. Toronto: University of Toronto Press.

Adrian, Melanie. 2015. "Outlawing the veil, banning the Muslim? Restricting religious freedom in France." *CrossCurrents* 65(3): 371–379.

Agrama, Hussein Ali. 2015. "Religious Freedom and the Bind of Suspicion in Contemporary Secularity." In *Politics of Religious Freedom*, edited by Winnifred F. Sullivan, Elizabeth Shakman Hurd, Saba Mahmood, and Peter G. Danchin, 301–313. Chicago: The University of Chicago Press.

Alghafli, Zahra, Loren D. Marks, Trevan G. Hatch, and Andrew H. Rose. 2017. "Veiling in fear or in faith? Meanings of the hijab to practicing Muslim wives and husbands in the USA." *Marriage & Family Review* 53(7): 696–716.

Alibhai, Zaheeda P. forthcoming. "The Boundaries of Religious Pluralism." In *Emergent Religious Pluralisms*, edited by Jan-Jonathan Bock, John Fahy, and Samuel Everett. Cham: Palgrave Macmillan.

Altglas, Véronique and Matthew Wood, eds. 2018. *Bringing Back the Social into the Sociology of Religion: Critical Approaches*. Leiden: Brill.

Alvi, Sajida Sultana, Homa Hoodfar, and Sheila McDonough, eds. 2003. *The Muslim Veil in North America: Issues and Debates*. Toronto: Women's Press.

Amien, Waheeda. 2015. "Postapartheid Treatment of Religious Freedom in South Africa." In *Politics of Religious Freedom*, edited by Winnifred Fallers Sullivan, Elizabeth Shakman Hurd, and Saba Mahmood, 179–193. Chicago: The University of Chicago Press.

Amiraux, Valérie. 2016. "Visibility, transparency and gossip: How did the religion of some (Muslims) become the public concern of others?" *Critical Research on Religion* 4(1): 37–56.

Amiraux, Valérie. 2018. "Citoyens, piété et démocratie. Réflexions sur l'occultation des corps croyants, l'intimité et le droit au secret." *Social Compass* 65(2): 168–186.

Amiraux, Valérie, Lori G. Beaman, Benjamin L. Berger, Simone Chambers, Ian Alexander Cuthbertson, Mohammad H. Fadel, Jean-François Gaudreault-DesBiens, Pamela Klassen, David Koussens, Jean-Michel Landry, Georges Leroux, Jocelyn Maclure, Ruth Marshall, Jeremy Stolow, Charles Taylor, Jeremy Webber and Daniel Weinstock. 2014. "The charter of Quebec values." *The Immanent Frame: Secularism, Religion, and the Public Sphere*, February 20, 2014. http://blogs.ssrc.org/tif/2014/02/20/the-charter-of-quebec-values/

Ammerman, Nancy T., ed. 2007. *Everyday Religion: Observing Modern Religious Lives.* Oxford: Oxford University Press.

Amoah, Jewel. 2011. "Religion vs Culture: Striking the Right Balance in the Context of Traditional African Religions in the New South Africa." In *Traditional African Religions in South African Law*, edited by T. W. Bennett, 37–62. Claremont: UCT Press.

Amsterdam, Anthony G., and Jerome Bruner. 2000. *Minding the Law.* Cambridge: Harvard University Press.

Anderson, Benedict. 2006. *Imagined Communities: Reflections on the Origin and Spread of Nationalism.* London: Verso.

Anderson-Levitt, Kathryn M. 2012. "Complicating the concept of culture." *Comparative Education* 48(4): 441–454.

Angus Reid Institute. 2015. "Prayer in Canadian public life: A nation divided." Angus Reid Institute, June 8, 2015. http://angusreid.org/public-prayer/

Angus Reid Institute. 2017. "A spectrum of spirituality: Canadians keep the faith to varying degrees, but few reject it entirely." Angus Reid Institute. April 13, 2017. http://angusreid.org/religion-in-canada-150/

Arden, Mary. 2015. *Common Law and Modern Society: Keeping Pace with Change.* Oxford: Oxford University Press.

Årsheim, Helge. 2015. "Lost in translation? Religion-making at four UN human rights committees, 1993–2013." PhD diss, University of Oslo, Norway.

Asad, Talal. 2003. *Formations of the Secular: Christianity, Islam, Modernity.* Stanford: Stanford University Press.

Asad, Talal. 2005. "Reflections on laïcité and the public sphere." *Items and Issues* 5(3): n.p.

Assemblée Nationale du Québec. n.d. "Salon de la race." Accessed October 1, 2019. http://www.assnat.qc.ca/fr/patrimoine/lexique/salon-de-la-race.html

Astor, Avi, Marian Burchardt, and Mar Griera. 2017. "The politics of religious heritage: Framing claims to religion as culture in Spain." *Journal for the Scientific Study of Religion* 56(1): 126–142.

Australian Bureau of Statistics. 2006. "1301.0—Year Book Australia, 2006: Religious Affiliation." Accessed August 25, 2016. http://www.abs.gov.au/ausstats/abs@.nsf/bb8db737e2af84b8ca2571780015701e/bfdda1ca506d6cfaca2570de0014496e!OpenDocument

Australian Bureau of Statistics. 2012. "2011 Census reveals Hinduism as the fastest growing religion in Australia." Accessed August 25, 2016. http://www.abs.gov.au/websitedbs/censushome.nsf/home/CO-61?opendocument&navpos=620

Australian Bureau of Statistics. 2017. "2016 Census data reveals 'no religion' is rising fast." Accessed September 26, 2019. http://www.abs.gov.au/AUSSTATS/abs@.nsf/mediareleasesbyReleaseDate/7E65A144540551D7CA258148000E2B85?OpenDocument

Bacquet, Sylvie. 2009. "Manifestation of belief and religious symbols at school: Setting boundaries in English courts." *Religion and Human Rights* 4(2–3): 121–135.

Bakht, Natasha. 2012. "Veiled Objections: Facing Public Oppositions to the Niqab." In *Reasonable Accommodation: Managing Religious Diversity*, edited by Lori G. Beaman, 70–108. Vancouver: UBC Press.

Barker, Fiona. 2010. "Learning to be a majority: Negotiating immigration, integration and national membership in Quebec." *Political Science* 62(1): 11–36.

Barras, Amélie. 2016. "Exploring the intricacies and dissonances of religious governance: The case of Quebec and the discourse of request." *Critical Research on Religion* 4(1): 57–71.

Barras, Amélie. 2017. "Secularism in France." In *The Oxford Handbook of Secularism*, edited by Phil Zuckerman and John R. Shook, 142–154. New York: Oxford University Press.

Basu, Tanya. 2015. "Who owns yoga?" *The Atlantic*, January 12, 2015. http://www.theatlantic.com/business/archive/2015/01/who-owns-yoga/384350/

Baubérot, Jean. 2008. *Une laïcité interculturelle: le Québec, avenir de la France?* Aube: La Tour d'Aigues.

Baubérot, Jean. 2013. *Histoire de la laïcité en France.* Paris: Presses universitaires de France.

Baubérot, Jean. 2014. "Laïcité and Freedom of Conscience in Pluricultural France." In *Secularism on the Edge: Rethinking Church-State relations in the United States, France, and Israel*, edited by Jacques Berlinerblau, Sarah Fainberg, and Aurora Nou, 103–112. New York: Palgrave MacMillan.

Baubérot, Jean. 2015. *Les Sept Laïcités françaises: Le modèle français de laïcité n'existe pas.* Paris: Éditions de la Maison des sciences de l'homme.

Bauder, Harald. 2008. "Media discourse and the new German immigration law." *Journal of Ethnic and Migration Studies* 34(1): 95–112.

Baum, Gregory. 2000. "Catholicism and Secularization in Quebec." In *Rethinking Church, State, and Modernity: Canada Between Europe and America*, edited by David Lyon and Marguerite Van Die, 149–165. Toronto: University of Toronto Press.

Bauman, Whitney A. 2015. "The Spatial Turn in Planetary Theologies: Ambiguity, Hope and Ethical Imposters." In *The Changing World Religion Map: Sacred Places, Identities, Practices and Politics*, edited by Stanley D. Brunn, 115–128. Dordrecht: Springer.

Bauman, Zygmunt. 2011. *Culture in a Liquid Modern World.* Translated by Lydia Bauman. Cambridge: Polity Press.

Bayart, Jean-François. 2005. *The Illusion of Cultural Identity.* Translated by Steven Rendall, Janet Roitman, Cynthia Schoch, and Jonathan Derrick. Chicago: The University of Chicago Press.

Bayefsky, Anne F., and Arieh Waldman. 2007. *State Support of Religious Education: Canada versus the United Nations.* Leiden: Martinus Nijhoff Publishers.

BBC News. 2009. "Italy school crucifixes 'barred'." BBC News, November 3, 2019. http://news.bbc.co.uk/2/hi/europe/8340411.stm

BBC News. 2015a. "Charlie Hebdo attack: Three days of terror." BBC News, January 14, 2015. http://www.bbc.com/news/world-europe-30708237

BBC News. 2015b. "Paris attacks: What happened on the night." BBC News, December 9, 2015. http://www.bbc.com/news/world-europe-34818994

BBC News. 2016. "Attack on Nice: Who was Mohamed Lahouaiej-Bouhlel?" BBC News, August 19, 2016. http://www.bbc.com/news/world-europe-36801763

BBC News. 2019. "Christchurch shootings: New Zealand MPs vote to change gun laws." BBC News, April 10, 2019. https://www.bbc.com/news/world-asia-47878042.

Beaman, Lori G. 2012/3. "Battles over symbols: The 'religion' of the minority versus the 'culture' of the majority." *Journal of Law and Religion* 28(1): 67–104.

Beaman, Lori G. 2013a. "Overdressed and underexposed or underdressed and overexposed?" *Social Identities* 19(6): 723–742.

Beaman, Lori G. 2013b. "The will to religion: Obligatory religious citizenship." *Critical Research on Religion* 1(2): 141–157.

Beaman, Lori G. 2014. "Deep equality as an alternative to accommodation and tolerance." *Nordic Journal of Religion and Society* 27(2): 89–111.

Beaman, Lori G. 2016a. "Namaste: The Perilous Journey of 'Real' Yoga." In *Constructions of Self and Other in Yoga, Travel, and Tourism: A Journey to Elsewhere*, edited by Lori G. Beaman and Sonia Sikka, 101–110. Switzerland: Palgrave Macmillan.

Beaman, Lori G. 2016b. "Universal and Foundational: Law's Constitution of an Ethic of Belonging for Nones." In *Sociology of Atheism*, edited by Roberto Cipriani and Franco Garelli, 17–35. Leiden: Brill.

Beaman, Lori G. 2017. *Deep Equality in an Era of Religious Diversity.* Oxford: Oxford University Press.

Beaman, Lori G. 2018. "Review of Leaving Christianity: Changing Allegiances in Canada since 1945, by Brian Clarke and Stuart Macdonald." *The Canadian Historical Review* 99(4): 664–666.

Beaman, Lori G., and Lisa Smith. 2016. "'Dans leur propre intérêt': La Charte des valeurs québécoises, ou du danger de la religion pour les femmes." *Recherches Sociographiques* 57(2–3): 475–504.

Beaman, Lori G., and Steven Tomlins, eds. 2015. *Atheist Identities—Spaces and Social Contexts.* Cham: Springer.

Beaman, Lori G., and Winnifred Fallers Sullivan. 2013. "Neighbo(u)rly Misreadings and Misconstruals: A Cross-Border Conversation." In *Varieties of Religious Establishment*, edited by Winnifred Fallers Sullivan, and Lori G. Beaman, 1–11. Farnham: Ashgate.

Beaman, Lori G., Jennifer A. Selby, Amélie Barras. 2017. "No Mosque, No Refugees: Some Reflections on Syrian Refugees and the Construction of Religion in Canada." In *The Refugee Crisis and Religion: Secularism, Security and Hospitality in Question*, edited by Luca Mavelli and Erin Wilson, 77–95. London: Rowman & Littlefield.

Becci, Irene, Marian Burchardt, and Mariachiara Giorda. 2017. "Religious super-diversity and spatial strategies in two European cities." *Current Sociology* 65(1): 73–91.

Beck, Ulrich. 2009. *World at Risk.* Translated by Ciaran Cronin. Cambridge: Polity Press.

Beckford, James A. 2003. *Social Theory and Religion.* Cambridge: Cambridge University Press.

Beckford, James A. 2012. "SSSR presidential address public religions and the postsecular: Critical reflections." *Journal for the Scientific Study of Religion* 51(1): 1–19.

Beckford, James A., ed. 2016a. *Migration and Religion.* Cheltenham: Edward Elgar.

Beckford, James A. 2016b. "Migration and religion: Changing problematics." Paper presented at the British Sociological Association Sociology of Religion Study Group Annual Conference. Lancaster University, UK. July 12–14, 2016.

Beckford, James A., Danièle Joly, and Farhad Khosrokhavar. 2005. *Muslims in Prison: Challenge and Change in Britain and France.* New York: Palgrave MacMillan.

Beckford, James A., and James T. Richardson, eds. 2003. *Challenging Religion: Essays in Honour of Eileen Barker.* London: Routledge.

Bellah, Robert N. 2005. "Civil religion in America." *Daedalus* 134(4): 40–55.

Bellah, Robert N., Richard Madsen, William M. Sullivan, Ann Swidler, and Steven M. Tipton. 1985. *Habits of the Heart: Individualism and Commitment in American Life.* Berkeley: University of California Press.

Bellah, Robert N., Richard Madsen, William M. Sullivan, Ann Swidler, and Steven M. Tipton. 1992. *The Good Society.* New York: Vintage Books.

Bender, Courtney. 2003. *Heaven's Kitchen: Living Religion at God's Love We Deliver.* Chicago: The University of Chicago Press.

Bennhold, Katrin. 2018. "Crosses go up in public offices. It's culture, Bavaria says, not religion." *The New York Times*, May 30, 2018. https://www.nytimes.com/2018/05/30/world/europe/bavaria-germany-crucifix-migrants.html

Berg, Linda, and Mikela Lundahl. 2016. "(Un-)veiling the West: Burkini-gate, Princess hijab and dressing as struggle for postsecular integration." *Culture Unbound. Journal of Current Cultural Research* 8(3): 263–283.

Berg, Thomas C. 2004. "Minority religions and the religion clauses." *Washington University Law Quarterly* 82(3): 919–1000.

Berg, Thomas C. 2006. "What's right and wrong with 'no endorsement'." *Washington University Journal of Law & Policy* 21(1): 307–322.

Berger, Benjamin L. 2013a. "Religious diversity, education, and the 'crisis' in state neutrality." *Canadian Journal of Law and Society* 29(1): 103–122.

Berger, Benjamin L. 2013b. "The Aesthetics of Religious Freedom." In *Varieties of Religious Establishment*, edited by Winnifred Fallers Sullivan, and Lori G. Beaman, 33–53. Farnham: Ashgate.

Berger, Benjamin L. 2015. *Law's Religion: Religious Difference and the Claims of Constitutionalism.* Toronto: University of Toronto.

Berlinerblau, Jacques, Sarah Fainberg, and Aurora Nou, eds. 2014. *Secularism on the Edge: Rethinking Church-State Relations in the United States, France, and Israel.* New York: Palgrave Macmillan.

Berman, Bruce J., Rajeev Bhargava, and André Laliberté, eds. 2013. *Secular States and Religious Diversity.* Vancouver: UBC Press.

Bernier, Lyne. 2015. "Les églises et les bâtiments à caractère religieux de Montréal: de la francisation à la patrimonialisation." PhD thesis, Université de Bretagne occidentale—Bres.

Beschle, Donald L. 2016. "Town of Greece and City of Saguenay: Non-establishment principles with or without an establishment clause." *First Amendment Law Review* 14 (3): 343–375.

Beyer, Peter. 2013. *Religion in the Context of Globalization: Essays on Concept, Form, and Political Implication.* London: Routledge.

Beyer, Peter. 2015. "From Atheist to Spiritual but Not Religious: A Punctuated Continuum of Identities among the Second Generation of Post-1970 Immigrants in Canada." In *Atheist Identities—Spaces and Social Contexts*, edited by Lori G. Beaman and Steven Tomlins, 137–151. Cham: Springer.

Beyer, Peter. 2019. "Religion in interesting times: Contesting form, function, and future." The Paul Hanly Furfey Lecture presented at the 81st Annual Meeting of the Association for the Sociology of Religion, New York City, New York. August 11–13.

Bild am Sonntag. 2018. "Deutsche gegen Kreuz-Pflicht in Behörden." *Bild am Sonntag*, April 28, 2018. https://www.bild.de/politik/inland/umfrage/deutsche-wollen-keine-kreuz-pflicht-55543370.bild.html

Black, Ian. 2004. "Christianity bedevils talks on EU treaty." *The Guardian*, May 25, 2004. https://www.theguardian.com/world/2004/may/25/eu.religion

Bleich, Erik, Irene Bloemraad, and Els de Graauw. 2015. "Migrants, minorities and the media: Information, representations and participation in the public sphere." *Journal of Ethnic and Migration Studies* 41(6): 857–873.

Bock-Côté, Mathieu. 2017. "Pourquoi le crucifix passionne-t-il autant?" *Le Journal de Montréal*, March 1, 2017. http://www.journaldemontreal.com/2017/03/01/pourquoi-le-crucifix-passionne-t-il-autant

Bosset, Pierre. 2009. "La 'crise' des accommodements raisonnables: regards d'un juriste sur le rapport Bouchard-Taylor." *Revue de droit parlementaire et politique* 3(2): 323–347.

Bouchard, Gérard. 2011. "What is interculturalism?" *McGill Law Journal* 56(2): 435–468.

Bouchard, Gérard, and Charles Taylor 2008. *Building the Future: A Time for Reconciliation.* Montreal: Government of Quebec.

Bouchard, Nancy, and Jacques Pierre. 2006. *Éthique et culture religieuse à l'école.* Québec: Presses de l'Université du Québec.

Bouchard, Nancy, and Marie-France Daniel, eds. 2010. *Penser le dialogue en éducation éthique.* Québec: Presses de l'Université du Québec.

Boudreau, Spencer. 2011. "From confessional to cultural: Religious education in the schools of Québec." *Religion & Education* 38(3): 212–223.

Bouma, Gary D., and Anna Halafoff. 2017. "Australia's changing religious profile—rising Nones and Pentecostals, declining British Protestants in superdiversity: Views from the 2016 census." *Journal for the Academic Study of Religion* 30(2): 129–143.

Bowen, John. 2007a. "A view from France on the internal complexity of national models." *Journal of Ethnic and Migration Studies* 33(6): 1003–1016.

Bowen, John R. 2007b. *Why the French Don't Like Headscarves: Islam, the State, and Public Space.* Princeton: Princeton University Press.

Bowen, John R. 2011. "How the French state justifies controlling Muslim bodies: From harm-based to values-based reasoning." *Social Research* 78(2): 325–348.

Boyarin, Daniel, and Jonathan Boyarin. 1993. "Diaspora: Generation and the ground of Jewish identity." *Critical Inquiry* 19(4): 693–725.

Bracke, Sarah, and Nadia Fadil. 2012. "'Is the headscarf oppressive or emancipatory?' Field notes from the multicultural debate." *Religion and Gender* 2(1): 36–56.

Bramadat, Paul, and David Seljak. 2013. "Between Secularism and Postsecularism: A Canadian Interregnum." In *Secular States and Religious Diversity*, edited by Bruce J. Berman, Rajeev Bhargava, and André Laliberté, 97–119. Vancouver: UBC Press.

Brean, Joseph. 2015. "More than half of Canadians agree with Supreme Court ruling that bans prayer in public life: poll." *National Post*, June 8, 2015. http://news.nationalpost.com/news/canada/more-than-half-of-canadians-agree-with-supreme-court-ruling-that-bans-prayer-in-public-life-poll

Brems, Eva, ed. 2014. *The Experiences of Face Veil Wearers in Europe and the Law.* Cambridge: Cambridge University Press.

Brighelli, Jean-Paul. 2014. "Brighelli: ce que cache l'interdiction des crèches de Noël." *Le Point*, December 9, 2014. http://www.lepoint.fr/invites-du-point/jean-paul-brighelli/brighelli-ce-que-cache-l-interdiction-des-creches-de-noel-09-12-2014-1888084_1886.php

Brockhaus, Hannah. 2018. "Italy proposes mandating display of crucifixes in public buildings." *Crux*, July 25, 2018. https://cruxnow.com/global-church/2018/07/25/italy-proposes-mandating-display-of-crucifixes-in-public-buildings/

Brown, David M. 2005. "Neutrality of privilege?: A comment on religious freedom." *The Supreme Court Law Review: Osgoode's Annual Constitutional Cases Conference* 29: 221–235.

Brown, Wendy. 2006. *Regulating Aversion: Tolerance in the Age of Identity and Empire.* Princeton: Princeton University Press.

Brownstein, Alan. 2014. "Constitutional myopia: The Supreme Court's blindness to religious liberty and religious equality values in *Town of Greece v. Galloway.*" *Loyola of Los Angeles Law Review* 48(2): 371–438.

Brubaker, Rogers. 2012. "Religion and nationalism: Four approaches." *Nations and Nationalism* 18(1): 2–20.

Bruce, Steve, and David Voas. 2010. "Vicarious religion: An examination and critique." *Journal of Contemporary Religion* 25(2): 243–259.

Brudnick, Ida A. 2011. "House and senate chaplains: An overview." Congressional Research Service, May 26, 2011. https://chaplain.house.gov/chaplaincy/ChaplainHistoryCRS.pdf

Buckingham, Janet Epp. 2014. *Fighting over God: A Legal and Political History of Religious Freedom in Canada*. Montreal & Kingston: McGill-Queen's University Press.

Burchardt, Marian. 2017. "Recalling modernity: How nationalist memories shape religious diversity in Quebec and Catalonia." *Nations and Nationalism* 23(3): 599–619.

Calhoun, Craig, Mark Juergensmeyer, and Jonathan Van Antwerpen, eds. 2011. *Rethinking Secularism*. Oxford: Oxford University Press.

Campbell, Colin. 1971. *Toward A Sociology of Irreligion*. London: Macmillan.

Canadian Press. 2011. "Quebec appeals court will hear bid by mayor who wants prayer before council." *iPolitics*, March 29, 2011. https://ipolitics.ca/2011/03/29/quebec-appeals-court-will-hear-bid-by-mayor-who-wants-prayer-before-council/

Carmella, Angela C. 2011. "Symbolic religious expression on public property: Implications for the integrity of religious associations." *Florida State University Law Review* 38(3): 481–536.

Caron, Anita. 2010. "L'éducation morale à l'école québécoise de 1966 à 2008: lieu de débats, de concertations, de recherché et d'ouverture à une société pluraliste." In *Penser le dialogue en education éthique*, edited by Nancy Bouchard, and Ronald Morris, 3–12. Québec: Presses de l'Université du Québec.

Carter, Azahara. 2012. *My Journey to the Fountain of Youth*. Bloomington: Trafford Publishing.

Caulcutt, Clea. 2014. "French court bans Christmas nativity scene." BBC News, December 4, 2014. http://www.bbc.com/news/world-europe-30326257

CBC News. 2015a. "Marilyn Kerton upset over top court's right-to-pray ruling." CBC News, April 16, 2015. https://www.cbc.ca/news/canada/new-brunswick/marilyn-kerton-upset-over-top-court-s-right-to-pray-ruling-1.3036006

CBC News. 2015b. "Stephen Harper explains 'old-stock Canadians' comment." CBC News, September 18, 2015. http://www.cbc.ca/news/politics/canada-election-2015-harper-debate-1.3233785

CBC News. 2015c. "Will Stephen Harper regret remark on niqabs?" CBC News, March 12, 2015. https://www.cbc.ca/news/canada/manitoba/will-stephen-harper-regret-remark-on-niqabs-1.2991721

CBC News. 2019a. "Côte Saint-Luc says it won't enforce religious symbol ban." CBC News, February 19, 2019. https://www.cbc.ca/news/canada/montreal/cote-saint-luc-religious-symbols-1.5024349

CBC News. 2019b. "Quebec City, Sherbrooke won't remove crucifixes from city hall chambers." CBC News, April 2, 2019. https://www.cbc.ca/news/canada/montreal/quebec-city-sherbrooke-won-t-remove-crucifixes-from-city-hall-chambers-1.5081279

Cesari, Jocelyne. 2011. "Islamophobia in the West: A Comparison between Europe and the United States." In *Islamophobia: The Challenge of Pluralism in the 21st Century*, edited by John L. Esposito and Ibrahim Kalin, 21–46. Oxford: Oxford University Press.

Chaland, Christophe. 2014. "Les crèches ont-elles leur place dans l'espace public?" *La Croix*. December 12, 2014. http://www.la-croix.com/Religion/Spiritualite/Les-creches-ont-elles-leur-place-dans-l-espace-public-2014-12-12-1252659

Chambraud, Cécile. 2016. "Les crèches de Noël dans les espaces publics autorisées sous certaines conditions." *Le Monde*, November 9, 2016. http://www.lemonde.fr/societe/article/2016/11/09/l-installation-de-creches-de-noel-dans-les-batiments-publics-autorisee-sous-certaines-conditions_5028188_3224.html

Chapman, Nathan S. 2015. "The establishment clause, state action, and Town of Greece." *William & Mary Bill of Rights Journal* 24(2): 405–450.

Chase, Steven. 2015. "Niqabs 'rooted in a culture that is anti-women,' Harper says." *The Globe and Mail*, March 10, 2015. https://www.theglobeandmail.com/news/politics/niqabs-rooted-in-a-culture-that-is-anti-women-harper-says/article23395242/

Chatterji, Angana P., Thomas Blom Hansen, and Christophe Jaffrelot, eds. 2019. *Majoritarian State: How Hindu Nationalism is Changing India*. New York: Oxford University Press.

Chaves, Mark. 1995. "On the rational choice approach to religion." *Journal for the Scientific Study of Religion* 34(1): 98–104.

Chelini-Pont, Blandine. 2005. "Religion in the public sphere: Challenges and opportunities." *Brigham Young University Law Review* 2005(3): 611–628.

Chemerinsky, Erwin. 2005. "Why Justice Breyer was wrong in *Van Orden v. Perry*." *William & Mary Bill of Rights Journal* 14(1): 1–16.

CHU de Québec. 2017. "Le CHU de Québec-Université Laval est victime d'une menace importante." CHU de Québec, February 28, 2017. https://www.chudequebec.ca/actualites/le-chu-de-quebec-universite-laval-est-victime-d%E2%80%99un.aspx

Clarke, Brian, and Stuart Macdonald. 2017. *Leaving Christianity: Changing Allegiances in Canada since 1945*. Montreal & Kingston: McGill-Queen's University Press.

Clarke, Lynda. 2013. *Women in Niqab Speak: A study of the niqab in Canada*. Gananoque: Canadian Council of Muslim Women.

Cominsky, John. 2015. "Chairman: Only Christian prayers welcome at Lincoln Co. meetings." *The Charlotte Observer*. May 9, 2015. https://www.charlotteobserver.com/news/local/community/news-alliance/wbtv-news/article20593905.html.

Connolly, William E. 1999. *Why I Am Not A Secularist*. Minneapolis: University of Minnesota Press.

Connolly, William E. 2011. *A World of Becoming*. Durham: Duke University Press.

Connolly, William E. 2013. *The Fragility of Things: Self-organizing Processes, Neoliberal Fantasies, and Democratic Activism*. Durham: Duke University Press.

Conseil d'État. 2016. "Display of Nativity scenes by public authorities." Conseil d'État, November 10, 2016. https://www.conseil-etat.fr/en/press-releases/display-of-nativity-scenes-by-public-authorities

Conseil d'État. n.d. "Quel est le rôle du rapporteur public?" Conseil d'État. Accessed May 16, 2018. http://www.conseil-etat.fr/Actualites/Communiques/Quel-est-le-role-du-rapporteur-public

Conservative Party of Canada. 2015. "Not the way we do things here." Accessed October 18, 2016. http://www.conservative.ca/cpc/not-the-way-we-do-things-here

Cooper, Betsey, Daniel Cox, Rachel Lienesch, and Robert P. Jones. 2015. "Anxiety, nostalgia, and mistrust: Findings from the 2015 American values survey." Public Religion Research Institute, November 17, 2015. https://www.prri.org/research/survey-anxiety-nostalgia-and-mistrust-findings-from-the-2015-american-values-survey/

Corbin, Caroline Mala. 2010. "Ceremonial deism and the reasonable religious outside." *UCLA Law Review* 57(6): 1545–1600.

Corbin, Caroline Mala. 2015. "Intentional discrimination in establishment clause jurisprudence." *Alabama Law Review* 67(1): 299–326.

Corbin, Caroline Mala. 2017. "Justice Scalia, the establishment clause, and Christian privilege." *First Amendment Law Review* 15(2): 185–220.

Côté, Pauline. 2008. "Québec and Reasonable Accommodation: Uses and Misuses of Public Consultation." In *Religion and Diversity in Canada*, edited by Lori G. Beaman and Peter Beyer, 41–66. Leiden: Brill.

Cover, Robert M. 1983. "The Supreme Court, 1982 term—Foreword: Nomos and narrative." Faculty Scholarship Series paper 2705. Available at: http://digitalcommons.law.yale.edu/fss_papers/2705

Cragun, Ryan T., Barry Kosmin, Ariela Keysar, Joseph H. Hammer, and Michael Nielsen. 2012. "On the receiving end: Discrimination toward the non-religious in the United States." *Journal of Contemporary Religion* 27(1): 105–127.

Cragun, Ryan, and Christel Manning. 2017. "Introduction." In *Organized Secularism in the United States: New Directions in Research*, edited by Ryan T. Cragun, Christel Manning, and Lori L. Fazzino, 1–12. Berlin: de Gruyter.

Cragun, Ryan T., Joseph H. Hammer, and Michael Nielsen. 2015. "The nonreligious-nonspiritual scale (NRNSS): Measuring everyone from atheists to Zionists." *Science, Religion, and Culture* 2(3): 36–53.

Criscione, Peter. 2015. "Peel region scraps prayer before council meetings." *Brampton Guardian*, April 16, 2015. http://www.bramptonguardian.com/news-story/5561098-peel-region-scraps-prayer-before-council-meetings/

Crop. 2017. *Les Canadiens, le populisme et la xenophobie, fevrier 2017.* Accessed October 1, 2019. http://ici.radio-canada.ca/nouvelles/special/2017/03/sondage-crop/Sondage%20CROP-Radio-Canada.pdf.

Crul, Maurice. 2016. "Super-diversity vs. assimilation: How complex diversity in majority-minority cities challenges the assumptions of assimilation." *Journal of Ethnic and Migration Studies* 42(1): 54–68.

CTV News Montreal. 2019. "National Assembly votes to remove crucifix." CTV News Montreal, March 28, 2019. https://montreal.ctvnews.ca/national-assembly-votes-to-remove-crucifix-1.4355860

Cusack, Christine L. 2015. "Religion in the classroom: Reflecting on ethics and values in 'secular' curricula." Paper presented at the Annual Meeting of the Society for the Scientific Study of Religion, Newport Beach, California, October 23–25.

Dabby, Dia, and Amélie Barras. 2018. "Bent out of shape: Fictions of yoga and religion before the courts." *Religion and Human Rights* 13(3): 270–296.

Davie, Grace. 2007. "Vicarious Religion: A Methodological Challenge." In *Everyday Religion: Observing Modern Religious Lives*, edited by Nancy T. Ammerman, 21–36. Oxford: Oxford University Press.

Davie, Grace. 2015. *Religion in Britain: A Persistent Paradox.* West Sussex: Wiley-Blackwell.

Day, Abby, Giselle Vincett, and Christopher R. Cotter, eds. 2013. *Social Identities between the Sacred and the Secular.* Farnham: Ashgate.

Day, Abby. 2011. *Believing in Belonging: Belief and Social Identity in the Modern World.* Oxford: Oxford University Press.

Day, Abby. 2017. *The Religious Lives of Older Laywomen: The Final Active Anglican Generation.* Oxford: Oxford University Press.

De Certeau, Michel, and Jean-Marie Domenach. 1974. *Le christianisme éclaté.* Paris: Éditions du Seuil.

Derrida, Jacques. 2013. "Avowing—The impossible: 'Returns,' Repentance, and Reconciliation." In *Living Together: Jacques Derrida's Communities of Violence and Peace*, edited by Elisabeth Weber, 18–41. New York: Fordham University Press.

Deutsche Welle. 2018. "Germany: Catholic cardinal rebukes Bavaria for ordering crosses in state buildings." *Deutsche Welle*, April 30, 2018. http://p.dw.com/p/2wsqK

Dias, Elizabeth. 2014. "Supreme Court Decision on official prayer will not end public debate." *Time*, May 5, 2014. http://time.com/88216/supreme-court-decision-on-official-prayer-will-not-end-public-debate/

Dickinson, John Alexander, and Brian J.Young. 2008. *A Short History of Quebec.* Montreal & Kingston: McGill-Queen's University Press.

Dot-Pouillard, Nicolas. 2007. "Les recompositions du mouvement féministe français au regard du hijab." *SociologieS* (online): http://sociologies.revues.org/document246.html

Dressler, Markus, and Arvind-Pal S. Mandair, eds. 2011. *Secularism and Religion-Making.* Oxford: Oxford University Press.

Drimonis, Toula. 2018. "The 'heritage' crucifix in Quebec's legislature is barely older than my mom's furniture." *Canada's National Observer*, October 16, 2018. https://www.nationalobserver.com/2018/10/16/opinion/heritage-crucifix-quebecs-legislature-barely-older-my-moms-furniture

Duhaime, Eric. n.d. "Sauvons le crucifix: Les Québécois se mobilisent pour le crucifix." TheRebel.media. https://www.therebel.media/sauvons_le_crucifix. Accessed June 12, 2019.

Dunbar-Ortiz, Roxanne. 2014. *An Indigenous Peoples' History of the United States.* Boston: Beacon Press.

Dunn, Andrew. 2015, "Lincoln County commissioner walks out during Muslim prayer." *The Charlotte Observer.* August 4, 2015. https://www.charlotteobserver.com/news/local/article29931514.html

Durham, W. Cole Jr. 2013. "State Reactions to Minority Religions: A Legal Overview." In *State Responses to Minority Religions*, edited by David M. Kirkham, 3–13. Surrey: Ashgate Publishing.

Eder, Klaus. 2013. "Public Sphere." In *The Wiley-Blackwell Encyclopedia of Social and Political Movements*, edited by David A. Snow, Donatella Della Porta, Bert Klandermans, and Doug McAdam, 530–531. Chichester: Wiley-Blackwell.

Edgell, Penny, Joseph Gerteis, and Douglas Hartmann. 2006. "Atheists as 'other': Moral boundaries and cultural membership in American society." *American Sociological Review* 71(2): 211–234.

Edgell, Penny, Douglas Hartmann, Evan Stewart, and Joseph Gerteis. 2016. "Atheists and Other Cultural Outsiders: Moral Boundaries and the Non-Religious in the United States." *Social Forces* 95(2): 607–638.

Edwards, Benjamin P. 2013. "When fear rules in law's place: Pseudonymous litigation as a response to systematic intimidation." *Virginia Journal of Social Policy & the Law* 20(3): 437–472.

Edwards, Korie L. 2019. "Presidential Address: Religion and power—A return to the roots of social scientific scholarship." *Journal for the Scientific Study of Religion* 58(1): 5–19.

Eff, Billy. 2017. "Un groupe se vante d'avoir remis un crucifix dans un hôpital de Québec." *Vice*, March 1, 2017. https://www.vice.com/fr_ca/article/vvjmej/un-groupe-se-vante-davoir-remis-un-crucifix-dans-un-hopital-de-quebec

Egerton, George. 2000. "Trudeau, God, and the Canadian Constitution: Religion, Human Rights, and Government Authority in the Making of the 1982 Constitution." In *Rethinking Church, State, and Modernity: Canada Between Europe and America*, edited by David Lyon and Marguerite Van Die, 90–113. Toronto: University of Toronto Press.

Epstein, Steven B. 1996. "Rethinking the constitutionality of ceremonial deism." *Columbia Law Review* 96(8): 2083–2174.

Estivalèzes, Mireille, and Solange Lefebvre. 2012. *Le programme d'éthique et culture religieuse. De l'exigeante conciliation entre le soi, l'autre soi.* Québec: Les Presses de l'Université Laval.

Eurostat. 2017. "Population on 1 January by sex, citizenship and broad group of country of birth." Accessed June 14, 2017. http://appsso.eurostat.ec.europa.eu/nui/show.do?dataset=migr_pop5ctz&lang=en

Evangelical Focus. 2018. "Two thirds of Protestants against displaying crosses in public buildings." *Evangelical Focus*, April 30, 2018. http://evangelicalfocus.com/europe/3459/Two_thirds_of_Protestants_against_crosses_in_public_building

Ewick, Patricia, and Susan S. Silbey. 1998. *The Common Place of Law: Stories from Everyday Life.* Chicago: The University of Chicago Press.

Ezzy, Douglas. 2000. "Illness narratives: time, hope and HIV." *Social Science & Medicine* 50(5): 605–617.

Ezzy, Douglas. 2004. "Geographical ontology: Levinas, sacred landscapes and cities." *The Pomegranate* 6(1): 19–33.

Fadil, Nadia. 2011. "Not-/unveiling as an ethical practice." *Feminist Review* 98: 83–109.

Fea, John. 2011. *Was America Founded as a Christian Nation? A Historical Introduction.* Louisville: Westminster John Knox Press.

Fédération nationale de la libre pensée. 2016. "Crèches chrétiennes dans les bâtiments de la République." *Fédération nationale de la libre pensée*, November 9, 2016. https://www.fnlp.fr/news/321/17/Creches-chretiennes-dans-les-batiments-de-la-Republique.html

Feldman, Stephen M. 1997. *Please Don't Wish Me a Merry Christmas: A Critical History of the Separation of Church and State.* New York: New York University Press.

Fernando, Mayanthi L. 2014. *The Republic Unsettled: Muslim French and the Contradictions of Secularism.* Durham: Duke University Press.

Ferrari, Alessandro. 2009. "De la politique à la technique: laïcité narrative et laïcité du droit. Pour une comparaison France/Italie." In *Le droit Ecclésiastique de la fin du XVIII, au milieu du XXe siècle en Europe*, edited by Basdevant Gaudement and François Jankowiak, 333–345. Leuven: Peeters.

Ferrari, Alessandro. 2016. "Religious Freedom and the Public-Private Divide: A Broken Promise in Europe?" In *Religion in Public Spaces: A European Perspective*, edited by Silvio Ferrari and Sabrina Pastorelli, 71–92. London: Routledge.

Ferrari, Silvio. 2010. "Introduction to European Church and State Discourses." In *Law and Religion in the 21st Century—Nordic Perspectives*, edited by Lisbeth Christoffersen, Kjell Å. Modéer, and Svend Andersen, 23–41. Copenhagen: DJØF Publishing.

Fletcher, Raquel. 2018. "National Assembly crucifix representing Quebec 'heritage' only 36 years old." *Global News*, October 31, 2018. https://globalnews.ca/news/4611900/36-years-national-assembly-crucifix/

Fofana, Balla. 2016. "Une crèche de Noël est-elle cultuelle ou culturelle?" *Libération*, October 20, 2016. https://www.liberation.fr/france/2016/10/20/une-creche-de-noel-est-elle-cultuelle-ou-culturelle_1523186

Fokas, Effie. 2015. "Directions in Religious Pluralism in Europe: Mobilisations in the Shadow of European Court of Human Rights Religious Freedom Jurisprudence." *Oxford Journal of Law and Religion* 4(1): 54–74.

Fokas, Effie. 2016. "Comparative Susceptibility and Differential Effects on the Two European Courts: A Study of Grasstops Mobilizations around Religion." *Oxford Journal of Law and Religion* 5(3): 541–574.

Fokas, Effie. 2017. "The European Court of Human Rights at the grassroots level: Who knows what about religion at the ECtHR and to what effects?" *Religion, State & Society* 45(3–4): 249–267.

Foucault, Michel. 1978. *The History of Sexuality, Volume 1: An Introduction.* New York: Pantheon Books.

Fountain, Jeff. 2010. *Deeply Rooted: The Forgotten Vision of Robert Schuman.* Heerde: Initial Media Global.

Fourneret, Jessica. 2006. "France: Banning legal pluralism by passing a law." *Hastings International and Comparative Law Review* 29(2): 233–250.

Fournier, Johanne. 2015. "Prière au conseil municipal: le maire de Cap-Chat se plie au jugement à contrecoeur." *Le Soleil.* May 29, 2015. https://www.lesoleil.com/actualite/priere-au-conseil-municipal-le-maire-de-cap-chat-se-plie-au-jugement-a-contrecoeur-40b5db1469707fd03b594dd4aab45ee4

Fournier, Pascale and Erica See. 2014. "The 'Naked Face' of Secular Exclusion: Bill 94 and the Privatization of Belief." In *Religion in the Public Sphere: Canadian Case Studies*, edited by Solange Lefebvre and Lori G. Beaman, 275–293. Toronto: University of Toronto Press.

Gallup. 2011. "Muslim Americans: Faith, freedom, and the future." Abu Dhabi Gallup Center, August 2011. https://news.gallup.com/file/poll/148931/Muslim%20American_2_NPC.pdf

Gallup International. 2012. *Global Index of Religiosity and Atheism: Press Release*. Switzerland.

Gallup International. 2015. "Losing our religion? Two thirds of people still claim to be religious." Accessed April 17, 2019. https://www.gallup-international.bg/en/33531/losing-our-religion-two-thirds-of-people-still-claim-to-be-religious/

Gamson, William A., and Andre Modigliani. 1989. "Media discourse and public opinion on nuclear power: A constructionist approach." *American Journal of Sociology* 95(1): 1–37.

Gauderault-DesBiens, Jean-François. 2016. "Religious Challenges to the Secularized Identity of an Insecure Polity: A Tentative Sociology of Québec's 'Reasonable Accommodation' Debate." In *Legal Practice and Cultural Diversity*, edited by Ralph Grillo, Roger Ballard, Alessandro Ferrari, André J. Hoekema, Marcel Maussen, and Prakash Shah, 151–176. London: Routledge.

Gauvreau, Michael. 2005. *The Catholic Origins of Quebec's Quiet Revolution, 1931–1970*. Montreal & Kingston: McGill-Queen's University Press.

Gergen, Kenneth J. 2015. "From mirroring to world-making: Research as future forming." *Journal for the Theory of Social Behaviour* 45(3): 287–310.

Gervais, Will M., Azim F. Shariff, and Ara Norenzayan. 2011. "Do you believe in atheists? Distrust is central to anti-atheist prejudice." *Journal of Personality and Social Psychology* 101(6): 1189–1206.

Gidney, R. D. 1999. *From Hope to Harris: The Reshaping of Ontario's Schools*. Toronto: University of Toronto Press.

Giorgi, Alberta, and Pasquale Annicchino. 2017. "'Genuine' religions and their arena of legitimation in Italy—the role of the ECtHR." *Religion, State, & Society* 45(3–4): 284–296.

Globe and Mail. 1938. "Alberta Moslems build first Canadian mosque in Edmonton." *Globe and Mail*, August 19, 1938.

Goldstein, Warren S., Rebekka King, and Jonathan Boyarin. 2016. "Critical theory of religion vs. critical religion." *Critical Research on Religion* 4(1): 3–7.

Göle, Nilüfer. 2016. "The Public Visibility of Islam and European Politics of Resentment: The Minarets-Mosques Debate." In *Toward New Democratic Imaginaries—İstanbul Seminars on Islam, Culture and Politics*, edited by Seyla Benhabib and Volker Kaul, 9–18. Switzerland: Springer.

Gorce, Bernard. 2014. "Le conseil général de Vendée privé de crèche de Noël." *La Croix*, December 2, 2014. https://www.la-croix.com/Actualite/France/Le-conseil-general-de-Vendee-prive-de-creche-de-Noel-2014-12-02-1246412

Gorce, Bernard. 2016. "Le conseil d'etat tranche sur les crèches de Noël." *Le Croix*, November 10, 2016. https://www.la-croix.com/Journal/Le-Conseil-dEtat-tranche-creches-Noel-2016-11-09-1100802099

Government of Canada. 2016. "Syrian Refugees Family Composition—Ad Hoc IRCC (Specialized Datasets)." Accessed May 8, 2017. http://open.canada.ca/data/en/dataset/ca243c40-a6d3-4a46-a578-b4fad4369df0?_ga=2.52652845.486735631.1494343039-2056400147.1494343038

Government of Canada. 2017. "Map of destination communities and service provider organizations." Accessed May 8, 2017. http://www.cic.gc.ca/english/refugees/welcome/map.asp

Government of Quebec. 2018. "Guidelines for dealing with requests for accommodations on religious grounds." Accessed October 1, 2019. https://www.justice.gouv.qc.ca/fileadmin/user_upload/contenu/documents/En__Anglais_/centredoc/publications/ministere/dossiers/neutralite/PL62-lignes-A.pdf

Graham-McLay, Charlotte. 2019. "Muslims in New Zealand say they have been sidelined in Christchurch inquiry." *The New York Times*, August 28, 2019. https://www.nytimes.com/2019/08/28/world/asia/christchurch-mosque-shootings-inquiry.html

Grant, Harriet. 1985. "Lynch v. Donnelly: The disappearing wall." *North Carolina Law Review* 63(4): 782–793.

Gravel, Stéphanie, and Solange Lefebvre. 2012. "Impartialité et neutralité autour du programme québécois Éthique et culture religieuse." In *Le programme d'éthique et culture religieuse. De l'exigeante conciliation entre le soi, l'autre soi*, edited by Mireille Estivalèzes and Solange Lefebvre, 191–213. Québec: Les Presses de l'Université Laval.

Green, Steven K. 2015. *Inventing a Christian America: The Myth of the Religious Founding*. Oxford: Oxford University Press.

Grewal, San. 2015. "Oshawa mayor plans to keep Lord's Prayer." *The Toronto Star*, April 15, 2015. https://www.thestar.com/news/gta/2015/04/15/oshawa-mayor-plans-to-keep-lords-prayer.html

Griffith, Andrew. 2015. *Multiculturalism in Canada: Evidence and Anecdote*. Anar Press.

Grigore, Monica. 2015. "The Aiud 'Prison Saints.' History, memory, and lived religion." *Eurostudia*, 10(1): 33–49.

Grigore Dovlete, Monica, and Lori G. Beaman. 2017. "Ghostly presence: An abandoned space and three religious communities in Parishville, Quebec." *Eurostudia* 12(1): 82–104.

Griswold, Wendy. 1987. "A methodological framework for the sociology of culture." *Sociological Methodology* 17: 1–35.

Griswold, Wendy. 1992. "The sociology of culture: Four good arguments (and one bad one)." *Acta Sociologica*, 35(4): 323–328.

Griswold, Wendy. 2013. *Cultures and Societies in a Changing World.* 4th edition. Los Angeles: Sage.

Grondin, Marie-Renée. 2017. "Crucifix retiré à l'hôpital: 'Aucun bon sens', dit Jean Tremblay." *Le Journal de Québec*, February 24, 2017. https://www.journaldequebec.com/2017/02/24/crucifix-retire-a-lhopital-aucun-bon-sens-dit-jean-tremblay

Gryboski, Michael. 2014. "Town of Greece decision may change how Supreme Court looks at first amendment." *The Christian Post*, June 26, 2014. https://www.christianpost.com/news/town-of-greece-decision-may-change-how-supreme-court-looks-at-first-amendment-122226/

Guénif-Souilamas, Nacira. 2006. "The other French exception: Virtuous racism and the war of the sexes in postcolonial France." *French Politics, Culture & Society* 24(3): 23–41.

Gunn, T. Jeremy. 2009. "Religion and law in France: Secularism, separation, and state intervention." *Drake Law Review* 57(4): 949–978.

Habermas, Jürgen. 1996. *Between Facts and Norms: Contributions to a Discourse Theory of Law and Democracy*. Translated by William Rehg. Cambridge: Polity Press.

Habermas, Jürgen. 2006. "Religion in the public sphere." *European Journal of Philosophy* 14(1): 1–25.

Hackett, Conrad. 2017. "5 facts about the Muslim population in Europe." Pew Research Center, November 29, 2017. http://www.pewresearch.org/fact-tank/2016/07/19/5-facts-about-the-muslim-population-in-europe/

Hall, David D., ed. 1997. *Lived Religion in America: Toward a History of Practice.* Princeton: Princeton University Press.

Hamilton, Graeme. 2013. "Muslim women in hijabs increasingly the target of insults since Quebec charter was introduced." *National Post*, October 2, 2013. http://news.nationalpost.com/full-comment/graeme-hamilton-despite-its-aim-of-gender-equality-quebec-values-charter-has-upset-a-lot-of-women

Hamilton, Graeme. 2017. "After outcry, Quebec hospital restores crucifix taken down in interest of 'religious neutrality'." *National Post*, March 1, 2017. https://nationalpost.com/news/canada/after-outcry-quebec-hospital-restores-crucifix-taken-down-in-interest-of-religious-neutrality

Hamilton, Graeme. 2018. "Barred from reading a prayer at council meetings, Quebec mayor tries O Canada instead." *National Post*, June 13, 2018. https://nationalpost.com/news/canada/barred-from-reading-a-prayer-at-council-meeting-quebec-mayor-tries-o-canada-instead

Hamilton, Marci A. 2013. "There is really only one issue in *Town of Greece v. Galloway*." *Verdict*. November 14, 2013. https://verdict.justia.com/2013/11/14/really-one-issue-town-greece-v-galloway

Hammer, Joseph H., Ryan T. Cragun, Karen Hwang, and Jesse M. Smith. 2012. "Forms, frequency, and correlates of perceived anti-atheist discrimination." *Secularism and Nonreligion* 1: 43–67.

Hansen, Hans Peter, Eric von Essen and Nadarajah Sriskandarajah. 2016. "Citizens, Values and Experts: Stakeholders and the Inveigling Factor of Participatory Democracy." In *Commons, Sustainability, Democratization: Action Research and the Basic Renewal of Society*, edited by Hans Peter Hansen, Birger Steen Nielsen, Nadarajah Sriskandarajah and Ewa Gunnarsson, 113–138. New York: Routledge.

Herberg, Will. 1955[1983]. *Protestant, Catholic, Jew: An Essay in American Religious Sociology*. Chicago: The University of Chicago Press.

Hersman, Nancy Blyth. 1985. "Lynch v. Donnelly: Has the lemon test soured?" *Loyola of Los Angeles Law Review* 19(1): 133–178.

Hervieu-Léger, Danièle. 2000. *Religion as a Chain of Memory*. Cambridge: Polity Press.

Hill, Jessie. 2010. "Of Christmas trees and Corpus Christi: Ceremonial deism and change in meaning over time." *Duke Law Journal* 59(4): 705–770.

Hinkson, Kamila, and Kalina Laframboise. 2017. "Canadians divided when it comes to immigration, poll suggests." CBC News, March 13, 2017. http://www.cbc.ca/news/canada/montreal/canadian-immigration-poll-quebec-1.4022664

Hjarvard, Stig. 2013. *The Mediatization of Culture and Society*. London: Routledge.

Hobsbawm, Eric, and Terence Ranger, eds. 1983. *The Invention of Tradition*. Cambridge: Cambridge University Press.

Hoodfar, Homa. 1997. "The Veil in Their Minds and on Our Heads: Veiling Practices and Muslim Women." In *The Politics of Culture in the Shadow of Capital*, edited by Lisa Lowe and David Lloyd, 248–279. Durham: Duke University Press.

Hooper, John. 2009. "Human rights ruling against classroom crucifixes angers Italy." *The Guardian*, November 3, 2009. https://www.theguardian.com/world/2009/nov/03/italy-classroom-crucifixes-human-rights

Horwitz, Paul. 2015. “The religious geography of Town of Greece v Galloway.” *Supreme Court Review* 2014(1): 243–295.

Howard, Erica. 2009. “School bans on the wearing of religious symbols: Examining the implications of recent case law from the UK.” *Religion and Human Rights* 4(1): 7–24.

Huggler, Justin. 2018. “German state orders all government buildings to display cross to reflect ‘cultural identity’.” *The Telegraph*, April 25, 2018. https://www.telegraph.co.uk/news/2018/04/25/german-state-orders-government-buildings-display-crucifix-reflect/

Hurd, Elizabeth Shakman. 2012. “International politics after secularism.” *Review of International Studies* 38(5): 943–961.

Hurd, Elizabeth Shakman. 2015. *Beyond Religious Freedom: The New Global Politics of Religion*. Princeton: Princeton University Press.

INED. 2017. “Immigration flows by continent of origin.” *Institut National d’étude démographique*. Accessed June 15, 2017. https://www.ined.fr/en/everything_about_population/data/france/immigration-flow/year-continent

INSEE. 2014. “Recent immigrants to France—Increasingly European immigration.” *National Institute of Statistics and Economic Studies*, November 28, 2014. https://www.insee.fr/en/statistiques/1283872

Institut français d’opinion publique. 2009. “ANALYSE: Le catholicisme en France en 2009.” Accessed July 15, 2018. http://www.ifop.com/media/pressdocument/43-1-document_file.pdf

Institut français d’opinion publique. 2010. “ANALYSE: Le catholicisme en France en 2010.” Accessed July 15, 2018. http://www.ifop.com/media/pressdocument/238-1-document_file.pdf

Institut français d’opinion publique. 2012. “L’image de l’Islam en France.” Accessed July 15, 2018. https://www.ifop.com/wp-content/uploads/2018/03/2028-1-study_file.pdf

Iovino, Alessandro. 2010. “On Europe, its Christian heritage and multiculturalism.” Paper presented at CESNUR2010 conference, Torino, Italy, September 9–11. http://www.cesnur.org/2010/to_iovino.htm

Jakobsen, Janet R., and Ann Pellegrini. 2003. *Love the Sin: Sexual Regulation and the Limits of Religious Tolerance*. New York: New York University Press.

Jakobsen, Janet R., and Ann Pellegrini, eds. 2008. *Secularisms*. Durham: Duke University Press.

Jedwab, Jack. 2017. “Quebec immigration today.” *The Association for Canadian Studies and the Canadian Institute for Identities and Migration*. Accessed November 10, 2017. https://acs-aec.ca/old/img/nouvelles/ACS-CIIM-2017EN-R309.pdf.

Jiwani, Nisara, and Geneviève Rail. 2010. “Islam, hijab and young Shia Muslim Canadian women’s discursive constructions of physical activity.” *Sociology of Sport Journal* 27: 251–267.

Johnson, Greg. 2013. “Varieties of Native Hawaiian Establishment: Recognized Voices, Routinized Charisma and Church Desecration.” In *Varieties of Religious Establishment*, edited by Winnifred Fallers Sullivan and Lori G. Beaman, 55–71. Farnham: Ashgate.

Johnston, Richard. 2012. “The Structural Bases of Canadian Party Preference: Evolution and Cross-National Comparison.” In *The Canadian Election Studies. Assessing Four Decades of Influence*, edited by Mebs Kanji, Antoine Bilodeau, and Thomas J. Scotto, 154–180. Vancouver: UBC Press.

Joppke, Christian. 2004. “The retreat of multiculturalism in the liberal state: Theory and policy.” *The British Journal of Sociology* 55(2): 237–257.

Joppke, Christian. 2018. “Culturalizing religion in Western Europe: Patterns and puzzles.” *Social Compass* 65(2): 234–246.

Joselit, Jenna Weissman. 2017. *Set in Stone: America's Embrace of the Ten Commandments.* New York: Oxford University Press.

Josephson, Jason Ānanda. 2012. *The Invention of Religion in Japan.* Chicago: The University of Chicago Press.

Josephson-Storm, Jason Ā. 2017. *The Myth of Disenchantment: Magic, Modernity, and the Birth of the Human Sciences.* Chicago: The University of Chicago Press.

Jouili, Jeanette S. 2011. "Beyond emancipation: Subjectivities and ethics among women in Europe's Islamic revival communities." *Feminist Review* 98: 47–64.

Kaell, Hillary, ed. 2017. *Everyday Sacred: Religion in Contemporary Quebec.* Montreal & Kingston: McGill-Queen's University Press.

Kaell, Hillary. 2015. "Quebec's Wayside Crosses and the Creation of Contemporary Devotionalism." In *The Long Shadow of Vatican II: Living Faith and Negotiating Authority since the Second Vatican Council*, edited by Lucas Van Rompay, Sam Miglarese, and David Morgan, 102–127. Chapel Hill: The University of North Carolina Press.

Kao, Grace Y., and Jerome E.Copulsky. 2007. "The pledge of allegiance and the meanings and limits of civil religion." *Journal of the American Academy of Religion* 75(1): 121–149.

Kazemipur, Abdolmohammad. 2014. *The Muslim Question in Canada: A Story of Segmented Integration.* Vancouver: UBC Press.

Kelly, Michael. 2017. "Laïcité and atheism in France." *French Cultural Studies* 28(1): 111–122.

Kettell, Steven. 2015. "The militant strain: An analysis of anti-secular discourse in Britain." *Political Studies* 63(3): 512–528.

Khan, Sheema. 2009. *Of Hockey and Hijab: Reflections of a Canadian Muslim Woman.* Toronto: TSAR Books.

Knott, Kim, Elizabeth Poole, and Teemu Taira. 2013. *Media Portrayals of Religion and the Secular Sacred: Representation and Change.* London: Ashgate.

Knox, Zoe. 2005. *Russian Society and the Orthodox Church: Religion in Russia after Communism.* London: RoutledgeCurzon.

Koenig, Matthias. 2015a. "Governance of Religious Diversity at the European Court of Human Rights." In *International Approaches to Governing Ethnic Diversity*, edited by Jane Boulden and Will Kymlicka, 51–78. Oxford: Oxford University Press.

Koenig, Matthias. 2015b. "Incorporating Muslim Migrants in Western Nation States—A Comparison of the United Kingdom, France, and Germany." In *After Integration: Islam, Conviviality and Contentious Politics in Europe*, edited by Marian Burchardt and Ines Michalowski, 43–58. Wiesbaden: Springer VS.

Korteweg, Anna C., and Gökçe Yurdakul. 2009. "Islam, gender, and immigrant integration: Boundary drawing in discourses on honour killing in the Netherlands and Germany." *Ethnic and Racial Studies* 32(2): 218–238.

Korteweg, Anna C., and Gökçe Yurdakul. 2014. *The Headscarf Debates: Conflicts of National Belonging.* Stanford: Stanford University Press.

Kosmin, Barry A. 2014. "The Vitality of Soft Secularism in the United States and the Challenge Posed by the Growth of the Nones." In *Secularism on the Edge: Rethinking Church-State relations in the United States, France, and Israel*, edited by Jacques Berlinerblau, Sarah Fainberg, and Aurora Nou, 35–50. New York: Palgrave MacMillan.

Koussens, David. 2009. "Neutrality of the state and regulation of religious symbols in schools in Quebec and France." *Social Compass* 56(2): 202–213.

Koussens, David. 2013. "Une mise en scène nationaliste de la laïcité en porte-à-faux avec la réalité des aménagements laïques canadiens: éléments du débat Québécois." *Revue de Droit de l'Université de Sherbrooke* 43(1–2): 183–204.

Koussens, David. 2015a. *L'épreuve de la neutralité. La laïcité française entre droits et discours.* Brussels: Bruylant.

Koussens, David. 2015b. "Les débats sur le voile intégral en Europe: vers une orthopraxie du 'vivre-ensemble'." In *Laïcité et symboles religieux à l'école*, edited by Denis Jeffrey, 93–105. Québec: Presses de l'Université Laval.

Kozlowska, Iga, Daniel Béland, and André Lecours. 2016. "Nationalism, religion, and abortion policy in four Catholic societies." *Nations and Nationalism* 22(4): 824–844.

Kruse, Kevin M. 2015. *One Nation Under God: How Corporate America Invented Christian America.* New York: Basic Books.

Kühle, Lene, Ulla Schmidt, Brian Arly Jacobsen, and Per Pettersson. 2018. "Religion and State: Complexity in Change." In *Religious Complexity in the Public Sphere: Comparing Nordic Countries*, edited by Inger Furseth, 81–136. Cham: Springer.

Kurien, Prema A. 2007. *A Place at the Multicultural Table: The Development of an American Hinduism.* New Brunswick: Rutgers University Press.

Kuru, Ahmet T. 2007. "Passive and assertive secularism: Historical conditions, ideological struggles, and state policies toward religion." *World Politics* 59(4): 568–594.

Kuru, Ahmet T. 2009. *Secularism and State Policies toward Religion: The United States, France, and Turkey.* Cambridge: Cambridge University Press.

Laborde, Cécile. 2008. *Critical Republicanism the Hijab Controversy and Political Philosophy.* Oxford: Oxford University Press.

Laborde, Cécile. 2012. "State paternalism and religious dress code." *International Journal of Constitutional Law* 10(2): 398–410.

Laborde, Cécile. 2013. "Political liberalism and religion: On separation and establishment." *The Journal of Political Philosophy* 21(1): 67–86.

Lachance, Sébastien. 2016. "Grand-Sault fait fi du jugement de la Cour suprême: la prière de retour au conseil municipal." *Acadie Nouvelle*, June 20 2016. http://www.acadienouvelle.com/actualites/2016/06/02/grand-sault-fi-jugement-de-cour-supreme-reunions-conseil-municipal-commenceront-priere/?pgnc=1

Langevin, Louis-de-Gonzague. 1992. *Risquer l'avenir.* Montreal: Éditions Fides.

Laniel, Jean-François. 2016. "What 'cultural religion' says about secularization and national identity: A neglected religio-political configuration." *Social Compass* 63(3): 372–388.

Laniel, Jean-François. 2018. "Religion and National Identity in Catholic Societies: The Quarrel between Religion and Culture." In *The Changing Faces of Catholicism*, edited by Solange Lefebvre and Alfonso Pérez-Agote, 21–42. Leiden: Brill.

Laplante, Benoît. 2014. "Normative groups: The rise of the formation of the first union through cohabitation in Quebec, a comparative approach." *Population Research and Policy Review* 33(2): 257–285.

Laprise, Maxime. 2017. "Le crucifix d'un Québec mythique." *leSoleil*, March 1, 2017. https://www.lesoleil.com/opinions/point-de-vue/le-crucifix-dun-quebec-mythique-82de5bedaeb1b6e53fe9e4222a555010

Larochelle Commission. 1992. Risquer l'avenir. Montreal: Fides.

Lavoie, Bertrand. 2016. "La foi musulmane et la laïcité en france et au québec, entre régulation publique et négociation quotidienne." PhD thesis, Université de Montréal and Université Panthéon-Assas Paris II.

Le Télégramme. 2016. "Crèches de Noël. Admises dans les lieux public?" *Le Télégramme*, October 21, 2016. http://www.letelegramme.fr/france/creches-de-noel-admises-dans-les-lieux-publics-21-10-2016-11263072.php

LeDrew, Stephen. 2013. "Discovering atheism: Heterogeneity in trajectories to atheist identity and activism." *Sociology of Religion* 74(4): 431–453.

Lee, Lois. 2012. "Talking about a revolution: Terminology for the new field of non-religion studies." *Journal of Contemporary Religion* 27(1): 129–139.

Lee, Lois. 2015. *Recognizing the Non-religious: Reimagining the Secular*. Oxford: Oxford University Press.

Lefebvre, Solange. 2008. "Between Law and Public Opinion: The Case of Québec." In *Religion and Diversity in Canada*, edited by Lori G. Beaman and Peter Beyer, 175–198. Leiden: Brill.

Lefebvre, Solange, ed. 2009. *Le Patrimoine religieux du Québec: Éducation et transmission du sens*. Québec: Les Presses de l'Université Laval.

Lefebvre, Solange. 2017. "National Commissions on Collective Identity and Diversity." In *Public Commissions on Cultural and Religious Diversity: Analysis, Reception and Challenges*, edited by Solange Lefebvre and Patrice Brodeur, 19–34. London: Routledge.

Lefebvre, Solange, and Guillaume St-Laurent, eds. 2018. *Dix ans plus tard: La Commission Bouchard-Taylor, succès ou échec?* Montréal: Québec Amérique.

Lefebvre, Solange, and Jean-François Breton. 2011. "Roman Catholics and Same-Sex Marriage in Quebec." In *Faith, Politics, and Sexual Diversity in Canada and the United States*, edited by David Rayside and Clyde Wilcox, 219–234. Vancouver: UBC Press.

Lefebvre, Solange, and Patrice Brodeur, eds. 2017. *Public Commissions on Cultural and Religious Diversity: Analysis, Reception and Challenges*. London: Routledge.

Leger. 2019. "Canadians' opinions on key issues." *The Canadian Press*, April 26, 2019. https://leger360.com/wp-content/uploads/2019/04/Federal-Politics-April-26-2019-hot-topics.pdf. Accessed June 7, 2019.

Lemieux-Lefebvre, Jasmin. 2017. "Retrait du crucifix: réponse du CHU et déclaration du cardinal Lacroix." *Église catholique de Québec*, February 28, 2017. http://www.ecdq.org/retrait-du-crucifix-reponse-du-chu-et-declaration-a-venir-du-cardinal-lacroix/

Levsque, Catherine. 2019. "Signes religieux: la communauté anglophone plus divisée qu'on pense, dit Christopher Skeete." *HuffPost*, April 4, 2019. https://quebec.huffingtonpost.ca/2019/04/04/signes-religieux-laicite-anglophone-anglais_a_23706492/

Litalien, Manuel. 2013. "The Changing State Monopoly on Religion and Secular Views in Thailand." In *Secular States and Religious Diversity*, edited by Bruce J. Berman, Rajeev Bhargava, and André Laliberté, 232–265. Vancouver: UBC Press.

Lithwick, Dahlia. 2014. "Majority rules." *Slate*, May 6, 2014. http://www.slate.com/articles/news_and_politics/jurisprudence/2014/05/town_of_greece_v_galloway_roanoke_virginia_already_seeing_the_effects_of.html

Loader, Colin. 2015. "Alfred Weber, 'the sociological concept of culture'." *Cultural Sociology* 9(2): 256–270.

Love, Erik. 2009. "Confronting Islamophobia in the United States: Framing civil rights activism among Middle Eastern Americans." *Patterns of Prejudice* 43(3–4): 401–425.

Lövheim, Mia. 2014. "Mediatization and Religion." In *Mediatization of Communication*, edited by Knut Lundby, 547–570. Berlin: De Gruyter Mouton.

Lundby, Knut, Henrik Reintoft Christensen, Ann Kristin Gresaker, Mia Lövheim, Kati Niemelä, Sofia Sjö, Marcus Moberg and Árni Svanur Daníelsson. 2018. "Religion and the Media: Continuity, Complexity, and Mediatization." In *Religious Complexity in the Public Sphere: Comparing Nordic Countries*, edited by Inger Furseth, 193–249. Cham: Springer.

Maclure, Jocelyn. 2016. "The Meaning and Entailment of the Religious Neutrality of the State: The Case of Public Employees." In *Religion and the Exercise of Public Authority*, edited by Benjamin L. Berger and Richard Moon, 11–22. Oxford: Hart Publishing.

Maclure, Jocelyn, and Charles Taylor. 2011. *Secularism and Freedom of Conscience*. Translated by Jane Marie Todd. Cambridge: Harvard University Press.

Mancini, Susanna. 2010. "The crucifix rage: Supranational constitutionalism bumps against the counter-majoritarian difficulty." *European Constitutional Law Review* 6(1): 6–27.

Manelli, Sophie. 2014. "Quand religion et République crèchent ensemble…" *La Provence*, December 10, 2014. https://www.laprovence.com/article/edition-marseille/3170549/quand-religion-et-republique-crechent-ensemble.html

Marans, Daniel. 2018. "Smear campaign against Michigan candidate shows how hard it is for Muslims to run for office." *HuffPost*, May 3, 2018. https://www.huffingtonpost.ca/entry/democrat-abdul-el-sayed-michigan-muslim-candidates-conspiracy-theories_n_5aeb27f6e4b0ab5c3d62baa7

Maries de France. 2015. "Laïcité: Le vade-mecum de l'AMF." Accessed July 6, 2018. http://www.amf.asso.fr/upload/fichiers/documents/AMF_14082_VADE_MECUM.pdf

Markoe, Lauren and Cathy Lynn Grossman. 2014. "Supreme Court approves sectarian prayer at public meetings." *The Washington Post*, May 5, 2014. https://www.washingtonpost.com/national/religion/supreme-court-approves-sectarian-prayer-at-public-meetings/2014/05/05/62c494da-d487-11e3-8f7d-7786660fff7c_story.html?utm_term=.754a8ca79c7e

Martin, David. 2000. "Canada in Comparative Perspective." In *Rethinking Church, State, and Modernity: Canada Between Europe and America*, edited by David Lyon and Marguerite Van Die, 23–33. Toronto: University of Toronto Press.

Martínez-Torrón, Javier. 2013. "Institutional religious symbols, state neutrality and protection of minorities in Europe." *Law & Justice* 171: 21–51.

Mauldin, Joshua T. 2016. "Contesting religious freedom: Impossibility, normativity, and justice." *Oxford Journal of Law and Religion* 5(3): 1–25.

May, Paul. 2016. "French cultural wars: Public discourses on multiculturalism in France (1995–2013)." *Journal of Ethnic and Migration Studies* 42(8): 1334–1352.

McDermott, Meaghan. 2013. "The women behind local Supreme Court case." *Democrat & Chronicle*, November 5, 2013. https://www.democratandchronicle.com/story/news/local/2013/11/04/greece-prayer-case-heads-to-supreme-court/3436417/

McGoldrick, Dominic. 2006. *Human rights and Religion: The Islamic Headscarf Debate in Europe*. Portland: Hart Publishing.

McGuire, Meredith B. 2008. *Lived Religion: Faith and Practice in Everyday Life*. Oxford: Oxford University Press.

McKenna, Kate. 2019. "Montreal church partners with circus company to help pay the bills." CBC News, February 17, 2019. https://www.cbc.ca/news/canada/montreal/montreal-church-circus-1.5022352

Mehta, Hemant. 2017. "Quebec hospital restores crucifix after complaints; now patients can see a dead man before surgery." *Friendly Atheist*, March 3, 2017. https://friendlyatheist.patheos.com/2017/03/03/quebec-hospital-restores-crucifix-after-complaints-now-patients-can-see-a-dead-man-before-surgery/

Meintel, Deirdre. 2016. "Religion, conviviality and complex diversity." *New Diversities* 18(1): 23–36.

Meissner, Fran, and Steven Vertovec. 2015. "Comparing super-diversity." *Ethnic and Racial Studies* 38(4): 541–555.

Merry, Sally Engle. 2001. "Changing Rights, Changing Culture." In *Culture and Rights: Anthropological Perspectives*, edited by Jane K. Cowan, Marie-Bénédicte Dembour, and Richard A. Wilson, 31–55. Cambridge: Cambridge University Press.

Meunier, Martin. 2016. "La Grande Noirceur canadienne-française dans l'historiographie et la mémoire québécoises. Revisiter une interprétation convenue." *Vingtième Siècle. Revue d'histoire* 129(1): 43–59.

Miedema, Gary R. 2005. *For Canada's Sake: Public Religion, Centennial Celebrations, and the Re-making of Canada in the 1960s*. Montreal & Kingston: McGill-Queen's University Press.

Milot, Micheline. 2002. *Laïcité dans le Nouveau Monde. Le cas du Québec*. Turnhout: Brepols Publishers.

Milot, Micheline. 2005. "Les principes de laïcité politique au Québec et au Canada." *Bulletin d'Histoire politique* 13(3): 13–27.

Milot, Micheline. 2010. "When religion disturbs. The debate over Secularism in Quebec." *Our Diverse Cities* 7(2010): 84–90.

Milot, Micheline. 2013. "Dualisme des conceptions de la laïcité au Québec et en France." *The Tocqueville Review/La revue Tocqueville* 34(1): 17–42.

Ministère de l'Éducation et de l'Enseignement supérieur. n.d. "The ethics and religious culture program." Accessed May 15, 2017. http://www.education.gouv.qc.ca/fileadmin/site_web/videos/campagnes/semaine_enseignants/depliantECR_ANG.pdf

Ministère de l'Immigration, de la Diversité et de l'Inclusion. 2015. "Recueil de statistiques sur l'immigration et la diversité au Québec." Accessed May 10, 2017. http://www.midi.gouv.qc.ca/publications/fr/dossiers/STA_ImmigrDiversite_Politique.pdf

Ministère de l'Immigration, de la Diversité et de l'Inclusion. 2016a. "Présence en 2016 des immigrants admis au Québec de 2005 à 2014." Accessed May 10, 2017. http://www.mifi.gouv.qc.ca/publications/fr/recherches-statistiques/PUB_Presence2016_admisQc.pdf

Ministère de l'Immigration, de la Diversité et de l'Inclusion. 2016b. "Statistiques refugies Syriens." Accessed May 10, 2017. http://www.immigration-quebec.gouv.qc.ca/publications/fr/divers/Statistiques_Refugies_Syriens.pdf

Ministry of AYUSH. 2015. "International day of yoga 21st June: Common yoga protocol." New Delhi: Government of India. Accessed August 6, 2015.

Mnookin, Robert H., and Lewis Kornhauser. 1979. "Bargaining in the shadow of the law: The case of divorce." *The Yale Law Journal* 88(5): 950–997.

Mohamed, Besheer. 2016. "A new estimate of the U.S. Muslim population." Pew Research Center. January 6, 2016. http://www.pewresearch.org/fact-tank/2016/01/06/a-new-estimate-of-the-u-s-muslim-population/

Montreal Gazette. 2017. "Disappointment, concern, but no surprise over immigration poll." *Montreal Gazette*. March 13, 2017. http://montrealgazette.com/news/local-news/disappointment-concern-but-no-surprise-over-immigration-poll

Moon, Richard. 2012. "Freedom of religion under the Charter of Rights: The limits of state neutrality." *U.B.C Law Review* 45(2): 497–550.

Moon, Richard, and Benjamin L. Berger. 2016. "Introduction: Religious Neutrality and the Exercise of Public Authority." In *Religion and the Exercise of Public Authority*, edited by Benjamin L. Berger and Richard Moon, 1–10. Oxford: Hart Publishing.

Moore, Kathleen M. 2007. "Visible through the veil: The regulation of Islam in American law." *Sociology of Religion* 68(3): 237–251.

Mossière, Géraldine. 2013. *Converties à l'islam: Parcours de femmes au Québec et en France*. Quebec: Presses de l'Université de Montréal.

Mudde, Cas. 2016. "Putting Canada in a comparative context: Still the multiculturalist unicorn." *Nationalism and Ethnic Politics* 22(3): 351–357.

Muñoz, Vincent Phillip. 2006. "Thou shalt not post the ten comandments? McCreary, Van Orden, and the future of religious display cases." *Texas Review of Law & Politics* 10(2): 357–400.

Myerhoff, Barbara G. 1978. "A Symbol Perfected in Death: Continuity and Ritual in the Life and Death of an Elderly Jew." In *Life's Career—Aging: Cultural Variations on*

Growing Old, edited by Barbara G. Myerhoff and Anrei Simić, 163–202. Newbury Park: Sage Publications.

Myers, Richard S. 1988. "The establishment clause and nativity scenes: A reassessment of *Lynch v. Donnelly*." *Kentucky Law Journal* 77(1): 61–116.

Myers, Daniel J., and Beth Schaefer Caniglia. 2004. "All the rioting that's fit to print: Selection effects in national newspaper coverage of civil disorders, 1968–1969." *American Sociological Review* 69(4): 519–543.

Neitz, Mary Jo. 2013. "Insiders, outsiders, advocates and apostates and the religions they study: Location and the sociology of religion." *Critical Research on Religion* 1(2): 129–140.

Newport, Frank. 2017. "2017 update on Americans and religion." Gallup, December 22, 2017. https://news.gallup.com/poll/224642/2017-update-americans-religion.aspx

Ng, Eddy S., and Irene Bloemraad. 2015. "A SWOT analysis of multiculturalism in Canada, Europe, Mauritius, and South Korea." *American Behavioral Scientist* 59(6): 619–636.

Norris, Pippa, and Ronald Inglehart. 2004. *Sacred and Secular: Religion and Politics Worldwide*. Cambridge: Cambridge University Press.

O'Neill, Maggie. 2010. *Asylum, Migration and Community*. Bristol: The Policy Press.

O'Toole, Roger. 2000. "Canadian Religion: Heritage and Project." In *Rethinking Church, State, and Modernity: Canada between Europe and America*, edited by David Lyon and Marguerite Van Die, 33–51. Toronto: University of Toronto Press.

Office for National Statistics. 2012a. "2011 Census: Key statistics for England and Wales, March 2011." Accessed September 26, 2019. http://www.ons.gov.uk/peoplepopulationandcommunity/populationandmigration/populationestimates/bulletins/2011censuskeystatisticsforenglandandwales/2012-12-11#religion

Office for National Statistics. 2012b. "Religion in England and Wales 2011." Accessed June 24, 2015. http://www.ons.gov.uk/ons/dcp171776_290510.pdf

Oliva, Javier Garcia. 2016. "Religious Dress Codes in the United Kingdom." In *Religion in Public Spaces: A European Perspective*, edited by Silvio Ferrari and Sabrina Pastorelli, 217–234. London: Routledge.

Orsi, Robert A. 2005. *Between Heaven and Earth: The Religious Worlds People Make and the Scholars Who Study Them*. Princeton: Princeton University Press.

Ouest-France. 2014. "Laïcité. Pas de crèche de Noël au conseil général de Vendée." OuestFrance.fr, December 5, 2014. http://www.ouest-france.fr/une-creche-au-conseil-general-de-vendee-le-tribunal-dit-non-3018928

Ozzano, Luca, and Alberta Giorgi. 2013. "The debate on the crucifix in public spaces in twenty-first century Italy." *Mediterranean Politics* 18(2): 259–275.

Palley, Howard A. 2006. "Canadian abortion policy: National policy and the impact of federalism and political implementation on access to services." *Publius: The Journal of Federalism* 36(4): 565–586.

Palmer, Susan J. 2011. *The New Heretics of France: Minority religions, la Republique, and the Government-Sponsored "War on Sects"*. Oxford: Oxford University Press.

Park, Keumjae. 2014. "Foreigners or multicultural citizens? Press media's construction of immigrants in South Korea." *Ethnic and Racial Studies* 37(9): 1565–1586.

Park, Richard S. 2016. "Christian and Islamic Conceptions of Public Civility: A Consideration of 'The Human Good'." In *Pathways for Inter-Religious Dialogue in the Twenty-First Century*, edited by Vladimir Latinovic, Gerard Mannion, and Peter C. Phan, 153–166. New York: Palgrave Macmillan.

Parliament of Australia. 2009. "Annotated standing orders of the Australian Senate." Accessed August 27, 2018. https://www.aph.gov.au/About_Parliament/Senate/Powers_practice_n_procedures/aso

Parliament of Canada. 2009. "House of Commons procedure and practice: Second Edition, 2009." Accessed September 27, 2019. http://www.parl.gc.ca/procedure-book-livre/document.aspx?sbdid=af057bd0-f018-4fb4-bd75-4a2200729f05&sbpidx=2

Parliament of New South Wales. 2005. "Bankstown City Council prayers." Accessed May 24, 2017. www.parliament.nsw.gov.au/prod/parlment/hansart.nsf/V3Key/LC20050524065

Peker, Efe. 2017. "The link between Quebec's niqab law and its sovereignty quest." *The Conversation*, October 29, 2017. https://theconversation.com/the-link-between-quebecs-niqab-law-and-its-sovereignty-quest-86200

Perisse, Marco. 2018. "Crocifisso in tutti gli uffici pubblici, scuole e università. La proposta di legge della Lega." *GQ*, July 25, 2018. https://www.gqitalia.it/news/2018/07/24/crocifisso-in-tutti-gli-uffici-pubblici-scuole-e-anche-nei-porti-la-proposta-di-legge-della-lega

Peritz, Ingrid. 2017. "Debate over wearing religious symbols returns to Quebec one week after mosque shooting." *The Globe and Mail*, February 7, 2017. https://www.theglobeandmail.com/news/national/debate-over-wearing-religious-symbols-returns-to-quebec-one-week-after-mosque-shooting/article33948284/

Perry, Barbara. 2015. "Disrupting the mantra of multiculturalism: Hate crime in Canada." *American Behavioral Scientist* 59(13): 1637–1654.

Pew Research Center. 2012a. "'Nones' on the rise." Accessed June 23, 2016. http://www.pewforum.org/2012/10/09/nones-on-the-rise/

Pew Research Center. 2012b. "The global religious landscape." Accessed August 17, 2016. http://www.pewforum.org/2012/12/18/global-religious-landscape-exec/

Pew Research Center. 2013. "The religious affiliation of U.S. immigrants: Majority Christian, rising share of other faiths." Pew Research Centre, May 13, 2013. http://www.pewforum.org/2013/05/17/the-religious-affiliation-of-us-immigrants/#muslim

Pew Research Center. 2017. "U.S. Muslims concerned about their place in society, but continue to believe in the American dream." Pew Research Center, July 26, 2017. https://www.pewforum.org/2017/07/26/findings-from-pew-research-centers-2017-survey-of-us-muslims/

Pew Research Center. 2018. "Being Christian in western Europe." Pew Research Center, May 29, 2018. https://www.pewforum.org/wp-content/uploads/sites/7/2018/05/Being-Christian-in-Western-Europe-FOR-WEB1.pdf

Pew-Templeton Global Religious Futures Project. 2015. "The future of world religions: Population growth projections, 2010–2050." Pew Research Center, April 2, 2015. https://www.pewforum.org/2015/04/02/religious-projections-2010-2050/

Pew-Templeton. 2015a. "Religions in France." Accessed July 15, 2017. http://www.globalreligiousfutures.org/countries/france#/?affiliations_religion_id=0&affiliations_year=2010&region_name=All%20Countries&restrictions_year=2015

Pew-Templeton. 2015b. "Sweden." Accessed April 17, 2019. http://www.globalreligiousfutures.org/countries/sweden#/?affiliations_religion_id=0&affiliations_year=2010&region_name=All%20Countries&restrictions_year=2016

Pew-Templeton. 2015c. "United States." Accessed October 3, 2019. http://www.globalreligiousfutures.org/countries/united-states#/?affiliations_religion_id=0&affiliations_year=2010&region_name=All%20Countries&restrictions_year=2016

Phelps Bondaroff, Teale N., Ian Bushfield, Katie E. Marshall, Ranil Prasad, and Noah Laurence. 2019. "Report: An analysis of prayer in the Legislative Assembly of British Columbia, 2003–2019." BC Humanist Association. https://d3n8a8pro7vhmx.cloudfront.net/bchumanist/pages/2639/attachments/original/1568097489/House_of_Prayer.pdf?1568097489

Philpott, Daniel, and Timothy Samuel Shah. 2016. "In defense of religious freedom: New critics of a beleaguered human right." *Journal of Law and Religion* 31(3): 380–395.

Poitras, Jacques. 2019. "Green MLA's motion aims to do away with daily Lord's Prayer." CBC News, April 2, 2019. https://www.cbc.ca/news/canada/new-brunswick/arseneau-higgs-austin-christian-prayer-legislature-1.5081671

Posner, Sarah. 2013. "Religious leaders split on prayer in government meetings." *Aljazeera America*, November 5, 2013. http://america.aljazeera.com/articles/2013/11/5/religious-leaderssplitonprayeringovernmentmeetings.html

Pottie-Sherman, Yolande, and Rima Wilkes. 2014. "Good code bad code: Exploring the immigration-nation dialectic through media coverage of the Hérouxville 'Code of Life' document." *Migration Studies* 2(2): 189–211.

Povinelli, Elizabeth A. 2011. *Economies of Abandonment: Social Belonging and Endurance in Late Liberalism*. Duke: Duke University Press.

Powers, Lucas. 2015. "Conservatives pledge funds, tip line to combat 'barbaric cultural practices'." CBC News, October 2, 2015. http://www.cbc.ca/news/politics/canada-election- 2015-barbaric- cultural-practices-law-1.3254118

Prélot, Pierre-Henri. 2017. "From Stasi (2003) to the Machelon Commission (2006): The Use of Commissions in Religious Regulation in France." In *Public Commissions on Cultural and Religious Diversity: Analysis, Reception and Challenges*, edited by Solange Lefebvre and Patrice Brodeur, 69–79. London: Routledge.

Prince Albert Daily Herald. 2015. "Moose Jaw sticking with prayer for now." *Daily Herald*, April 25, 2015.

Putnam, Robert D. 2000. *Bowling Alone: The Collapse and Revival of American Community*. New York: Simon & Schuster Paperbacks.

Quack, Johannes. 2014. "Outline of a relational approach to 'nonreligion'." *Method and Theory in the Study of Religion* 26(4–5): 439–469.

Quack, Johannes, and Cora Schuh, eds. 2017. *Religious Indifference: New Perspectives from Studies on Secularization and Nonreligion*. Cham: Springer.

Quillen, Ethan G. 2018. *Atheist Exceptionalism: Atheism, Religion, and the United States Supreme Court*. London: Routledge.

Quinio, Dominique. 2014. "La bataille des crèches." *La Croix*. December 5, 2014. http://www.la-croix.com/Editos/La-bataille-des-creches-2014-12-05-1248380

Radin, Jessica L. 2016. "Review of *Politics of Religious Freedom*, edited by Winnifred Fallers Sullivan, Elizabeth Shakman Hurd, Saba Mahmood, and Peter G. Danchin." *Middle East Law and Governance* 8(1): 105–118.

Radio-Canada. 2017a. "Le crucifix de retour à l'hôpital du Saint-Sacrement." Radio-Canada, March 2, 2017. https://ici.radio-canada.ca/nouvelle/1019915/crucifix-reinstalle-hopital-du-saint-sacrement-quebec-controverse

Radio-Canada. 2017b. "Les Canadiens, le populisme et la Xénophobie." Accessed October 8, 2019. https://ici.radio-canada.ca/nouvelles/special/2017/03/sondage-crop/Sondage%20CROP-Radio-Canada.pdf

Ravitch, Frank S. 1999. *School Prayer and Discrimination: The Civil Rights of Religious Minorities and Dissenters*. Boston: Northeastern University Press.

Razack, Sherene H. 2008. *Casting Out: The Eviction of Muslims from Western Law and Politics*. Toronto: University of Toronto Press.

Read, Jen'nan Ghazal, and John P. Bartkowski. 2000. "To veil or not to veil? A case study of identity negotiation among Muslim women in Austin, Texas." *Gender & Society* 14(3): 395–417.

Redfield, Robert. 1956. *Peasant Society and Culture: An Anthropological Approach to Civilization*. Chicago: The University of Chicago Press.

Reid, Michelle Siobhan. n.d. "Access by province." *The Morgentaler Decision: A 25th Anniversary Celebration*. Accessed May 8, 2017. http://www.morgentaler25years.ca/the-struggle-for-abortion-rights/access-by-province/

Republican Integration Contract. n.d. "Welcome to France." *Ministry for Employment, Social Cohesion, and Housing and National Agency for the Welcome of Foreigners and Migrations*. Accessed May 16, 2018. http://travail-emploi.gouv.fr/IMG/pdf/cai_anglais.pdf

Retailleau, Bruno. 2014. "Crèche de Vendée: oui au principe de laïcité, non au principe d'absurdité!" LeFigaro.fr, December 4, 2014. http://www.lefigaro.fr/vox/societe/2014/12/03/31003-20141203ARTFIG00415-creche-de-vendee-oui-au-principe-de-laicite-non-au-principe-d-absurdite.php

Richardson, James T. 2015. "Managing religion and the judicialization of Religious Freedom." *Journal for the Scientific Study of Religion* 54(1): 1–19.

Richardson, James T., and Marat S. Shterin. 2008. "Constitutional courts in post-communist Russia and Hungary: How do they treat religion?" *Religion, State & Society* 36(3): 251–267.

Richardson, James T., and Massimo Introvigne. 2004. "'Brainwashing' theories in European parliamentary and administrative reports on 'cults' and 'sects'." *Journal for the Scientific Study of Religion* 40(2): 143–168.

Riga, Andy. 2017. "Quebec mosque shooting suspect Alexandre Bissonnete changes lawyer." *Montreal Gazette*, March 30, 2017. http://montrealgazette.com/news/local-news/quebec-mosque-shooting-suspect-alexandre-bissonnette-back-in-court

Riis, Ole, and Linda Woodhead. 2010. *A Sociology of Religious Emotions*. Oxford: Oxford University Press.

RMC Radio. 2014. "Crèches de noël: 'On a affaire à des ayatollahs de la laïcité', dit Robert Ménard." RMC Radio. December 5, 2014. https://rmc.bfmtv.com/mediaplayer/video/creches-de-noel-on-a-affaire-a-des-ayatollahs-de-la-laicite-dit-robert-menard-366172.html

Rocher, François, and Bob W. White. 2014. "L'interculturalisme québécois dans le contexte du multiculturalisme canadien." Montreal: Institut de recherche en politiques publiques.

Rosenberger, Wendy M. 1982. "Anonymity in civil litigation: The 'Doe' plaintiff." *Notre Dame Lawyer* 57(3): 580–597.

Roseneil, Sasha, and Stephen Frosh, eds. 2012. *Social Research after the Cultural Turn*. Hampshire: Palgrave Macmillan.

Ross, Melissa. 2016. "Jacksonville City Council allows first-ever secular invocation." *Florida Politics*, March 23, 2016. http://floridapolitics.com/archives/205367-jacksonville-city-council-allows-first-ever-secular-invocation

Ross, Ryan. 2015. "No end to prayer at legislature." *The Guardian*, April 19, 2015. https://www.theguardian.pe.ca/news/local/no-end-to-prayer-at-legislature-99011/

Rothenberg, Celia E. 2004. *Spirits of Palestine: Gender, Society, and Stories of the Jinn*. Lanham: Lexington Books.

Rousseau, Louis. 2011. "Prière et démocratie municipale." *Éthique publique* 13(2): 1–5. https://doi.org/10.4000/ethiquepublique.862

Rousseau, Louis, ed. 2012. *Le Québec après Bouchard-Taylor: Lles identités religieuses de l'immigration*. Québec: Presses de l'Université du Québec.

Roy, Eleanor Ainge. 2019. "'Real leaders do exist': Jacinda Ardern uses solace and steel to guide a broken nation." *The Guardian*, March 19, 2019. https://www.theguardian.com/world/2019/mar/19/real-leaders-do-exist-jacinda-ardern-uses-solace-and-steel-to-guide-a-broken-nation

Roy, Olivier. 2013. *Holy Ignorance: When Religion and Culture Part Ways.* Translated by Ros Schwartz. Oxford: Oxford University Press.

Rubin, Alissa J. 2016. "French 'burkini' bans provoke backlash as armed police confront beachgoers." *The New York Times*, August 24, 2016. https://www.nytimes.com/2016/08/25/world/europe/france-burkini.html

Rukavina, Steve. 2018. "Charles Taylor slams CAQ plan to ban religious symbols for some civil servants." CBC News, October 18, 2018. https://www.cbc.ca/news/canada/montreal/charles-taylor-slams-caq-plan-to-ban-religious-symbols-for-some-civil-servants-1.4868901

Ryan, Phil. 2016. "Does Canadian multiculturalism survive through state repression?" *Nationalism and Ethnic Politics* 22(3): 342–350.

Ryder, Bruce. 2005. "State neutrality and freedom of conscience and religion." *The Supreme Court Law Review: Osgoode's Annual Constitutional Cases Conference* 29 (2005): 169–199.

Sahgal, Neha. 2018. "10 key findings about religion in Western Europe." Pew Research Center, May 29, 2018. https://www.pewresearch.org/fact-tank/2018/05/29/10-key-findings-about-religion-in-western-europe/

Sandberg, Russell. 2014. *Religion, Law and Society.* Cambridge: Cambridge University Press.

Scheffer, Paul. 2011. *Immigrant Nations.* Translated by Liz Waters. Cambridge: Polity Press.

Schmidt, Leigh Eric. 2016. *Village Atheists: How America's Unbelievers Made Their Way in a Godly Nation.* Princeton: Princeton University Press.

Schultz, Colin. 2013. "Yoga a 'distinctly American cultural phenomenon,' California judge decrees." Smithsonian.com, July 2, 2013. https://www.smithsonianmag.com/smart-news/yoga-a-distinctly-american-cultural-phenomenon-california-judge-decrees-5739356/

Scott, Joan Wallach. 2007. *The Politics of the Veil.* Princeton: Princeton University Press.

Scott, Marian. 2019. "Montreal unanimously adopts bipartisan declaration opposing Bill 21." *Montreal Gazette*, April 16, 2019. https://montrealgazette.com/news/local-news/city-council-to-oppose-bill-21

Sehat, David. 2011. *The Myth of American Religious Freedom.* Oxford: Oxford University Press.

Selby, Jennifer A. 2014a. "Un/veiling women's bodies: Secularism and sexuality in full-face veil prohibitions in France and Quebec." *Studies in Religion/Sciences Religieuses* 43(3): 439–466.

Selby, Jennifer A. 2014b. "France." In *The Oxford Handbook of European Islam*, edited by Jocelyne Cesari, 23–63. Oxford: Oxford University Press.

Selby, Jennifer A., Amélie Barras, and Lori G. Beaman. 2018. *Beyond Accommodation: Everyday Narratives of Muslim Canadians.* Vancouver: UBC Press.

Seljak, David. 1996. "Why the Quiet Revolution was 'quiet': The Catholic Church's reaction to the secularization of nationalism in Quebec after 1960." *Historical Studies* 62: 109–124.

Seljak, David. 2000. "Resisting the 'No Man's Land' of Private Religion: The Catholic Church and Public Politics in Quebec." In *Rethinking Church, State, and Modernity: Canada between Europe and America*, edited by David Lyon and Marguerite Van Die, 131–149. Toronto: University of Toronto Press.

Seljak, David. 2012. "Protecting religious freedom in a multicultural Canada." *Canadian Diversity* 9(3): 8–11.

Seljak, David. 2016. "Post-secularism, multiculturalism, human rights, and religion in Ontario." *Studies in Religion/ Sciences Religieuses* 45(4): 542–565.

Senato della Repubblica. 2019. "Att Camera n. 387." Senato della Repubblica. http://www.senato.it/leg/18/BGT/Schede/Ddliter/49215.htm

Shakeri, Esmail. 2000. "Muslim Women in Canada: Their Role and Status as Revealed in the Hijab Controversy." In *Muslims on the Americanizaton Path?*, edited by Yvonne Yazbeck Haddad and John L. Esposito, 129–144. Oxford: Oxford University Press.

Shingler, Benjamin. 2017. "Crucifix restored to wall of Quebec City hospital after thousands object to its removal." CBC News, March 2, 2017. https://www.cbc.ca/news/canada/montreal/quebec-city-hospital-threat-crucifix-arrest-1.4006197

Shingler, Benjamin. 2018. "Judge suspends Quebec face-covering ban, says it appears to violate charter." CBC News, June 28, 2018. https://www.cbc.ca/news/canada/montreal/quebec-bill-62-face-covering-july1-1.4724863

Sikka, Sonia. 2012. "Moral relativism and the concept of culture." *Theoria: A Journal of Social and Political Theory* 59(133): 50–69.

Sikka, Sonia. 2019. "Unpacking religion: Faith, identity and reason." *India International Centre Quarterly*, 46(2): 31–41.

Simpson, John H. 2000. "The Politics of the Body in Canada and the United States." In *Rethinking Church, State, and Modernity: Canada between Europe and America*, edited by David Lyon and Marguerite Van Die, 263–283. Toronto: University of Toronto Press.

Smart, Carol. 1989. *Feminism and the Power of Law*. London: Routledge.

Smith, Dorothy E. 1987. *The Everyday World as Problematic: A Feminist Sociology*. Toronto: University of Toronto Press.

Solyom, Catherine. 2015. "Quebec bill to ban face coverings sparks mixed reaction." *Montreal Gazette*, June 10, 2015. http://montrealgazette.com/news/quebec/bill-to-ban-face-coverings-sparks-mixed-reaction

Somekh, Simone. 2018. "Pope adviser blasts pro-crucifix bill in Italy: 'Hands off!'" *Crux*, July 26, 2018. https://cruxnow.com/vatican/2018/07/26/pope-adviser-blasts-pro-crucifix-bill-in-italy-hands-off/

Soon, Judith A., Marc Levine, Brenda L. Osmond, Mary H. H. Ensom, and David W. Fielding. 2004. "Provision of emergency contraceptives by pharmacists." *Canadian Pharmacists Journal* 137(6): 23–29.

Spiteri, Ray. 2014. "Does religion belong in municipal councils?" *Fort Erie Times*, October 9, 2014. https://www.niagarafallsreview.ca/news-story/8448193-does-religion-belong-in-municipal-councils-/

Stark, Rodney, and Roger Finke. 2000. *Acts of Faith: Explaining the Human Side of Religion*. Berkeley: University of California Press.

Stasi, Bernard. 2003. *Commission de réflexion sur l'application du principe de laïcité dans la République: Rapport au président de la République*. Paris: La Documentation Française. https://www.ladocumentationfrancaise.fr/var/storage/rapports-publics/034000725.pdf

Statistics Canada. 2011. "Religion (108), Immigrant Status and Period of Immigration (11), Age Groups (10) and Sex (3) for the Population in Private Households of Canada, Provinces, Territories, Census Metropolitan Areas and Census Agglomerations, 2011 National Household Survey." Accessed September 26, 2019. http://www12.statcan.gc.ca/nhs-enm/2011/dp-pd/dt-td/Rp-eng.cfm?LANG=E&APATH=3&DETAIL=0&DIM=0&FL=A&FREE=0&GC=0&GID=0&GK=0&GRP=0&PID=105399&PRID=0&PTYPE=105277&S=0&SHOWALL=0&SUB=0&Temporal=2013&THEME=95&VID=0

Statistics Canada. 2013a. "2011 National Household Survey: Immigration, place of birth, citizenship, ethnic origin, visible minorities, language and religion." Accessed September 26, 2019. http://www.statcan.gc.ca/daily-quotidien/130508/dq130508b-eng.htm

Statistics Canada. 2013b. "Immigration and ethnocultural diversity in Canada." Accessed September 26, 2019. http://www12.statcan.gc.ca/nhs-enm/2011/as-sa/99-010-x/99-010-x2011001-eng.pdf

Statistics Canada. 2017. "Marital Status (13), Age (16) and Sex (3) for the Population 15 Years and Over of Canada, Provinces and Territories and Census Metropolitan Areas, 1996 to 2016 Censuses - 100% Data." Accessed August 10, 2018. http://www12.statcan.gc.ca/cen

sus-recensement/2016/dp-pd/dt-td/Rp-eng.cfm?LANG=E&APATH=3&DETAIL=0&DIM=0&FL=A&FREE=0&GC=0&GID=0&GK=0&GRP=1&PID=109650&PRID=10&PTYPE=109445&S=0&SHOWALL=0&SUB=0&Temporal=2016&THEME=117&VID=0&VNAMEE=&VNAMEF=

Stokes, Bruce. 2017. "What it takes to truly be 'one of us'." Pew Research Center, February 1, 2017. http://www.pewglobal.org/2017/02/01/what-it-takes-to-truly-be-one-of-us/

Straughn, Jeremy Brooke, and Scott L. Feld. 2010. "America as a 'Christian nation'? Understanding religious boundaries of national identity in the United States." *Sociology of Religion* 71(3): 280–306.

Sullivan, Winnifred Fallers. 1994. *Paying the Words Extra: Religious Discourse in the Supreme Court of the United States.* Cambridge: Harvard United Press.

Sullivan, Winnifred Fallers. 2005. *The Impossibility of Religious Freedom.* Princeton: Princeton University Press.

Sullivan, Winnifred Fallers. 2009. "We are all religious now. Again." *Social Research: An International Quarterly* 76(4): 1181–1198.

Sullivan, Winnifred Fallers. 2013. "Law's prayer: Town of Greece v Galloway." *Reverberations: New Directions in the Study of Prayer*, November 5, 2013. http://forums.ssrc.org/ndsp/2013/11/05/laws-prayer-town-of-greece-v-galloway/

Sullivan, Winnifred Fallers. 2014. *A Ministry of Presence: Chaplaincy, Spiritual Care, and the Law.* Chicago: The University of Chicago Press.

Sullivan, Winnifred Fallers, Elizabeth Shakman Hurd, Saba Mahmood, and Peter G. Danchin. 2015. "Introduction." In *Politics of Religious Freedom*, edited by Winnifred F. Sullivan, Elizabeth Shakman Hurd, Saba Mahmood, and Peter G. Danchin, 1–9. Chicago: The University of Chicago Press.

Szekely, Reka. 2015. "Oshawa drops Lord's Prayer from council meetings." Durhamregion.com. April 29, 2015. http://www.durhamregion.com/news-story/5592285-oshawa-drops-lord-s-prayer-from-council-meetings/

Tabet, Marie-Christine. 2014. "La crèche dépasse la sphère religieuse." *Le Journal du Dimanche*, December 21, 2014. http://www.lejdd.fr/Societe/Religion/Creches-de-Noel-La-creche-depasse-la-sphere-religieuse-707826

Takaki, Ronald. 1993. *A Different Mirror: A History of Multicultural America.* Boston: Little, Brown & Company.

Tallmadge, Katherine. 2011. *Diet Simple: 195 Mental Tricks, Substitutions, Habits & Inspirations.* Washington: LifeLine Press.

The Association for Canadian Studies. 2019. "Restrictions on religious signs in Quebec on the basis of linguistic identification." Accessed October 1, 2019. https://qcgn.ca/wp-content/uploads/2019/05/Survey-Results-on-Bill-21-1.pdf

The Canadian Press. 2019. "Quebec bans religious symbols for state workers in new law." *Global News*, June 16, 2019. https://globalnews.ca/news/5397857/quebec-religious-symbol-ban-passed/

The Christian Institute. 2017. "Christian politician shares Easter message in Canadian Parliament." *The Christian Institute*, April 12, 2017. http://www.christian.org.uk/news/christian-politician-shares-easter-message-canadian-parliament/

The Chronicle Journal. 2017. "Crucifix to be back on view at Quebec City hospital following removal." *The Chronicle Journal*, March 1, 2017. http://www.chroniclejournal.com/news/national/crucifix-to-be-back-on-view-at-quebec-city-hospital/article_d1e9c19b-037a-5b3f-b814-f272987f88f0.html

The Florida Senate. 2018. "CS/HB 7055: Education." Accessed June 11, 2019. https://www.flsenate.gov/Session/Bill/2018/7055/

The Globe and Mail. 2017. "The Quebec City mosque attack: What we know so far." *The Globe and Mail*, January 30, 2017. http://www.theglobeandmail.com/news/national/quebec-city-mosque-shooting-what-we-know-so-far/article33826078/

The Guardian. 2019. "Jacinda Ardern on the Christchurch shooting: 'One of New Zealand's darkest days'." *The Guardian*, March 15, 2019. https://www.theguardian.com/world/2019/mar/15/one-of-new-zealands-darkest-days-jacinda-ardern-responds-to-christchurch-shooting

Time. 1974. "Beating the Blahs." *Time* 104(15): 123.

Tomlins, Steven and Spencer Culham Bullivant. 2017. "Canada: Insights Derived from the Atheist Bus Campaign on the Status of Atheism in Canada's Multicultural Mosaic." In *The Atheist Bus Campaign: Global Manifestations and Responses*, edited by Steven Tomlins and Spencer Culham Bullivant, 81–113. Leiden: Brill.

Toronto Star. 2015. "Readers' letters: Thoughts on prayer ruling." *Toronto Star*, April 26, 2015. https://www.thestar.com/opinion/letters_to_the_editors/2015/04/26/thoughts-on-prayer-ruling.html

Toronto SUN. 2017. "Canadians like values and dislike M103." *Toronto Sun*, March 14, 2017. http://www.torontosun.com/2017/03/13/canadians-like-values-and-dislike-m103

Trépanier, Antoine. 2016. "Prière à Grand-Sault: le maire de Saguenay appuie le maire Deschênes." Radio-Canada, June 1, 2016. http://ici.radio-canada.ca/regions/atlantique/2016/06/16/004-acadie-nouveau-brunswick-rencontre-conseil-municipal-grand-sault-priere-jean-tremblay.shtml

Troper, Michel. 2016. "Republicanism and Freedom of Religion in France." In *Religion, Secularism, & Constitutional Democracy*, edited by Jean L. Cohen and Cécile Laborde, 316–337. New York: Columbia University Press.

Truth and Reconciliation Commission of Canada. 2015. *Truth and Reconciliation Commission of Canada: Calls to Action*. Winnipeg: Truth and Reconciliation Commission of Canada. http://trc.ca/assets/pdf/Calls_to_Action_English2.pdf

Turgeon, Laurier, ed. 2005. *La Patrimoine Religieux du Québec: Entre le cultuel et le culturel*. Québec: Presses de l'Université Laval.

Turner, Graeme. 2012. *What's Become of Cultural Studies?* London: SAGE Publications.

Tutton, Michael. 2019. "New Brunswick debates ending Christian prayers in legislature." *Global News*, April 8, 2019. https://globalnews.ca/news/5141612/christian-prayer-nb-legislature/

Urry, John. 2010. "Mobile sociology." *The British Journal of Sociology* 61(1): 347–366.

Valiante, Giuseppe. 2019. "Quebec removes crucifix from legislature as government defends secularism law in court." *The Star*, July 9, 2019. https://www.thestar.com/news/canada/2019/07/09/muslim-civil-liberties-groups-begin-court-battle-against-quebec-secularism-law.html

Vallois, Thirza. 2014. "The santons of Provence: A history." *France Today*, December 14, 2014. https://www.francetoday.com/culture/the_santons_of_provence/

Van Arragon, Leo. 2015. "Religion and Education in Ontario Public Education: Contested Borders and Uneasy Truces." In *Issues in Religion and Education: Whose Religion?*, edited by Lori G. Beaman and Leo Van Arragon, 34–58. Leiden: Brill.

Van Dijk, Teun A. 1993. "Principles of critical discourse analysis." *Discourse & Society* 4(2): 249–283.

Vertovec, Steven. 2007. "Super-diversity and its implications." *Ethnic and Racial Studies* 30(6): 1024–1054.

Vertovec, Steven. 2019. "Talking around super-diversity." *Ethnic and Racial Studies* 42(1): 125–139.

Vertovec, Steven, and Susanne Wessendorf, eds. 2010. *The Multiculturalism Backlash: European Discourses, Policies and Practices.* London: Routledge.

von Stuckrad, Kocku. 2010. "Reflections on the limits of reflection: An invitation to the discursive study of religion." *Method and Theory in the Study of Religion* 22(2–3): 156–169.

Wahlquist, Calla. 2019. "Ardern says she will never speak name of Christchurch suspect." *The Guardian*, March 19, 2019. https://www.theguardian.com/world/2019/mar/19/new-zealand-shooting-ardern-says-she-will-never-speak-suspects-name.

Wald, Kenneth D., and Allison Calhoun-Brown. 2011. *Religion and Politics in the United States.* 6th Edition. Lanham: Rowman & Littlefield Publishers.

Waldman, Paul. 2019. "Supreme Court maintains special status for Christianity." *The Washington Post*, June 20, 2019. https://www.washingtonpost.com/opinions/2019/06/20/supreme-court-maintains-special-status-christianity/?noredirect=on

Wallace, Michael, Bradley R. E. Wright, and Allen Hyde. 2014. "Religious affiliation and hiring discrimination in the American south: A field experiment." *Social Currents* 1(2): 189–207.

Wallis, Simeon. 2014. "Ticking 'no religion': A case study amongst 'young nones'." *Diskus* 16(2): 70–87.

Warner, R. Stephen. 1993. "Work in progress toward a new paradigm for the sociological study of religion in the United States." *American Journal of Sociology* 98(5): 1044–1093.

Waterton, Emma, and Steve Watson. 2013. "Framing theory: Towards a critical imagination in heritage studies." *International Journal of Heritage Studies* 19(6): 875–909.

WCTV Eyewitness News. 2018. "Tallahassee Atheists group responds to 'In God We Trust' law." WCTV.tv, August 6, 2018. https://www.wctv.tv/content/news/Tallahassee-Atheists-group-responds-to-In-God-We-Trust-law-490171911.html

WDRB. 2017. "Gov Matt Bevin publicly signs bill allowing Kentucky's public schools to teach the Bible." WDRB.com. June 27, 2017. http://www.wdrb.com/story/35761799/gov-matt-bevin-publicly-signs-bill-allowing-kentuckys-public-schools-to-teach-the-bible

Weins, W. Jesse. 2007. "A problematic plurality precedent: Why the Supreme Court should leave marks over *Van Orden v. Perry*." *Nebraska Law Review* 85(3): 830–874.

Welborne, Bozena C., Aubrey L. Westfall, Özge Çelik Russell, and Sarah A. Tobin. 2018. *The Politics of the Headscarf in the United States.* Ithaca: Cornell University Press.

Wenger, Tisa. 2017. *Religious Freedom: The Contested History of an American Ideal.* Chapel Hill: The University of North Carolina Press.

Westbrook, Tom. 2019. "'New Zealand mourns with you. We are one,' PM tells Christchurch Muslims near shooting site." *Global News*, March 21, 2019. https://globalnews.ca/news/5083465/jacinda-ardern-new-zealand-mourns/

Westfall, Aubrey, Bozena Welborne, Sarah Tobin, and Özge Çelik Russell. 2016. "The complexity of covering: The religious, social, and political dynamics of Islamic practice in the United States." *Social Science Quarterly* 97(3): 771–790.

Wexler, Jay. 2019. *Our Non-Christian Nation: How Atheists, Satanists, Pagans, and Others Are Demanding Their Rightful Place in Public Life.* Stanford: Redwood Press.

Whittington, Les. 2015. "Stephen Harper skeptical of Ukraine ceasefire." *The Star*, February 12, 2015. https://www.thestar.com/news/canada/2015/02/12/stephen-harper-skeptical-of-ukraine-ceasefire.html

Wilkins-Laflamme, Sarah. 2016. "The changing religious cleavage in Canadians' voting behaviour." *Canadian Journal of Political Science* 49(3): 499–518.

Wilkins-Laflamme, Sarah. 2017. "Religious-secular polarization compared: The cases of Quebec and British Columbia." *Studies in Religion/Sciences Religieuses* 46(2): 166–185.

Willaime, Jean-Paul. 2008. "The Paradoxes of Laïcité in France." In *The Centrality of Religion in Social Life: Essays in Honour of James A. Beckford*, edited by Eileen Barker, 41–54. Farnham: Ashgate.

Williams, Melissa S. 2009. "The Politics of Fear and the Decline of Multiculturalism." In *The Ties that Bind: Accommodating Diversity in Canada and the European Union*, edited by John Erik Fossum, Johanne Poirier, and Paul Magnette, 53–76. Brussels: P.I. E. Peter Lang.

Williams, Rhys H. 2015. "Religion and multiculturalism: A web of legal, institutional, and cultural connections." *The Sociological Quarterly* 56(2015): 607–622.

Williams, Rhys H., and Gira Vashi. 2007. "Hijab and American Muslim women: Creating the space for autonomous selves." *Sociology of Religion* 68(3): 269–287.

Wilson, Erin. 2014a. "'But that's culture, not religion': The politics of Christianity as cultural heritage." Building Bridges Presented at the University of Ottawa, April 3, 2014.

Wilson, Erin. 2014b. "'Culture' or 'religion'? Understanding the popularity of the passion." ReligionFactor, April 17, 2014. https://www.rug.nl/research/centre-for-religious-studies/religion-conflict-globalization/blog/culture-or-religion-understanding-the-popularity-of-the-passion-17-04-2014

Winter, Elke. 2011. *Us, Them and Others: Pluralism and National Identities in Diverse Societies.* Toronto: University of Toronto Press.

Winter, Elke. 2015. "Rethinking multiculturalism after its 'retreat': Lessons from Canada." *American Behavioral Scientist* 59(6): 637–657.

Woodhead, Linda. 2011. "Five concepts of religion." *International Review of Sociology* 21(1): 121–143.

Woodhead, Linda. 2016a. "The rise of 'no religion' in Britain: The emergence of a new cultural majority." *Journal of the British Academy* 4: 245–261.

Woodhead, Linda. 2016b. "Is no religion the new religion?" Paper presented at the annual meeting for the Association for the Sociology of Religion, Seattle, Washington, August 19–21.

Yamane, David. 2007. "Symposium on the 20th anniversary of habits of the heart." *Sociology of Religion* 68(2).

Yelle, Robert A. 2013. *The Language of Disenchantment: Protestant Literalism and Colonial Discourse in British India.* Oxford: Oxford University Press.

YouGov. 2015. "YouGov/University of Lancaster survey results." Accessed June 23, 2016. https://d25d2506sfb94s.cloudfront.net/cumulus_uploads/document/m6imjuukrf/UniversityofLancasterResults_151222_ChurchBuildings_LifeStages_website.pdf/

Zubrzycki, Geneviève. 2016. *Beheading the Saint: Nationalism, Religion, and Secularism in Quebec.* Chicago: The University of Chicago Press.

Zuckerman, Phil. 2008. *Society without God: What the Least Religious Nations Can Tell Us About Contentment.* New York: New York University Press.

Zuckerman, Phil. 2012. *Faith No More: Why People Reject Religion.* New York: Oxford University Press.

Zuckerman, Phil, and John R. Shook, eds. 2017. *The Oxford Handbook of Secularism.* New York: Oxford University Press.

Case law and legislation

(R-26. 2. 01, section 16)

Allen v. Renfrew (County), 2004. 69 O.R. (3d) 742 (Ont. Sup. Ct. J.).

Bill 60, Charter affirming the values of State secularism and religious neutrality and of equality between women and men, and providing a framework for accommodation requests. 1st reading November 7, 2013. 40th Legislature, 1st Session, 2013.

Bill 62, An Act to foster adherence to State religious neutrality and, in particular, to provide a framework for religious accommodation requests in certain bodies. 1st Reading, June 10, 2015. 41st Legislature, 1st Session, 2015.

Bill 94, An Act to establish guidelines governing accommodation requests within the Administration and certain institutions. 1st Reading, March 24, 2010, 39th Legislature, 1st Session, 2010.

Bill C-75: An Act to amend the Citizenship Act and to make a consequential amendment to another Act. 1st Reading, June 19, 2015, 41st Legislature, 2nd Session, 2015.

Brief for Unitarian Universalist Association et al. as Amici Curiae Supporting Respondents, at p. 12.

BVerfG, 1 BvR 1087/91 vom 16.05.1995.

Canada (Attorney General) v. Bedford, 2013. SCC 72, [2013] 3 S.C.R. 1101.

Capitol Square Review & Advisory Board v. Pinette, 1995. 515 U.S. 753.

Carter v. Canada (Attorney General), 2015. SCC 5, [2015] 1 S.C.R. 331.

Cha'are Shalom Ve Tsedek v. France, 2000. [GC], no. 27417/95, § 73, ECHR 2000-VII.

Conseil d'État, 9 novembre 2016, N° 395122, Publié au recueil Lebon.

County of Allegheny v. American Civil Liberties Union Greater Pittsburgh Chapter, 1989. 492 U.S. 573.

Cour administrative d'appel de Paris, 1ère chambre, 8 October 2015, n° 15PA00814, Inédit au recueil Lebon.

Doe v. Stegall, 1981. 653 F.2d 180, 181–182 (5th Cir. 1981).

E.E.O.C. v. Abercrombie & Fitch Stores, 2015. 575 U.S. ____.

El Morsli v. France, 2008. (Dec), no. 15585/06, March 4, 2008.

Erazo v. Dufferin-Peel Catholic District School Board, 2014. ONSC 2072.

Freitag v. Penetanguishene (Town), 1999. CanLII 3786 (ONCA).

Galloway v. Town of Greece, 2010. 732 F. Supp. 2d 195, 241–243 (W.D.N.Y. 2010).

Galloway v. Town of Greece, 2012. 681 F.3d 20 (2d Cir. 2012).

Immigration, Refugees and Citizenship Canada Operational Bulletin 359—December 12, 2011, Requirements for candidates to be seen taking the Oath of Citizenship at a ceremony and procedures for candidates with full or partial face coverings.

Ishaq v. Canada, 2015. (Citizenship and Immigration), FC 156.

La cour administrative d'appel de Nantes, 13 October 2015, n° 14NT03400 [Crèche CA].

Lautsi and others v. Italy, 2011. ECHR. No. 30814/06.

Law v. Canada (Minister of Employment and Immigration), 1999. 1 S.C.R. 497.

Lemon v. Kurtzman, 1971. 403 U.S. 602.

Lynch v. Donnelly, 1984. 465 U.S. 668.

Mouvement laïque québécois v. Saguenay (City), 2015. SCC 16 [2015] 2 S.C.R. 3.

National Council of Canadian Muslims (NCCM) c. Attorney General of Québec, 2018. QCCS 2766, at para. 80.

Newdow v. United States, 2013. 13 CV 741 (HB).

Palau-Martinez v. France, 2003. (no. 64927/01, § 43, ECHR 2003-XII).

Phull v. France, 2005. (Dec), no. 35753/03, ECHR 2005-I.

R v. Big M Drug Mart Ltd, 1985. 1 S.C.R. 295.

R v. Edwards Books and Art Ltd., 1986. 2 S.C.R. 713.

R.C. v. District School Board of Niagara, 2013. HRTO 1382.

R-26.2.01, Section 10.

Reference re Same-Sex Marriage, 2004. 3 S.C.R. 698, 2004 SCC 79.
S.A.S. v. France, 2014. [GC] (CEDH, n. 43835/11).
Saguenay (Ville de) v. Mouvement laïque québécois, 2013. QCCA 936.
Santa Fe Independent School Dist. v. Doe, 2000. 530 U.S. 290.
Sch. Dist. of Abington Twp., Pa., v. Schempp, 1963. 374 U.S. 203.
Sedlock v. Baird, 2013. No. 37201300035910-CU-MC-CTL (Cal Super Ct CD).
Sedlock v. Baird, 2015. 235 Cal. App. 4th 874.
Simoneau v. Tremblay, 2011. QCTDP 1.
The American Legion v. American Humanist Association, 2019. No. 17–1717, 588 U.S. ___.
Town of Greece v. Galloway, 2014. 572 U.S. ___.
Tribunal Administratif de Nantes, 14 novembre 2014, Fédération de Vendée de la Libre Pensée, n° 1211647.
United States v. Essex County, 2010.
United States v. New York Metropolitan Transit Authority, 2004.
United States v. Washington Metropolitan Area Transit Authority, 2018.
Van Orden v. Perry, 2005. 545 U.S. 677.
Vendée (N° 395223), 2016.
Waldman v. Canada, 1999. No. 694/1996.
Zylberberg v. Sudbury Board of Education, 1988.

Index